FABULOUS

To Stuart!

Happy Christmas!

I know I was meant to loan my
own copy but now you have your
own!

I love you lots and lots!

Here's to our first Christmas

love
Owen
x

Yale UNIVERSITY PRESS NEW HAVEN AND LONDON

Christmas 2018!

MADISON MOORE

FABULOUS

THE RISE OF THE BEAUTIFUL ECCENTRIC

Yale University Press books may be purchased in quantity for educa-
tional, business, or promotional use. For information, please e-mail
sales.press@yale.edu (U.S. office) or sales@yaleup.co.uk (U.K. office).

Designed by Sonia L. Shannon.
Set in Futura type by Tseng Information Systems, Inc.
Printed in the United States of America.

Library of Congress Control Number: 2017957274
ISBN 978-0-300-20470-4 (hardcover : alk. paper)

This paper meets the requirements of ANSI/NISO Z39.48-1992 (Permanence of Paper).

10 9 8 7 6 5 4 3 2 1

CONTENTS

the story of fabulousness was on my mind way before I knew it vii
would become a whole book. It was on my mind when I rushed to Casa
Magazines on the corner of 8th Avenue and 12th Street in New York City
every month to get the latest issues of French and Italian *Vogue.* It was on
my mind when I saw my grandmother get all dressed up for church or the
casino—wigs, broaches, sequins, and all. And as a teenaged gay boy I
locked myself in my bedroom and plugged into this book as I danced to
Prince and Lenny Kravitz, two black men who fascinated me because they
could wear leather pants, fringe, and high heels, and nobody seemed to
mind all that much. "How do they do it?" I wondered. Almost twenty years
later here I am, posing the same question.

There are some books you read that really stick with you over
the course of your lifetime, and for me *The Theory of the Leisure Class,* a
canonical book by the Yale-trained economist Thorstein Veblen, published
in 1899, is one of those books. It's a breezy, satirical portrait of the white,
straight, new-moneyed elite of the Gilded Age, the book that birthed the
term *conspicuous consumption.* Today, Veblen's little book seems as relevant in Trump's America as it did more than a hundred years ago, as the
Minnesotan author was primarily interested in, or more like disgusted
by, grotesque displays of wealth. He understood the conspicuousness of
luxury, fancy clothes, big houses, and decadent feasts as limitless, never-
ending examples of power and financial prowess. Sound familiar? But
the story of conspicuousness I'm telling here is much more brown, much
more queer, and a lot more fun. The pursuit of fun and pleasure are political gestures too. This bedazzled revision of Veblen is about how fashion,
glitter, and sequins, things I can't get enough of, are not only shiny, conspicuous, and look great on Instagram, but they underscore the pleasure
and power of creativity for queer and marginalized people and other
social outcasts. The story I'm telling is about fabulousness as a queer aesthetic, an essence that allows marginalized people and social outcasts to
regain their humanity and creativity, not necessarily to boast about power
or influence.

Veblen's original text is, at its heart, about the wasteful nature of
capitalism and the leisure class that spills out of it. He was curious about

how the conspicuous consumption of goods was used to wield financial prowess over people of considerably less influence and social value. Think, for instance, of the nineteenth-century socialite Caroline Schermerhorn Astor, *the* Mrs. Astor, who threw exclusive parties at her home on Fifth Avenue, ruled the New York social scene, and was rumored to keep a List of 400—the only four hundred people in all of the city who mattered. These parties were definitely about performing a certain kind of conspicuous consumption. But were there any brown people at the functions?

In revising Veblen's original ideas about conspicuous consumption and power I want to tell a different side of the story. I want to talk about how fabulousness is not about money but about opening doors to brand-new dimensions, creating a separate space in the here and now. The challenge of telling the story of fabulousness is that there is no single, traditional archive specifically dedicated to it. There is no single university or museum that holds the definitive record on material related to fabulousness as it has spread and been experienced across time, communities, and space. Fabulousness is everywhere, but it is not necessarily right in front of us at all times. It flashes before our eyes for brief moments at a time, seducing us emotionally. That's what makes it exciting. It's a type of creative engagement we can find everywhere: from Balzac's realist fiction and writings on fashion, like his 1836 novel *Old Goriot* or his 1830 *Treatise on Elegant Living,* to the more contemporary cultural forms of performance art, voguing, and club culture.

Fabulous: The Rise of the Beautiful Eccentric is not a manifesto. Not everyone needs to be fabulous all the time, and there are certainly millions of people who don't want to or can't be fabulous for one reason or another. But what is compelling about fabulousness are the people who consciously chose the harder route, the *risk* and the *rise* of living as a "spectacle," when it would be so much easier—though no less toxic—to just follow the rules and blend in. This book tells their stories.

1.
The Rise of the Beautiful Eccentric

i will never forget the day I saw the Juilliard-trained queer virtuoso violinist Amadéus Leopold (formerly Hahn-Bin) live in concert. It was his first downtown show, a special performance handpicked by Lou Reed and Laurie Anderson at a tiny experimental music and performance art venue in New York called the Stone. At the time, Leopold, who had studied violin with the legendary Itzhak Perlman at Juilliard, pumped around the classical music, fashion, and art worlds in New York City, making a splash with his blend of unquestionable virtuosity, his thrilling sense of performance, his fashion and creative strangeness. He took classical music from Alice Tully Hall to MoMA and from the catwalk to the nightclub. I'd been assigned to write a story about him for *Interview* magazine, and the fashion diva and classical music nerd in me was eager to see him in action. It's hard to convey how much Leopold's art spoke to me: I also grew up in the violin world of orchestra, summer music camps, recitals, and competitions, even earning a full ride to a school of music for violin performance. But in my two decades of studying violin I always felt something wasn't quite right. Where was the diversity? America's homegrown heartthrob virtuoso Joshua Bell is great, and so are other star performers like Midori and Anne-Sophie Mutter. But where was the fabulous brown queen behind the violin?

As soon as I learned about Amadéus Leopold I exhaled. At last, an unapologetically queer classical violin virtuoso! What drew me to Leopold wasn't just that he had studied with Perlman at Juilliard, so he must be good. It was that he really knows how to *work a look*. Take one glance at Leopold and you'll see that fashion is just as much a part of his art as the music he plays. When I got to meet him for the *Interview* story, I asked if it was difficult to play sixty-fourth notes—some of the fastest notes on the violin—in gravity-defying high heels. "It's a struggle," he told me, "but the shoes and everything I wear is really part of the art. It's not an option for me to take them off."[1] Now that's a balancing act.

That evening at the Stone, Leopold was a breath of fresh air. Not only were his interpretations of standard violin concert pieces like Pablo de Sarasate's *Zigeunerweisen* remarkable, but his creatively strange looks—

3

the dramatic makeup, particularly around the eyes, the tight leopard-print pants, red ankle boots, and hair piled atop his head like a swirl of black ice cream—added an extra surge of creativity to the spectacle. In a 2011 *Today Show* interview Leopold described himself as a "performance artist who speaks through the language of the violin," welding together theater, fashion, dance, and classical music. When asked how he's received by traditional classical music audiences Leopold remarked, somewhat humorously, "I think that the classical music world has sort of been taking a nap, and I'm here to wake them up! People said, 'You can't go to Carnegie Hall looking like this!'" But when you are queer, of color, and gender nonconforming, what does it mean to look like "this"? Queer and gender-nonconforming people are often reduced to "this" or "that" by haters, homophobes, and transmisogynists while simply walking down the street: "What is *that*?" they'll say. Not even human—a "thing." The moment Leopold steps out onstage, perhaps the only "safe" space, audiences typically respond with an audible gasp, he noted, and for him that gasp circles the way fabulousness changes the energy in a room. That's when the real performance begins.[2]

"My parents—everybody—would tell me that I'm a boy, I have to act this way, you can't wear these things," he told me. "You can't put on makeup. And so for me, fashion and the visual expression of myself became a way to claim self-love. Every time I put on lipstick, every time I drape myself, I become my own self rather than what everybody else would rather have me be."[3] Leopold's art pinpoints in no uncertain terms that fabulousness is something embodied and queer—an aesthetic— one rooted in certain kinds of creative agency, where extravagant self-expression is a dangerous political gesture.

Nearly every story about fabulousness I've learned in the course of writing this book begins with such a turning point, a shedding of a past way of living in favor of living for oneself in another dimension in the here and now. Fabulousness may look great on the outside, and beautiful eccentrics may seem confident and well put together, but underneath the surface lurks a story of struggle, survival, and resistance, even if the story is still being written. The watershed moment of fabulousness occurs when marginalized people and other social outcasts get fed up with the pressures to conform to norms that never had them in mind in the first place and respond to that suffering and exhaustion by taking the risk to live exactly the way they see fit. This is what Francesca Royster encourages us to think of as "the freedom to be strange."[4] "I don't think I would have gone the length to find the truest form of visual identity," Leopold remembers, "had I not suffered through the boundaries that had been present in my former environments."[5] With all its pomp and circumstance, fabulousness sees norms and resists them, twists them and makes them abstract, taking them on face-to-face, no holds barred. Perhaps one of the greatest creative gifts of marginalized people and social outcasts is that power of abstraction—the ability to see through the here and now and to live dangerously through radical style, art, music, and ideas.

"This kid is FABULOUS!"

"WERRRRKKKKKK hahahah"

"LOVES IT!!!! SO CREATIVE!!"

"Send that boy some eyelashes!!!!!!!"

"That's a lot of talent with little resources."

"Just stepped out the mini fridge, feeling gorgeous. Werk."[6]

They're talking about Apichet "Madaew Fashionista" Atirattana, a teenager from the Khon Kaen province of northeastern Thailand who became a viral Internet sensation in 2015 by posting creative photos of himself on Instagram and Facebook. But these are not just any photos or selfies. They are creatively *strange*. "Newest Fashionista Famous for WTF Factor," one Thai blog wrote.[7] The "WTF Factor" of Madaew's photos is that he creates his looks out of everyday—but unusual—materials, things that are just lying around his family's market stall, like chicken wire, concrete blocks, or dyed cabbage leaves. In a 2016 *Time* magazine profile, Atirattana expressed that he wants "people to see that ugly things that don't seem to go together can become something beautiful . . . and that looking good doesn't depend on money."[8] In one look, for instance, "liked" by nearly sixty thousand people on Facebook, Madaew stands unusually tall because he's wearing three sheets of corrugated metal that he has arranged just so, working the metal pieces as a "dress" and posing to eternity. In another shot he stands barefoot, out in an open field, wearing a look made entirely of toilet paper. The camera is positioned in a way that dramatizes the toilet paperness of the look, just in case we didn't get it. And in one of my favorite looks Madaew poses at the top of a highway overpass—the photo is shot from the bottom of the stairs—wearing a dress made of a reddish-pink Thai checkered cloth with a train that must be at least thirty feet long. The train, his ponytail, cascades dramatically all the way down the stairs. It's fabulous.

In 2015 Indonesian-American drag queen Raja Gemini, winner of season 3 of *RuPaul's Drag Race*, shared a video on Facebook of Madaew posing outdoors. "I'm obsessed with this!" he said. "Basically this is me everyday."[9] In the clip Madaew poses in the flawless self-made looks we're used to seeing him in, but what's different is that now we get to see him in action. We get to see him work it. The video is composed of several brief vignettes, each narrated around a single look and accompanied by a Beyoncé soundtrack. Madaew builds anticipation by treating each pose as a surprise performance. In every vignette Madaew hides and the camera quickly pans the space as if to ask, "Where is he?" and then—*boom!*—there he is, posing, ready for us to take in his newest look, each one more fabulous than the last. At one moment he pops out of a mini fridge in full regalia. In another he hides in a giant pile of hay only to burst out, climb to the top, and strike a pose as if, as the art critic Craig Owens might say, he is *"already a picture."*[10]

Madaew is fabulous, and his story is evidence of certain unique traits of fabulousness we will explore in *Fabulous: The Rise of the Beautiful Eccentric*. But first, a caveat. When most of us think about something fabulous we usually think about the visual excesses of luxury: endless wealth, huge mansions, fur coats, diamond rings, and limousines. When I mention to anyone that I've been writing a book about fabulousness, for instance, the first examples anyone brings up almost always point to film divas like Marilyn Monroe or Marlene Dietrich—"They are fabulous!" people tell me. Sure they are. As theorists of commodities and celebrity culture from

Adorno and Horkheimer to Richard Dyer have shown, celebrities and pop stars make countless millions of dollars a year as part of an industrialized entertainment system and cultural industry. They benefit from an entire machinery designed to make them fabulous. They have agents to help secure top movie roles and advertising campaigns. They have stylists, makeup artists, and access to the best wigs in town. They have Photoshop and airbrushing. They get free clothes from all the top fashion houses and they are paid to look good for us. Take a peek at the cover of a fashion magazine, which usually features only one person, and ask yourself how many people are in the image. It's a trick question because we may be looking at one person but there are actually countless interns, camerapeople, assistants, stylists, agents, art directors, creative directors, editors, and even designers on-site. This is a whopping industrial apparatus most of us don't typically get to access.

I'm interested in a different biography of fabulousness. This story is not about pop stars, celebrities, or Hollywood glamour—that's a book that has already been written many times. *Fabulous* is about how eccentric style is staged in performance as well as in everyday and everynight life by club kids, creatives, artists, and other people like Madaew Fashionista and Amadéus Leopold. This book is also about people like Natalie, a lawyer/floating vision of sickeningness I met one summer afternoon at a club in Berlin. I love club fashion—not only figuring out what to wear but seeing how other people get all dressed up too. Natalie worked a bold green blazer, white sneakers, and long hair don't care. I told her I was writing a book about fabulousness and her eyes lit up. "I wake up every day and think, 'What would Diana Ross and Grace Jones do?'" she said. The answer? "Be fierce and fabulous and realize that every day is Oscar day. You better turn up like you're going to win something!"

All told, I'm interested in queer and other people forced to the margins who create themselves for themselves and who don't have access to top celebrity stylists, who aren't on the covers of magazines, but who *are* fashion or art students and other creative types who make or improvise their own looks. These fabulous creative renegades don't have a team of people working for them around the clock and, importantly, their personal styling almost always bends the rules of socially accepted appearance.

Here are the four basic traits of fabulousness that are the basis of this book: (1) Fabulousness does not take a lot of money. You can achieve creative brilliance with very few resources; (2) It's an aesthetic that requires high levels of creativity, imagination, and originality, but there is no blueprint for fabulousness; (3) Fabulousness is dangerous, political, confrontational, risky, and largely (but certainly not only) practiced by queer, trans, and transfeminine people of color and other marginalized groups; and (4) Finally, it's about making a spectacle of yourself not merely to be seen but because your body is constantly suppressed and undervalued. Fabulousness can light up a room and that means it's easy to frame it as a simple narrative of triumph—feel bad, look great—but it's much more complicated than that. Fabulous people struggle and fight for air every single day.

Great style is never simply style for style's sake. It isn't just about looking good and feeling confident. It's also a form of protest, a revolt against the norms and systems that oppress and torture us all every day, things like white supremacy, misogyny, transmisogyny, patriarchy, toxic masculinity, gender policing, and racism. Let me put it this way: when you tell someone on the street, at the coffee shop, or at the club they look fabulous, something many of us do all the time, know that the person you're talking to didn't simply arrive at fabulousness by accident. Know it was a solid choice because fabulousness is always an embrace of yourself when you're constantly reminded that you don't deserve to be embraced. Know that the style and presence you're commenting on is the direct result of all sorts of trauma, depression, and anxiety, not to mention verbal and physical street violence. When you tell someone they are "sickening" or that they are "slaying" a look (as in looking really, really good), know that there are folks out there who do think that people forced to the margins *are* sick, a problem, and, as much as someone may be "slaying" a look, realize that there are people who want to (and do) physically slay them on the streets. This constellation of beauty and pain, of virtuosic creativity and risk, is central to how fabulousness operates: society wants nothing more than for us to play by its rules, and we're punished for it when we don't. The fact that beautiful eccentrics put themselves on the line every day despite the odds shows how important they are not only as aesthetic geniuses but as political activists too.

Fabulous: The Rise of the Beautiful Eccentric explores the allure of effervescent style as an embodied queer aesthetic that appears in everyday and everynight life. In theory circles the word queer is typically thought of as a resistance to "the norm" as well as to "regimes of the normal."[11] Indebted to thinkers like Richard Wright, who believed that "no theory of life can take the place of life," throughout this book I position fabulousness as theory from the streets, a visual, mobile theory that just happens to look great.[12] In 1898 the Austrian architect and style icon Adolf Loos asked, "Who does not desire to be well-dressed?" and in 2008 Simon Doonan, the creative director at large for Barneys New York, wondered, "Why the hell wouldn't you want to be one of the fabulous people, the life enhancers, the people who look interesting and smell luscious and who dare to be gorgeously more fascinating than their neighbors?"[13] As a book that tells the story of fashion, appearance, and self-styling, Fabulous is not a militant manifesto of appearance. I'm not arguing that all people need to get fabulous right now or suffer the consequences (and look terrible too). Fabulousness would be boring if everyone did it. So no, I'm afraid this book will not make you fabulous. Some of us don't want to (or can't) be fabulous—and others, very often queer people, do. Fabulousness almost always stems from a turning point: the moment we realize that suppressing our full selves by trying to fit in does us more harm than good, that it just isn't working, even if sometimes we are forced to blend in to feel safe. Instead of thinking about how this book could make us fabulous, I'd prefer we recognize the ways we suppress ourselves and the toll that has on our emotional well-being. Fabulousness isn't just about sequins: it's what happens the second we stop trying to fit in and start daring to inhabit space on our own terms.

This is a very personal book. There have been days in my life when I've felt like an outsider, a black queer error, and it seemed like I couldn't go on without completely falling apart. I get bogged down by the stresses of living while black, working while black, and loving while black, but just when I felt like there was no way out of the depression, with its usual ebbs and flows, fashion and style were always there to lift me up. A little turquoise sequined jacket here, a black floor-length maxi skirt there. Every day fashion and style help me remember that my voice matters. I don't get dressed because I want to be stared and pointed at on the subway or while walking down the street. I would love to live in a world where I could wear whatever I wanted without getting verbally harassed, being followed, or fearing for my safety. But that's not the world we live in. Our world constantly reminds me that I shouldn't exist, so I dress the way I do to scream that I am here. Style lets me tell you about my vision of the world and my dreams for the day, even if the structures that produce my depression don't evaporate just because I'm wearing my favorite sequined jacket. At least I can wear it and say to myself: Today is going to be a good day.

The stories in this book take solace in the creative and think clearly about how marginalized people rise up out of the ashes. Sarah Lewis, a cultural critic and curator based at Harvard, argues in *The Rise: Creativity, the Gift of Failure, and the Search for Mastery* that all forms of creative brilliance emerge from a sort of improbable rise. "Brilliant inventions," she writes, "involve a path aided by the possibility of setbacks and the inestimable gains that experience can provide."[14] "You may trod me in the very dirt," the poet Maya Angelou wrote in *Still I Rise*,

> **But still, like dust, I'll rise**
> **Does my sassiness upset you?**
> **Why are you beset with gloom?**
> **'Cause I walk like I've got oil wells**
> **Pumping in my living room.**[15]

Here is a beautiful poem that is as much about the richness and expansive creativity of black people as it is about rising up out of the ashes and turning that journey into something beautiful. It centers on the optimism of never allowing yourself to be reduced to the dirt we get dragged through day by day, because the moment we lower our heads, give in and suppress ourselves, the system wins. When we give up, the system is reified.

The thing I always say about marginalized people is that we are not actually marginal. Social codes, laws, norms, and other pathologies beat up on us and take us out of the center. But even as systems get scared and throw us to the margins, we use imagination as the best revenge. Following Maya Angelou and Sarah Lewis, I'm articulating an optimistic, real-time cultural theory that privileges possibility over impossibility and creative expression over victimhood. Robin D. G. Kelley aims for the utopian, creative possibilities of blackness as a "revolution of the mind." For Kelley, it's important that brown bodies are not simply victimized because of the turbulence and unbridled violence of living while black. The revolution he imagines is one of creativity and dreaming. "I am talking about an unleashing of the mind's most creative capacities," he writes, "catalyzed by participation in struggles for change." For Kelley, the creative is a political act.[16] I'm in line with Greg Tate, who writes poetically that black people are "damaged goods, a people whose central struggle has been overcoming the nonperson status we got stamped and stomped into." For Tate, the upside to being "damaged goods" is that black people are inspired to take the oppressions of everyday life and "re-create the world anew every Goddamn day."[17] And I agree with Francesca Royster, whose work on black eccentricity paves the way for thinking about how black artists use creative agency to make a place for themselves when a place in real life isn't always given. "Through acts of spectacular creativity," she writes, "the eccentric joins forces with the 'queer, 'freak,' and 'pervert' to see around corners," and by doing so they "push the edges of the present to create a language not yet recognized: new sounds, new dances, new configurations of self—the makings of a black utopia."[18] I don't want to overlook the struggles and violence of living while brown, queer, or trans, but I am interested in how people forced to the margins assert themselves anyway despite the dangers and the odds. Fabulousness is about rising up out of the ashes, flipping the bird to the norms that have burned us, and excelling as the best possible revenge.

One common misconception about fabulousness is that it is just

A performance image of Portland-based drag queen Faun Dae, winner of Critical Mascara: A Post-Realness Drag Extravaganza as part of the Time-Based Art Festival at the Portland Institute for Contemporary Art in September 2015. (Courtesy of Faun Dae and Sophia Wright Emigh.)

about gay men channeling femininity. That's because in a post–*RuPaul's Drag Race* moment men in drag are seemingly more visible than ever. When we say fabulousness is simply men in drag we're really promoting an essentialist idea that femininity belongs to women and masculinity belongs to men, case closed. This is the source of much transphobic violence, to be sure, but it also obscures the glorious powers of abstraction, eccentricity, fantasy, futurism, and even the wild nature of a fabulous aesthetic. Drag queens like the San Francisco-based performance artist Fauxnique, the London-based artist Victoria Sin, and the Portland-based Faun Dae show that not all interrogations of femininity are practiced by cisgender gay men. All forms of drag practiced by all genders and nonbinary people are equally potent critiques of gender.

Victoria Sin, for instance, is deeply inspired by the New York nightlife icon Amanda Lepore, who herself is inspired by both Marilyn Monroe and the cartoon figure Jessica Rabbit. In *Define Gender: Victoria*

Sin, a 2017 video portrait of the artist directed by Amrou Al-Kadhi, Sin speaks powerfully about the ways in which femininity exalts them. "It's not that I'm shy or that I don't know how to assert myself," they narrate in the video portrait. "It's that I'm tired of pushing back against subtle violations of my femininity. As femmes we often change ourselves and adjust our behavior to carry the weight of how femme bodies are treated in society." In a world that relegates femmes to the margins every day, femme bodies often move through the social world in less amplified ways, all in the name of safety. The beauty of Sin's drag persona and art practice is in how "femininity," filtered and constructed as it is, sits absolutely at the center, and it all boils down to the wig. "When I put on my wig," Victoria narrates, "I am taller. My wig is huge. It is in your way. Its presence makes you step aside." "My wig is enormous," they continue, and "the bigger the hair, the larger the space I occupy. It was always my space, but now you are aware that you are in it, and you move aside. My wig is huge. It helps me to take up space so that you cannot not see me. You cannot dismiss me."[19]

There is a long history in Western capitalist societies of women being looked at and spectacularized in ways that oppress them. For the British film theorist Laura Mulvey, women are framed "to connote to-be-looked-at-ness, meaning men actively look whereas women are styled in visual media specifically to be looked at."[20] I'm reminded here of the so-called Hooters for Intellectuals live performance events of contemporary artist Vanessa Beecroft, a work like *vb46* from 2007, in which an army of white-haired women stand completely nude except for heels.[21] Part live high-fashion photographic event, part critique of "to-be-looked-at-ness," Beecroft's performances feature women who seem unavailable, even bored. Thorstein Veblen, who was an early theorist of how women's fashion was less about personal style and more about allowing men to show that they owned women, felt that fashion guaranteed women were seen as prize trophies for those men who succeeded at capitalism, even offering one of the first definitions of the "trophy wife."[22]

Instead of strictly adhering to or circulating hard-edged notions of "male" or "female," I'm convinced that fabulousness wants us to get past gender, to abstract it, to end it altogether. I follow thinkers like Susan

Stryker, who positions gender as porous, permeable, and open-ended, and David Getsy, who feels that abstraction offers a less determined way to think about our relationship to gender.[23] Taking a cue from artists like Alok Vaid-Menon, I think fabulousness offers a fourth space, a separate dimension where gender meets an end and where bodies are abstracted. "How do we actually *end gender,*" they ask in an interview that follows this chapter, "so that we don't actually have to have such a reductive conversation of 'gay man' 'performing femininity' and instead have 'person' 'being transcendental'?" For Alok, boredom is one of the most oppressive aspects of not doing fabulousness. "I always say let's add *boring* to our list of oppressor identities: cis, white, straight, *boring* men. The truth is I don't want to dress this way not just because I'm trans. It's because I don't want to be *boring!*" Banishing boredom is the difference fabulousness makes. When queer and trans people of color do fabulousness, they rarely look bored. Think again of the low-key performances of Madaew Fashionista. He finds joy in the pose and in rejecting masculinity. He is saved from the strict confines of patriarchal masculinity, a dominant force in straight culture that is even more oppressive in mainstream contemporary gay male culture, as seen in the obsession with "masculinity" on gay sex apps like Grindr. The brilliance of fabulousness as an embodied aesthetic is in how it actually exposes the bland, boring nature of rote masculinity.

Fabulousness lets us tap out of toxic masculinity, and that means it's less about upholding or adhering to any gender norms and more about ending gender through what I'll call "creative strangeness." At its heart, creative strangeness is simple: it is a style that surprises because it makes fashion out of things that are not made for fashion, or it merges things together in unexpected ways. You're supposed to burn wood, not wear it. Your hair should be brown, not teal with black roots. Purple eyebrows? Wow! A creatively strange look is edgy. It doesn't make sense because being creatively strange means taking something from one context and suddenly giving it a fashion meaning, much as Madaew Fashionista turned pots and pans into a full look, even posing with a spoon to maximize the oomph. Creative strangeness, a fashion aesthetic/event you'll find everywhere from club kids and other eccentrics to vogue balls and high-fashion editorials, is about confusion, neither male nor female, and its strangeness has to do with how it messes things up or creates a kind of chaos. Creative strangeness is disorienting, not unlike the way the artist T. L. Cowan uses glitter as a resistant, disorienting quality. The whole point of glitter, she writes in the GLITTERfesto, "is to transform public space into a funhouse mirror room full of tiny disco balls."[24] Glitter disorients, creates a kaleidoscope, and spins rapidly. Creative strangeness, another arm of glitter theory, disorients and puts us on the cutting edge of identity—the cutting edge of something that is already unstable. You can see it in a popular look in the 1970s and 1980s known as "gender fuck." As fashion historian Shaun Cole has shown, gender fuck is a style of drag that puts male and female clothing together in a way that actually confuses or waters down the way gender is read from the clothes, the point being that they're just clothes. Gender fuck was not about doing femininity but was more a way to "get away from the hard-edged definitions of gendered dress" and it used "conflicting signals to challenge and confuse heterosexual society."[25]

I'm thinking of an image like *RuPaul Is Everything!,* a 1986 photograph of the famous drag queen shot in Atlanta, Georgia, in which RuPaul works a mohawk and is nude except for one black fishnet glove, a pair of high worker boots, football shoulder pads, and a jockstrap, effortlessly worn with a black belt on top. This image is certainly not about femininity. It is about creative strangeness, taking something "masculine" like football shoulder pads and giving them a new high-concept fashion meaning. The point of a fabulous style, the American fashion photographer Bill Cunningham said in 1983, "is to mix unexpected elements into a highly original and aesthetic design worn with enormous personal style and dash. This world of free-spirited fashion is not for shy, timid souls; nor is it for those concerned with their neighbors' comments."[26] This kind of creative strangeness describes the young black queer club kid I saw waiting to get into the Boom Boom Room nightclub at the Standard Hotel in New York on a summer evening in 2010. He wore a straitjacket, fishnet stockings, a pair of heels, and no pants. Who wears a straitjacket as fashion? Someone fabulous, that's who.

All forms of beautiful eccentricity put the body on the cutting edge of identity, and this is why it is a meaningful aesthetic. It is a way of working (*snap!*) the self, despite the odds, and for maximum emotional impact. Anthropologist Martin Manalansan IV, in new research on "fabulosity," tells the story of a group of queer undocumented immigrants in Queens, New York, whom he calls "the Queer 6," who use fabulousness as a process of "ethical self-making." In his words, "Fabulosity is creating and realizing a self through and despite an existence on the fringes of low pay, drudgery of public transportation, and inhabiting dingy apartments. It is about storymaking and narration, the act of narrating selves in these forms of contingency."[27] The most important thing about fabulousness, I find, is that it is a special kind of embodied creative genius largely expressed by people who do not fit in, who have been forced to the margins, and who are not cisgendered, white, male, and straight. It is no wonder that the people most inclined to do fabulous performance almost always emerge from marginalized backgrounds—they are poor, gay, lesbian, or trans, outcasts, of color—and they splash on glitter and sequins to parade themselves in the club, on the street, and in photographs. Echoing Manalansan's theory of fashion as ethical self-making, *beautiful eccentrics* look forward to every new chance they get to use fashion and performance to say that they are not their marginalization. Fabulousness, as the fashion theorist Carol Tulloch might say, offers an agency that shows how selves are created through a range of craft-making practices that are applied directly to the body.[28]

But why *not* just fit in? Why not just be "normal"? In 2014 clothing retailer Gap ran a global brand campaign asking its customer base to "Dress Normal." David Fincher, the brains behind *The Social Network* and the $100 million Netflix series *House of Cards,* directed a number of sexy, celebrity-studded TV commercials for the campaign, all shot in black and white. Tag lines included phrases like "Simple clothes for you to complicate" and "Dress like no one's watching." On September 18, 2014, the brand even tweeted, "Let your actions speak louder than your clothes."[29] Unfortunately, the campaign failed despite the red-hot sex appeal and A-list celebrity charge surrounding the ads. November 2014 sales for the brand dropped 4 percent and media outlets uniformly slammed the clothes as too boring.[30] "Dress like no one's watching? More like, sell like no one's shopping," *New York* magazine sassed.[31] *Jezebel* called the clothes "blah," and *Buzzfeed* said they were "way too normal."[32] The lesson here is that, as much pressure as there is to be normal, to fit in and blend in, from a purely numbers perspective normal does not always sell.

What can I say? It pays to be fab. As an embodied aesthetic category, one that is not about fitting in but about creating what Sianne Ngai has called "a distinctive kind of aesthetic subject," fabulousness appeals to us because it is exciting, interesting. When we find something interesting it means stumbling on the unexpected and looking at it again and again. For Ngai, "Interest has the capacity for duration and is fundamentally recursive, returning us to the object for another look." It is "a dynamic that makes the interesting not just about the unexpected but also about the familiar, not just about difference but also about repetition."[33] In its invitation to *look*, fabulousness becomes "interesting" because it seduces the senses, encouraging repeated glances. But if being normal is about blending in and if fabulousness is about the exciting and interesting, what does it take to look *fabulous?* Does it mean wearing a certain type of gown or the design of a big-name fashion house? Is it a trendy haircut or an expensive handbag?

Patricia Field, the iconic downtown New York fashion stylist and costume designer known for her work on *Sex and the City,* told me that fabulousness is not something you can purchase: "Fabulousness is something that catches the eye. The reason it catches the eye is that it is unique and has not been seen before. If you see 1 million pairs of jeans and a polo shirt it's not fabulous. You've seen it before. Fabulousness is creating a story, a narrative, a meaning around the way you present yourself as to who you are and what you are presenting. Jeans and polo shirts are not presenting anything. They're just covering their bodies because it's our custom not to go running around naked."[34] For Field, fabulousness means creating a story, telling a narrative about who we are. It is a specialness, a uniqueness that arrests us visually because we have not seen anything like it.

This is the point where Field, whose fashion styling is celebrated for its embrace of theatricality, joins the influential theater historian Herbert Blau, who knew there was a deep relationship between fashion and performance. He used examples from the theater to show how fashion is a mode of performance we usually write off as ridiculous, an "insubstantial pageant," as "nothing coming of nothing," when in fact people love fashion and costume because they feed the eyes. Fashion tells a story. It is an exciting system of pleasure that we enjoy because of the way it forces us to look at and notice one another, what Blau thinks of as dressing to "incite the look"—or what I would describe as simply turning heads, "working it."[35]

Fabulousness is important because it shows how marginalized bodies create art and beauty in states of duress—a creativity from the margins. That duress highlights the violence brown, queer, and other disenfranchised bodies face as they figure out how to survive within a system of power that keeps whiteness, heterosexuality, masculinity, and patriarchy intact. As T. L. Cowan writes powerfully in the *GLITTERfesto*, glitter is fabulous because it wants "to create a queer space where white supremacy and male supremacy are rendered ridiculous." Now that's a world I'd like to live in! As a confrontational form of self-presentation, fabulousness is a practice of everyday life that black, queer, and other people forced to the margins have used to protect some form of autonomy in their day-to-day experience. I may be disempowered by capitalism, but I will empower myself through my ideas and creativity. Black feminist theorist Cathy Cohen sees an important difference between *defiant* acts and *merely deviant* ones. In one study on the power of rebellion as resistance, Cohen wrote that not all acts of deviance are strategies of resistance to oppression and duress. You might make a choice that pressures against cultural rules, but "every counter normative defiant act is not political, either in intent, result, or both, where political resistance is the intent to defy laws, interactions, obligations, and normative assumptions viewed as systematically unfair."[36] Her point is fair enough. For instance, fabulousness itself will not change laws to protect trans kids. Fabulousness does not pay the rent or put food on the table. You can't say to your landlord, "I don't have any rent money this month but hey, I'm fabulous!" So no, not every defiant act will rustle the cultural order or have immediate or lasting power, but I think what Cohen overlooks is the effect that defiant acts of *fashion* have on people. There is serious risk involved when we choose to present ourselves in public in a way that is decidedly outside of the established cultural order, a risk that can often lead to homophobic or transphobic violence.

At the heart of fabulousness is a philosophy of creativity that has many things in common with the gay sensibility of camp, in particular its commitment to style and extravagance. But there is a major difference. As Susan Sontag famously wrote, "Camp is a certain mode of aestheticism. It is one way of seeing the world as an aesthetic phenomenon. That way, the way of Camp, is not in terms of beauty, but in terms of the degree of artifice, of stylization."[37] Even Jack Babuscio, in an article reclaiming the gayness of camp, which he felt Sontag purposefully omitted from her essay, shows how camp is "a view of art; a view of life; and a practical tendency in things or persons."[38] The difference is that fabulousness is never there just for the sake of being fabulous. It is never just art for art's sake, nor is it style over content. When you are brown, queer, and eccentric in appearance, fabulousness *is* the political content. Fabulousness is art created in states of duress, and this is its political edge. When you are brown, queer, or an outcast—already a moving target—fabulousness *is* the politic. It is glitter as defiance—think of glitter bombing—and this sense of confrontation separates it from camp, which Sontag described as apolitical.

Being fabulous in public space is risky. When Leo GuGu, a New York City–based black queer nightlife personality, hails a cab, all while serving a strong look, he is a defiant apparition, whether he intended to be political or not. Even if he had no interest in using fashion to stage a commentary about gender, race, sexuality, or disenfranchisement—even *if* it was just pure creative expression, a "show"—he is still giving a powerful performance, perhaps a dangerous one, a danger that is amplified when he is dressed in a way that encourages physical and verbal kinds of homophobic violence.

At the heart of all this is self-styling, a term often used in fashion discourse to describe how we dress for the social world. But fabulousness does not come easy. Nobody "woke up like this," as Beyoncé suggests in her 2014 single "***Flawless." The labor that goes into stories of fabulousness requires talent—an "eye"—and the look must be thought about and conceptualized, tweaked and edited. As a queer aesthetic category, fabulousness requires aesthetic labor and "work," or what I have come to think of as work with an "e" (*snap!*).

The art critic John Berger once said that seeing might establish our place in the world, but as soon as we can see we also learn that other people are looking at us.[39] Seeing means more than looking—it's knowing how to look. That's why fabulousness does more than just style the self. New York nightlife impresario Susanne Bartsch told me that for her, fashion is *self-couture*, "a visual form of self-expression. Part stylist, part fashion design, part tailor, part makeup artist, part hairstylist, part milliner, part manicurist, part taxidermist, part shock art, part haute couture."[40] Self-couture here means being a one-person theatrical production: you create every aspect of the look from scratch, inhabiting multiple creative roles at the same time. Making your own headpieces, doing your own makeup, finding looks, or creating your own clothes, constantly adorning yourself. Thinking about fabulousness as self-couture helps us understand the labor that goes into producing a single *look*. But self-couture also means a *couturing* of the self, where the word *couture* also suggests exclusivity—insurance that what we are seeing is unusual, one of a kind.

I'd like to point out one last trait of fabulousness: *critical mascara*. This is a term I learned from Pepper Pepper, a Portland, Oregon–based art house drag queen and performance artist who ran an epic party called Critical Mascara, a yearly drag ball that was always the highlight of the Time-Based Art Festival at the Portland Institute for Contemporary Art. If fabulousness is about how art and beauty are created in states of duress, then *critical mascara* is the end product of fabulousness. It is *critical* because it uses fashion, creativity, and the body to revise and reshape prescribed gender roles. It is critical because it critiques both white supremacy and the patriarchy—it abstracts and does away with them altogether. As Dick Hebdige has written, style is always significant because of the way it challenges "the myth of consensus." When style confronts hegemony the challenge is issued "obliquely, in style" and done so in a way to "offend the silent majority."[41] *Mascara*, on the other hand, is one tool of fabulousness, a single brush stroke that facilitates self-couture. With strokes of *critical mascara*, it's possible to be critical and look great too!

In September 2014 Pepper invited me to be a "celebrity guest judge" at Critical Mascara, an extravaganza that is part competition, part dance party, and part queer spectacle. The only panels I'd been on until then were academic, so I was really excited and immediately started panicking about what to wear. I arrive by taxi in my "boy" clothes (#safety) and head straight to the greenroom, where I get changed into my actual look: an oversized, bright yellow blazer with big pads in the shoulders. I love a shoulder pad. I found the blazer at a Goodwill in Carbondale, Illinois, for $2, a steal. I'm bold and decide to wear black boxer briefs as pants—actually three pairs so I don't expose myself *too* much—fishnet thigh-highs (I'm careful not to puncture any holes in the fishnets with my toes or else the look is ruined), no shirt (though I have splashed blue glitter all over my chest), and pointy black stiletto pumps with platinum silver heels. I'm cocoa-buttered from here to eternity, and when I walk out of the greenroom into a pre-event reception a black queer comrade sees me and shakes his head in excitement, an affirmation. "Mmm hmm! Mmm hmm! You better slay!" he says.

There is no centralized physical archive of fabulousness, no major author, no all-in-one site to see and study it because it is a quality that moves across time, media, and space. That's why this book is not a *history* of fabulousness but a *theory* of fabulousness as a form of creativity from the margins. It's one thing to "be" fabulous or "look" fabulous, but it's another to understand where fabulousness comes from. And you can't understand fabulousness unless you get that it emerges from trauma, duress, exclusion, exhaustion, and depression, and that in some ways being fabulous is the only thing that can get us out of bed in the morning. Sometimes that little jolt of creativity is all we've got.

The stakes of fabulous eccentricity are that at the same time that brown, queer, and trans bodies express, feel good about, and expand ourselves through fabulousness and self-styling, that joy is subject to surveillance, torture, and ridicule by homonormative, heteronormative, misogynist, and patriarchal systems every single day, from the workplace to our living rooms and from the dating app to the sidewalk. Read this part again if you need to, because these are the political stakes of fabulousness. It isn't about looking amazing or utopian aspiration. Fabulousness is always a unique set of aesthetic properties engaged by people who take the risk of making a spectacle of themselves—to stretch out and expand—when it would be much easier, though no less toxic, to be normative, as when Alok Vaid-Menon asks, "What feminine part of yourself did you have to kill to survive in this world?" If fabulous eccentrics played by the rules and fit in, then they wouldn't have to worry about being harassed or feeling unsafe on the sidewalks. At the end of the day, the question fabulousness asks all of us is: When can we have a world where it will be safe to just be me, where I don't have to be depressed because my body doesn't fit in with norms and ideals that never had me in mind in the first place?

I want us to bring Pepper's term *critical mascara* into the way we think about style, identity, and queer aesthetics. Critical mascara offers more than simply utopian aspiration. It comes with risk, and the main point I'll stress throughout this book is that style and fashion are always political choices. Knowing you could get in trouble for what you wear and doing it anyway—this is the dangerous act of fabulousness as a type of critical mascara. Critical/mascara—an adjective and a noun that, taken together as a theoretical concept, spell out the urgency of fabulousness as an embodied queer aesthetic practice. The "critical" part means being skeptical of body or gender norms and having a demonstrated commitment to using art, media, performance, and the body to destabilize them. "Mascara," on the other hand, is a tool of fabulousness, one of many, a metaphor about how style is used to expand and exaggerate. The "critical" in *critical mascara* is an undoing; the "mascara" is about the pleasure of style.

Spectacular style is not necessarily about parading financial status or posturing a heightened social position. The implications of "fabulousness" as a type of creative outlet become clear when looking at the origins of the word *fabulous*. The etymology of the term is *fabulosus*, Latin for "fable." One definition of fabulous is "of a person (or anything personified): Fond of relating fables or legends, given to fabling."[42] Another definition of fabulous is "such as is met with only in fable; beyond the usual range of fact; astonishing, incredible." By 1546 the English dramatist John Bale had already used the term *fabulouse* in *The Acts of Englysh Votaryes*, and in Shakespeare's play *Henry VI*, a bit of news is described as "fabulous and false."[43] Today, scholars like Tavia Nyong'o have developed concepts of "fabulation" as a way to capture "the not yet, the people who are missing."[44] What is notable is that all these uses of the word are related to stories, to make-believe and fables, and this shows how fabulousness is about using fashion to tell a one-of-a-kind narrative.

I think fabulousness is mythical because it lives way beyond the expanse of the believable and what the mind has been prepared to process. "Fabulousness," the *OED* says, is "the quality or state of being fabulous . . . proneness to fiction or invention."[45] What this means is that fabulousness is already on the outskirts of normalcy and social custom because of the way it is already exaggerated beyond belief. It is about how people craft intricate selves in contemporary everyday life. Not unlike tall tales themselves, beautiful eccentrics use their bodies and imaginations to tell big stories and to create their own myths. Fabulousness radiates an otherworldly, nonconforming, alien, and mythical self that startles and captivates us aesthetically because it stretches what we think is possible.

If the word *fabulous* is about bodies and mythmaking it is also an umbrella term that captures an entire lexicon of catchphrases that enunciate the visceral nature of spectacular looks: "work!" "fierce," "you *better* work," "working it," "giving me life," "it," "glamorous," "serving a look," "working a look," "conspicuous consumption," "gagging," "letting them have it," "living," "I live," "pseudo-events," "legendary," "serving," "sickening," "yaaass!" "slay," "amazing," "flawless," "the performance of leisure," "eat it!" "luxurious," "status panic," "everything," and "the currency of fabulousness." The majority of these terms were born in black gay culture. Both E. Patrick Johnson's masterful oral history *Sweet Tea: Black Gay Men of the South* and Marlon Bailey's deeply important *Butch Queens Up in Pumps: Gender, Performance and Ballroom Culture in Detroit* include a glossary of terms like these and describe how they are used in black queer spaces. Today, these phrases have been popularized, if not entirely gentrified, by mainstream popular culture and media hot spots like *RuPaul's Drag Race* and *Buzzfeed,* which in 2013 ran a listicle titled "22 Animals Who Are Like YAAAAAAAS!"[46] The article is funny because the images show animals with their mouths wide open—picture it—sort of like they're saying, "Yaaaaaas!" Number 6 in the article (a picture of a llama) seemed to have the most punch: "Oh you are workin' those shoes, honey, YAAAAAAAAS!"

Because these terms emerge from black gay culture, and particularly from the social world of voguing, we have the linguistic proof that people forced to the margins invest in looking fabulous as an expressive need when living under socioculturally induced states of duress.[47] These words are more about expression than economics and are certainly more nonconformist than conforming. Phrases like these are most effective as positive metaphors for the *joy* of living, such as "I'm *living!*" and "I *live!*," typically used when we are moved by a great outfit or look. "I'm living!" is especially telling because it celebrates life despite the escalating rate of trans violence, queer violence, and police brutality against brown bodies—in other words, people who in fact do *not* always get to live.

If you look closely you will find examples of fabulousness in nearly every pocket of contemporary popular, media, and visual culture. In the 2003 cult film *Party Monster,* a docu-movie about the lives and horrors of fabulous club life in New York City, Michael Alig's character desperately asks James St. James, then the queen of New York nightlife, to teach him how to be fabulous. *As if.* In 2006 former model and American businesswoman Kimora Lee Simmons wrote *Fabulosity: What It Is and How to Get It,* a self-help guide geared toward finding your best, most confident self (and then, no surprise, she trademarked the term *fabulosity*).[48] In London, bold ads for Wahanda, the UK's largest hair, makeover, and beauty book-

"Book Yourself Fabulous," a shot of the advertisement for Treatwell, formerly Wahanda, on the London Underground.

ing website, are splashed around the London Underground, telling commuters to "Book Yourself Fabulous."[49] And on television, popular shows like *Absolutely Fabulous, Sex and the City, America's Next Top Model, Make Me a Supermodel,* and now especially *RuPaul's Drag Race* have introduced fabulousness to the mainstream.

YouTube is one arena where fabulousness is visible and endlessly replayable. Take Chris Koo, a young dancer known online for his spot-on dance covers of pop songs. His most clicked video by far, with more than 5 million views, is his living room recording of Beyoncé's 2003 single "Crazy in Love," a clip that shows how tightly he has perfected the choreography while also adding his own "sickening" twists.[50] Then there's B. Scott, the biracial transgender North Carolina–bred YouTuber cum mainstream pop culture personality whose confessional videos cover everything from relationships and beauty to his time as a student at the University of North Carolina. One of my favorite videos is 2008's "I Went to the Doctor Today!," where going to the doctor is a metaphor for getting a hot new hairstyle, in this case a chin-hugging silky bob with razor sharp edges:

> **Do you like my style? Mmm, aaah. *Yes,* baby! I got a nice little haircut. Do y'all see it? Do you see it, baby? I had to go to the doctor today, *I had to go to the doctor!* Yes. And not because I had the flu but *none other* because I had to fix this hair, honey. I had to give you something *else.* Look at it [*he swings his freshly pressed hair, admires it*], it . . . oooh. I can't get my hands off of it. Ladies, have you ever been that way? When you get a new style you just wanna touch it? You just wanna feel it? And check out the back, baby [*he turns around to show the back*]. Oh, it is werking, it is *werking.* Let me say this, can I go ahead and say this? *Legendary.*[51]**

He looks great, and what I love about this performance is how in his "feminine" hairstyle he is an unapologetic spectacle of black queerness. His monologue is really about the joy of loving the way you look and of knowing that you are expressing yourself just the way you feel. You-Tube performances of fabulousness are unique because they are more about personal confession and creating a platform to showcase uniqueness, particularly in a studio and network system that still privileges whiteness and masculinity and usually does not make space for brownness and queerness.

But I also love the way B. Scott says "It is *werking*" as he gives us a glimpse of his new hairstyle. There is a crucial difference between *work* and *werk,* a term that gets used all the time in queer popular culture. That little "e" is the distance between the stuff we don't want to do but have to in order to live and pay our bills (work) and the love and labor we do because we want to (werk). This is one of the most circulated slang terms in contemporary black gay male culture, one that Henry Louis Gates might see as a kind of "signifyin(g)."[52] In Jennie Livingston's *Paris Is Burning*, a well-known documentary about the New York voguing scene in the 1980s, for instance, one of the first words we hear is "*Werk!*" which an off-camera personality screams at the top of his lungs for Pepper LaBeija as she strolls down the catwalk in a golden, futuristic look that would give Lady Gaga a run for her money. This opening moment of the film has always struck me for the ways it suggests the joy of working hard to look fabulous. By 1993 American celebrity drag queen RuPaul brings "Werk!" to households everywhere with her chart-topping club single "Supermodel (You Betta Work!)." Even her 2010 autobiographical style manual is titled *Workin' It*. When RuPaul tells us we "Betta Work," what are we actually supposed to do? What are we working? And what does it mean in this context to tell a brown body, a body frequently exploited for labor, to work?

Werk taps into what Yale performance theorist Joseph Roach calls "reclaimed labor."[53] All told, werk is about creativity, virtuosity, and a certain kind of mastery. Werk is a type of aesthetic labor actually seen on the body, and it highlights the effort that goes into making memorable aesthetic moments happen. In queer spaces "Werk!" is almost always meant as a compliment to an aesthetic situation—a look, a hairstyle, a dance move. In an early essay on the black gay male subcultural practice of "reading," even performance theorist E. Patrick Johnson shows how "work" is exciting because of how it responds positively to creativity. To say that someone is *werking* is to say, "Girl you are wearin' that dress! SNAP! . . . Work, girl. Work! (SNAP! SNAP! SNAP!)."[54] Werk, even when it is not produced in ideal situations, and even when it involves sweat and bruises, means the investment of time, love, and skill into one's own work and, to line up with Roach, this type of reclaimed labor gives creative people "an exhilarating kind of freedom."[55]

For queer people, werk is an articulation of self in everyday life. It's what Carol Tulloch sees as "style narratives," personal style moments that "expound an autobiography of oneself through the clothing choices an individual makes."[56] When I asked RoRo Morales, a New York–born, Portland-based chef, fashion designer, and former NYC club kid to describe to me the first time he felt fabulous, he came for my wig because the question implied there was a day in his life he was not fabulous: "I've always been *fabulous*. I work looks *everywhere*. I won't walk out of the house unless I'm in *something*. When I was thirteen and twelve and eleven I would wear fishnets to . . . school. I didn't give a fuck. I just never thought it was strange. My family just embraced me as I was. So the fabulous part, I feel, has always been there. I have pictures of myself at twelve and thirteen, full face of makeup, fishnet stockings, six-inch high heels, and I'm going to *school*."[57] For RoRo, there was never a question that he would be anything but fabulous. Why should he act in a way that masks how he really feels? As a queer Puerto Rican boy who grew up in Queens, New York, fabulousness was an aesthetic essence he felt inside from a fairly young age. But it was also a method of survival. Instead of conforming to masculine gender ideals during the day and sneaking into fishnets and a face full of makeup in secret, RoRo one-upped his social position and used fabulousness as a way to claim back his personhood. For RoRo, style was an affirmation of self and a flight from social conformity.

Any "theory" of eccentric style needs to think about how it works as lived experience—how it is actually done—but not in a way that takes lived experience as the last word. Obviously our lived experience offers a rich, personal archive of everyday life, but we should also be sensitive to the ways those experiences are produced and framed. And this means thinking about the systems that create the experiences we have.[58] Lived experience transforms fabulousness from a heady, abstract theory into something that happens right before our eyes and that wields certain real-time consequences. I agree with Sianne Ngai, for whom writing about aesthetic categories is not just about "exotic philosophical abstractions," as fun as it can be to think big and play with abstract concepts, but instead a part of the fabric of the everyday. Thinking about aesthetics allows us to share and confirm our experiences with others.[59]

Though there are many theaters where fabulousness comes to life—restaurants, red carpet ceremonies, beauty pageants, drag shows, and church services—my search for fabulousness has led me to certain specific social worlds: the street, the selfie, the nightclub, and the vogue ball. Each of these spaces is a creative scene, an alternative world built around specialized knowledge of what's "hot" in that world. These scenes show that fabulousness is a mode of creative expression, an aesthetic need that is typically employed by people responding to oppressive or otherwise restrictive sociocultural conditions. Being fabulous works against the fear of irrelevance, boredom, impermanence, and invisibility in a postmodern culture of hyper-visibility, immediate sensations, and instantaneous connectivity.

Fabulousness, at its heart, is an expression of visibility for people who are made invisible. Yet some have warned against too much visibility. "Visibility is a trap," performance theorist Peggy Phelan once observed, and the performance artist Alok Vaid-Menon picks up on her claim when they ask, "Do trans people have to be fabulous to matter?"[60] Increased visibility does not necessarily bring increased power with it. Disenfranchised bodies—now made fully visible—will not suddenly feel at ease the moment they see their images in representational media. If this were the case, "then almost-naked young white women should be running Western culture," Phelan wrote humorously. Heightened visibility is a trap: as an imagined, discursive form, vision itself is always already flawed because it encourages surveillance, framing, fetishism, and voyeurism.[61] If I can see you, then I can also keep tabs on you. But what happens when we take control of our own image as a way of returning the gaze, not to be passively looked at but to do the looking ourselves?

We are talking about how art and beauty are created in duress, and I have found that the people most likely to do fabulous performance are either those who, though well-off, feel hemmed in by conservative conditions or, alternatively, those who have in some way faced historically conditioned, systemic oppression. Although ethnic, gendered, and sexual marginalization are more visible, other kinds of other restrictive containments can give rise to beautiful eccentricity too. Bad girl and Andy Warhol's muse Edie Sedgwick, for instance, whom he often described as "fabulous," was notoriously kicked out of her family when she refused to follow the path of a wealthy heiress. She retaliated by going out in fur coats, oversized earrings, underwear, and T-shirts—almost nude and without pants. Contemporary heiresses such as Daphne Guinness are evidence of the ways that being freed from a limited space makes us prone to finally be ourselves. The thirst for freedom is a very human quality. When we get out of a bad relationship, for instance, we feel liberated to finally do all the things we didn't feel able to do. In the catalogue for *Daphne Guinness*, an exhibition of her stunning wardrobe held at the Fashion Institute of Technology in 2011, Guinness describes being locked in an oppressive marriage and how she blossomed into her own once she was untangled from it.[62] As amazing as Edie Sedgwick and Daphne Guinness are, and as impeccable as they look, there's no denying that they are nonetheless tied to a system of privilege, wealth, whiteness, and resources that makes the thrust of their eccentricity less potent than someone with creativity from the margins, even if their expressions of creativity have the same impact in a room. Not all beautiful eccentrics are brown, queer, or trans, but there's a safety built into white and heteronormative expressions of eccentricity that brown, queer, and trans bodies do not get to access.

For them, the articulation of self is urgent for survival in everyday life in a society that constantly says you shouldn't exist. This was the point of Rebecca Walker's anthology on black cool, which includes a powerful essay that captures the essence of fabulous appearance as a mode of combat for disenfranchised bodies. In "Resistance," image activist Michaela angela Davis writes that "black style is an intelligence of the soul." It was the one thing that did not get kicked, choked, or raped out of black people. "It couldn't be burned up or shot up or locked up. You can't fuck it up." Black style is a kind of genius that is indestructible and oppression only makes it stronger.[63] Defiant, fabulous appearances are usually a direct response to these kinds of restrictive conditions. Voguing or house ball culture, for instance, looks like people dressing in outrageous looks and dancing in a unique style that often evokes the fluidity of model poses. But it emerged out of the desire on the part of black and Latino gay youths to form their own familial units in the face of homophobia and to live the imagined life of models and movie stars, even if only for a moment. This is a merging of fashion, self-couture, creative labor, and performance not merely out of status panic, but as an exhilarating, expressive need.

Style is almost always about possibility. Given all the options of what to wear tonight, what will I choose? "It is my belief that minoritarian subjects," the late queer theorist José Muñoz once wrote, "are cast as hopeless in a world without utopia."[64] What he means is that without utopia, people forced to the margins are stuck with the systems that oppress us in our daily lives. Utopias may not overhaul systems of oppression, but at the very least they give us something to look forward to, and they allow us to work toward other possibilities in the here and now. In a world that denies people forced to the margins nearly everything, without possibility, dreams, nightclubs, fashion, music, good food, good sex, and good community, there's almost nothing left. For Muñoz, utopia is the one thing that allows marginalized people to imagine a different kind of future, a future full of possibility. When we think about people who dress up in wild outfits, seek solace in the nightclub, and are celebrated for their larger-than-life presence, we see how ordinary people reshape the raw material of daily life to produce new aesthetic forms in response to the terribleness of the everyday. This helps us understand how people refuse to accept the laws of the social world at face value, turning to art to create separate possibilities and dimensions in the here and now.

Every book has a jumping-off point, a theoretical idea, a text or an artwork that sparks the imagination and gets the ideas up and moving. For me, that point was embodied in the turn-of-the-twentieth-century social economist Thorstein Veblen, a Yale University–trained academic whose ideas I discovered as a Yale graduate student and who helped set my ideas about spectacle in motion. Actually, you could say two theorists shaped my ideas: Veblen and RuPaul. If you've heard the term *conspicuous consumption* or seen a person carry a designer handbag with the logo scrawled across the front in a giant font, you already know a lot about Veblen. He was best known for a book published in 1899 called *The Theory of the Leisure Class* in which he lays out his claims about the ways that conspicuousness, spectacle, and over-the-topness connect to power. The book was published less than two years after the opening of the sumptuous Waldorf Astoria Hotel in New York City. *The Theory of the Leisure Class* made such a splash that it inspired of-the-moment novelists like Edith Wharton, Theodore Dreiser, Henry James, and Marcel Proust to write fictional illustrations of Veblen's teachings about the role of appearance. One critic described Veblen's book as "an opportunity for American fiction," a chance for writers to fictionalize Veblen's economic theories.[65] His ability to see beyond the dazzling surface of things shows how he was able to offer up a theory of the leisure class, and it is telling that the boldest analysis of wealth and its patterns of consumption was written by a critic who was the child of immigrants and who grew up in a simple agrarian household where luxuries were not tolerated. As Veblen's fictional mother Kari Bunde Veblen says in the economist Leonard Silk's posthumous 1966 satirical play *Veblen: A Play in Three Acts*, "All those Yankee women are good for is to dress up."[66]

The narrative of *The Theory of the Leisure Class* goes like this: leisure is the only job of the wealthy class, as opposed to the working or middle classes, so all the leisure class has to do is appear, exist. That's their only task. Of course, this is all wrapped up into a spirit of capitalism that rewards those who are able to seize the most, as if barbarians in a jungle. For Veblen, one of the defining features of the leisure class is the need to always look really rich, where looking that rich highlights a competitive ability to get more and better and bigger things than anybody else.[67] Under capitalism man hunts but he also requires physical evidence of his conquests, evidence that takes the form of "trophies"—stuff—that show off his prowess. He beats his chest and yells in triumph, and as he screams and yells, gold coins pour out of his mouth.

Veblen's theory of the leisure class is an alluring one because it is all about appearance. Clothes are the most visual artifacts available to convey messages about social standing. A high-society portrait like John Singer Sargent's *Mrs. Hugh Hammersley* (1892) gets straight to the point: a well-heeled woman of means luxuriates in a reddish-pink couture gown with ruffles around her neck. She crosses her legs, pointy gold shoes on. The rug is opulent, as is the chaise she gracefully leans on. There is an abundance of abundance in this image: an abundance of gold cloth behind her, framing her portrait, and the dress itself is so voluminous that the whole thing couldn't even be captured within the frame of the painting. No finger is lifted—not even one—and here the painting tells us, in unmistakable terms, that Mrs. Hugh Hammersley doesn't work. She is not only posing for the painter; she has the leisure to do so. Here's what Veblen would have said to Mrs. Hammersley if he had stormed into the room during her portrait sitting: "Our dress . . . should not only be expensive, but it should also make plain to all observers that the wearer is not engaged in any kind of productive labor."[68] Or, put plainly, Mrs. Hammersley is a show-off, bragging about her pocketbook and her luxury.

Fancy clothes are restrictive, binding, and otherwise totally ridiculous for everyday tasks. We can look at this painting of Mrs. Hammersley, which is ultimately a trophy, and feel certain that she is not about to mow the lawn in that dress. It's the clothes that drive home the message. Indeed, Veblen was always interested in the binding powers of clothing and once taught a seminar at the University of Chicago on the history of high heels, arguing that they were intended to bind women as yet another trophy item for men while also demonstrating the man's ability to pay.[69] Think of the stunning photo-realistic paintings of the contemporary American artist Marilyn Minter, a work like *Strut* (2005), a blown-up image of a dirty, bruised foot struggling to walk in a glamorous, diamond-laced Christian Dior heel. For Veblen, the high heel is added evidence of enforced leisure, an object that places women under house arrest. It is "obviously unfit for work."[70] While such apparel may make women attractive and expensive-looking, the trade-off is that it incapacitates the wearer, making her conspicuously exempt from manual labor and turning her into an object in the process.

Veblen focused on how fashion is used to communicate power by showing off, but what he missed is that when you are forced to the margins, drawing attention to yourself is an act of self-love. Veblen wrote about wealthy people who already have power, and that's fair enough. But using the effervescence of creative agency, style, and fabulousness allows marginalized people to empower themselves as a triple act of defiance, confidence, and self-love. For the fabulous, those beautiful eccentrics, a group of rogue creative individuals linked together by sensational style, the body is the canvas for creative expression, but it's never just style for style's sake. Eccentrics see norms but then use their bodies and aesthetics to displace and expose them.

Fabulous is a form of currency, there's no doubt about it. The catch is that a sickening outfit doesn't pay the rent. You can't give your landlord twenty thousand Instagram likes instead of the rent—cash money, honey! This kind of currency falls into what Elizabeth Currid-Halkett has called "the Warhol economy," an economic world of creativity where being at the right party or fashion show at the right time is just what you need to advance in the creative industries.[71] In our social media era, the more followers you have and the bigger the splash you can make online, the more chance you have to turn those followers' admiration into paid opportunities. More "likes" means more attention, which can often be translated into other forms of cultural and economic capital. If we can figure out how to get the attention of consumers and other passersby long enough to make them interested in a specific product, idea, or experience, then knowing how to get attention becomes an important type of currency.[72]

That's why fabulousness is a kind of "symbolic capital," a term the philosopher Pierre Bourdieu used to describe any alternative, nonmonetary form of capital that pops up and assumes value in a social group.[73] Symbolic capital works in all kinds of subcultural groups. Think of the secret gay hankie codes of the 1970s, whereby handkerchiefs of a certain color placed in a specific pocket indicated interest in a specific kind of sex—but only to those in the know. For Bourdieu, the sex appeal of symbolic capital lies in its world-making power and its ability to create alternate universes and systems of value.[74] The thing about these kinds of alternate universes is that the real world and the alternate universe both exist at the same time.

You don't need money to be fabulous. I can't give you a box of fabulousness, and there is no "poof—just add water!" product that can deliver instant fabulousness, even if it promises it can, so beware! Fabulousness is certainly a currency, as performance theorist Fiona Buckland has written. "In a queer life world," Buckland wrote in an important study of queer nightlife in New York during the 1990s, "being fabulous was hard currency. It was exchanged for belonging to a peer group, for being loved and desired, and for self-esteem."[75] Buckland was interested in how gay male clubbers used a "currency of fabulousness" to build community. Building off of Buckland, I would describe fabulousness this way: an idea-based creative transaction that is experienced in fleeting moments between people on the street, on the bus, or at the club. You can't buy it or transfer it but you can be fascinated by the thing. When the black queer downtown New York performer Leo GuGu puts on his ten-inch-high, gravity-defying, heel-less shoes and a giant glitter wig and rides the subway, he fascinates everyone. That moment of fascination, of inspiration, can't be bought or transferred. GuGu can inspire and fascinate, but fascination itself is not tangible. You can't hold a box of fascination. And when the iconic disco club Studio 54 opened in New York City in 1977 one theater producer said you had to be *fabulous* just to get past the velvet rope. Here the symbolic capital of fabulousness resulted in admission to the nightclub—you give me fabulousness and I let you in—but fabulousness can't be handed out like tote bags to everyone on the street.

Fabulousness is an intangible aura, a glow. But to pry an object from its shell, as Walter Benjamin once put it, is to destroy its aura.[76] This is key for thinking about fabulous appearances as unique, unbreakable auras that we can see, experience, and document, but which cannot be pried from the original source. The idea that someone's aura could be extracted perplexed even Andy Warhol, who once described how a brand approached him to buy his aura. "They didn't want my product. They kept saying, 'We want your aura.' I never figured out what they wanted. But they were willing to pay a lot for it. So then I thought that if somebody was willing to pay that much for my it, I should try to figure out what it is."[77]

All told, I think it helps to see fabulousness as a *gift*. In his 1923 essay *The Gift*, French sociologist Marcel Mauss explores the nature of gift-giving by challenging the long-held idea that we give gifts because we want to, without hoping for something in return. For Mauss, gift-giving is a bond of exchange. If I give you a token, then I have power over you until you give me something even better. These rites of exchange control the circulation of gifts, and Mauss even sees gift refusal as a declaration of war—"it is a refusal of friendship and intercourse."[78] For Mauss, gifts are based on capitalist exchange and are never simply given out of free will. We always want something back in return. What I love about fabulousness is that when we encounter it in the public sphere, it totally awakens our senses. We are taken aback, wowed, surprised, and inspired, and this is how it gets exchanged. Great style is a gift, an offering, and when we think about it this way we learn that having great style means constantly gifting away key parts of our nature but also that when we notice great style or compelling aesthetics, we're actually taking in that person's essence too.[79] Being eccentric means constantly giving a piece of yourself away, but it also means learning from others as a way to ramp up our own creative juices.

Honoré de Balzac's 1835 novel *Old Goriot* is the story of Eugène de Rastignac, a handsome boy from the south of France, who tells his parents that he wants to move to Paris to study law. But, like most teenagers, he has an ulterior motive: all he wants is to become a fixture of Parisian high society. If only it were that simple. Rastignac, who came from nothing, needs to look like a fashionable, well-dressed man if he really wants to make it. As Balzac wrote in his *Treatise on Modern Stimulants,* being fashionable was the only way to look civilized in a big, booming city like Paris. In Balzac's novels, fashion is a central narrative device used to highlight a character's personality as well as their motives and he took fashion so seriously that his *Human Comedy,* a series of interlinked novels and short stories written between 1830 and 1848, contains at least 375 clothing portraits.[80]

The first time the penniless yet ambitious Rastignac shows up at a fancy ball hosted by a high-powered distant relative, Madame la Vicomtesse de Beauséant, he discovers she is one of the most fashionable, connected women in all of nineteenth-century Paris. And with that, he is well on his way. "Being admitted to those glittering salons was tantamount to a certificate of the highest nobility," Balzac wrote. "By appearing in such company, the most exclusive of all, he had gained the right to go anywhere." Despite the fact that Rastignac is a poor student who lives in a hostel, everyone believes he belongs to the noble class. At the party he meets Madame Anastasie de Restaud and mentions he is related to Madame de Beauséant. Impressed, she invites him to stop by. Rastignac is excited. "What it is to be young, to have a thirst for the world, to be hungry for a woman and to see two grand houses open up to you! To have a foot in the door of the Vicomtesse de Beauséant's house in the Faubourg Saint-Germain and a knee in that of the Comtesse de Restaud in the Chaussé d'Antin!"[81]

Rastignac is technically a student of law but the reality is that he is a student of appearances. When he goes to Madame de Restaud's house he puts on his most elegant clothes, which are nice but frankly not all that nice, and he walks there from the hostel. Along the way he takes "a thousand precautions to avoid being spattered with mud." Getting spattered with mud in nineteenth-century Paris was a dead giveaway that you were part of the working class. A respectable member of the leisure class would have traveled exclusively by horse carriage. Splashed in mud and not wanting to ruin his chance for upward mobility, Rastignac stops at the Palais-Royal to have his boots polished and trousers cleaned, but traces of mud remain—when he arrives at the courtyard of the Maison de Restaud his cover is blown. Madame de Restaud's servants assume he is a nobody because he arrived on foot. They are reluctant to let him inside, and when they finally do he makes matters worse by pretending he knows his way around the house. Obviously he doesn't, and "stumbled clumsily into a room filled with lamps, sideboards and a contraption for heating bath towels."[82] Better luck next time, young Rastignac. The lesson we learn is that appearance is everything.

No one can opt out of the visual world or the laws of appearance because that's how social worlds are managed. Fashion theorist Susan Kaiser believes that styling the body is an important part of understanding who we are and how we express the intersectionalities of our identities.[83] But being is always a two-way street: as soon as you are aware that you can see, you will also know that you can be seen—and judged. What Rastignac does not realize is that it's not enough simply to act as though he belongs in the house. Everyone else needs to believe he does. As a student of appearance, Rastignac has been outed as an impostor, and as one influential social theorist has said, that happens when the impostor has no business doing what he is doing.[84] Rastignac may have the right to pretend to be noble, but the lesson is that as a student of appearances and modern living, he can fake it until he makes it—*if* he can fake it.

Many say that appearance is irrelevant because of its connection to artifice, pleasure, and rituals of vanity. Research on appearance usually emphasizes how surfaces are "naturally" deceptive. Appearances are fake because they highlight the artificial rather than the natural, the ornamental instead of the substantial. Carolyn Cooper, a scholar of Jamaican dance hall culture, reminded me of the meaningless association between seriousness, plainness, frivolousness, and the superficial when she told me she often wears "party clothes" to work:

> **I might wear very bright colors, as opposed to people who are going to work in navy blue or brown. And I wear jewelry that people would not consider "work" jewelry. I remember one day I was at work and I had on a jumpsuit. One of my friends is a designer and she had done a sort of jumpsuit thing, off the shoulder, shoulders bare. One of my colleagues said to me, "Carolyn Cooper! Instead of wearing your clothes on the wrong side why don't you go home and write a paper?" I said, "But I *am* writing papers." Why is that stopping me if I wear my clothes on the wrong side?**[85]

The Nigerian author Chimamanda Ngozi Adichie, in an essay called "Why Can't a Smart Woman Love Fashion?," wrote of her frustration that women in Western culture who want to be taken seriously need to show an indifference to appearance: "I hid my high heels. I told myself that orange, flattering to my skin tone, was too loud. That my large earrings were too much. I wore clothes I would ordinarily consider uninteresting, nothing too bright or too fitted or too unusual. I made choices thinking only about this: How should a serious woman writer be? I didn't want to look as if I tried too hard."[86] Indeed, why is it that if you care about fashion, style, and being a bit flashy, then somehow your work is unserious? Why does wearing a sequined caftan to a department meeting make you unproductive and incompetent? I agree with Jack Halberstam, who wrote in *The Queer Art of Failure* that "being taken seriously means missing out on the chance to be frivolous, promiscuous, and irrelevant." The problem with "seriousness" is that we don't get the chance to follow "visionary insights or flights of fancy."[87]

In 1991 fashion historian Valerie Steele wrote, very humorously, that "academics may be the worst-dressed middle-class occupational group in the United States," not because they are roundly incapable of fashion, but because they have been trained to associate an interest in surfaces with frivolity, inappropriate to their practices of close reading, deep interpretation, and analysis, all tools that aim to dig beneath the surface. In the essay Steele explains how her dissertation on fashion history was received by the Department of History at Yale with scorn and suspicion. "Academics implicitly believe that fashion is frivolous, vain, and politically incorrect."[88] The issue is why certain people believe that fashion is not worth pursuing, intellectually or aesthetically. The answer to this hostility to fashion, for the art critic Hal Foster, might be that we are in an age of "total design"; in the megastore of commodities, packaging is more important than what's inside. This culture of superficial appearances is "all image and no interiority."[89] If only we could get rid of surfaces once and for all, the suggestion seems to be, then we would finally be liberated from the chains of capitalism and able to enjoy a truly democratic social world.[90]

Appearance matters, so much so that the French philosopher Guy Debord once said, "All social life is mere appearance."[91] As early as ancient Egypt, laws were in place to rigidly define who could wear what kinds of clothing. At the time, only the upper classes were allowed to wear sandals, and later in Rome only a citizen could go out in a toga. In medieval Europe both church and state viewed luxurious clothing as an indication of the excesses of vanity. As citizens aimed to outdo their neighbors in the ballet of appearances the church retaliated by inaugurating sumptuary laws that defined how members of a given social rank could dress, essentially sifting them out by controlling *how* they could appear. At one point it was illegal for lower classes to wear clothes that were above their social class even if they could afford them.[92] The whole point was to prevent confusion between the upper class and the lower class. What these laws tell us is that appearances matter enough that large-scale institutions, like the church and the government, have intervened to manage how people look.[93]

By 1750 Jean-Jacques Rousseau railed against the emptiness and vanity of luxury and the pursuit of appearance, advocating for a more naturalist state of humankind. "There would be neither vanity nor luxury" in his vision of an idealized, definitely unfabulous Christian society, because such artifice places emphasis on the external rather than on the qualities of one's character.[94] In 1792 Mary Wollstonecraft took it further, describing women who follow the whims of fashion as slaves. "The soul is left out," she felt, "and none of the parts are tied together by what may properly be termed character. This varnish of fashion, which seldom sticks very close to sense, may dazzle the weak; but leave nature to itself, and it will seldom disgust the wise."[95] Wollstonecraft believed that the artifice of fashion blinds the weak, whereas the truly wise do not feel a need to enhance the natural. Here again is the association of fashion and appearance with artifice and deception, wherein the naturalness of the body automatically means the display of truth.

Despite church- and government-backed sumptuary laws and intellectual efforts to control appearances up through at least the late eighteenth century, the boom in industrialization and the rise of commodity culture in the nineteenth century ushered in a heightened role for appearance, shifting the focus away from the body as an expression of truth and toward external appearance as a manifestation of personal character. Take the volume of novels, realist fiction, fashion journals, and etiquette guides published in the nineteenth century, such as Stephane Mallarmé's 1874 fashion journal *La dernière mode* as well as writings by Zola, Balzac, Charles Baudelaire, Barbey d'Aurevilly, and Oscar Wilde on the dandy as a creature of cultivated appearance.[96] As Lord Henry memorably tells Dorian Gray in Wilde's *The Picture of Dorian Gray*, "It is only shallow people who do not judge by appearances. The true mystery of the world is the visible, not the invisible."[97] But the emphasis on appearances and new ways of looking that exploded in the nineteenth century, which included things like world exhibitions, arcades, fashion, the display of commodities, and the flâneur, did not mean that appearances were finally emancipated from theories of deception. Negative critiques of appearance increasingly led to what one historian called "conspiratorial theories of mass deception," or the ways skeptical critics argue against the value of spectacle, fashion, and ornamentation.[98]

In 1904 the German sociologist Georg Simmel argued against fashion because he felt it differentiated groups at the same time as it actually created a certain unity within them, at least temporarily. The evolution of fashion was largely about keeping the class boundaries intact. "Just as soon as the lower classes begin to copy their style, thereby crossing the line of demarcation the upper classes have drawn and destroying the uniformity of their coherence, the upper classes turn away from this style and adopt a new one, which in its turn differentiates them from the masses; and thus the game goes merrily on."[99] Fashion, for Simmel, is a line of demarcation that visually solidifies unity and membership within a social class. This is still true today: the moment a red-hot fashion item becomes all the rage, the trend is over. Trends are less about class status and more about subcultural status and an access to cool. The reason fashions change so quickly is essentially to make sure that a higher class status is not given in error to someone like Rastignac who can afford to purchase the status symbols of a particular class but isn't actually a part of it.

For what it's worth, I don't actually believe in "trends." Trends do happen, of course, but I'm of the mind that having a personal look, a signature style, is a much more interesting way to go about fashion. A signature look means you are you all the time, no matter what's going on in the fashion world. I will always love black leather pants and big hoop earrings, whether or not they are "in." Period. Have you ever seen Anna Wintour with a different haircut? Or Lady Bunny? Even as you hold down the fort of your personal look, the fashion system will still move at a break-neck pace, but having style is timeless.

No matter how much or how little you're interested in fashion, whether you're invested in the latest trends or if you march to the beat of your own drum, and even if you think fashion doesn't impact you, know that it does. I have a pair of spiked wedge shoes that are always a conversation piece when I wear them out. They are my favorite thing, and I would be totally depressed if I lost them somehow. Whenever people see them in my room they always ask to try them on. Everyone does this—male, female, heterosexual, gay. They try them on for the fun of it and they love the feel-ing the shoes give them. But then they say: "I could never wear those," a phrase we have all used to describe an item of clothing that makes us un-comfortable or that we don't see ourselves in because it goes against the image we have already constructed for ourselves. But who actually says we can't wear it?

The power of appearance, that's "who."

Fashion naysayers are often people who are "uncomfortable with taking full responsibility for their own looks," Anne Hollander tells us, "who either fear the purely visual demands of social life—'appearance' or 'appearances'—or don't trust the operation of their own taste," which means in the end that they "feel threatened and manipulated by fash-ion."[100] Negative theories of appearance emerge out of a nervousness and anxiety about one's own way of looking, which coincidentally works to reinforce the power of appearance. When Rastignac puts on his best clothes and shows up at the house of Madame de Restaud he believes he is entitled to be there. The influential sociologist Erving Goffman, who

Spiked, gravity-defying "heel-less" wedges are the ultimate conversation piece and icebreaker at any party.

used theater as a metaphor to explain everyday social interactions, also believed that as soon as we walk into a room we are already busy trying to understand details about a person's background, things like his or her class status, trustworthiness, and sense of self.[101] Appearance prompts a close reading of other people, a reading strategy meant to tease out biographical and contextual information.

Everyone has a ritual of appearance. When we groom ourselves and choose what to wear for different social occasions we are already performing a specific version of ourselves. Even choosing not to groom, wearing the same thing every day, or saying things like "I don't care about fashion!" is still a confirmation of appearance. It is still a *look*. There are ways of dressing up for job interviews, going shopping, first dates, and gym class that are different from going to a concert, getting into exclusive nightclubs, attending a vogue ball, or working at avant-garde fashion boutiques. No matter the given socio-theatrical situation, people are always subject to the laws of appearance. This is what the American drag icon RuPaul meant when in his 1995 autobiography *Lettin' It All Hang Out* he said, "You're born naked and the rest is drag," a significant comment because it implicates everyone in the act of getting dressed.[102]

Drawing from embodied practice, personal narrative, media, and visual culture, *Fabulous: The Rise of the Beautiful Eccentric* explores narratives of style, creativity, and fabulousness as they appear in a variety of spaces. We'll take a stroll down an East London sidewalk, pump down a catwalk, and wait in line at a popular nightclub in Berlin. Acknowledging yet ultimately moving beyond studies that consistently describe an interest in the surface of fashion and self-styling as about pointless vanity, deception, and the mindless search for status, I argue that fabulousness is creative labor, a type of "self-couture," where our bodies become the site of artistic expression and creativity. Fabulousness, I show, is an enabling mode of performance that in particular allows people forced to the margins to assert themselves through radical self-styling/self-couturing. Fabulous presentations of self in everyday life are activated by the specific rejection of normative ways of looking—but also by the simple joy of wanting to be beautiful.

The point of having personal style, any kind of thoughtful, personal style, is that it makes things much more interesting. This is what the critic Virginia Postrel meant when she wrote that our current cultural moment is an age of aesthetics in which style and design impact every level of consumerism. Take a look around. Today it is impossible to make a consumer choice that is not in some way also an aesthetic choice. From designer computers to designer bathrooms, in an age of aesthetics what looks great on the outside typically outsells the ugly and the commonplace. Postrel's critiques of the aesthetic recall Hal Foster's thinking that in a culture of "total design," packaging is more important than the product itself. The difference between them is that Postrel does not see design as a crime. "It is an essential form of human self-expression." We are visual creatures. Our "real selves [are] the ones wearing make-up and high heels. . . . We care about surfaces."[103] Postrel is one of the few academics to emphasize the creative possibilities that fabulousness opens up. Fashion is, after all, about possibility. Appearance gives us the power to reinvent ourselves and to create new relationships.

But fabulousness is also the opportunity to work against the sameness of things. Life is boring, and as a philosophy of creativity fabulousness lets us see the world with our "third eyes rather than in the desolation that surrounds us." For the philosopher Carol S. Gould fabulousness adds "aesthetic interest to the human experience, both for those who observe it and the self that possesses it."[104] I believe fabulousness can make a difference in the shape of our everyday lives as it drives us to break free from the matrix and to question the kinds of people we aspire to be as well as the sorts of lives we want to live. Style *is* political, a theory of a poetic self. More than anything, fabulousness is political glitter—a glitter-bomb through everyday life.

"I Don't Want to Be Boring!"
A Conversation with Alok Vaid-Menon

ALOK VAID-MENON is a transfeminine multimedia performance artist. They are known internationally for their incisive spoken-word poetry, their quirky aesthetic, and the way they link fashion to gender, politics, and activism in the fight against transmisogyny. I first came across Alok on Instagram, where they regularly publish succulent outfit posts that look great on the one hand, but that tell the story of trauma and transmisogyny on the other. Alok is a prime example of the political nature of fabulousness and style as asserting personhood, with the caveat that we live in a world where simply asserting yourself as a marginalized person comes at a very high price.

I want to start by asking you about Madaew Fashionista, the young Thai boy who became a viral sensation in 2015 because of Instagram photos in which he displayed amazing ingenuity and aesthetic genius by creating strong, high-fashion looks out of nothing. For me, that's what an aesthetics of fabulousness is about: creating beauty and genius from scratch. How did you feel the first time you saw these images?

47

I think there was an incredible sense of recognition where I was like, "Oh, my god! I totally did that growing up." When I was younger I used to stage proto–drag show/stripper/belly dance sessions for my local Indian community in Texas. I would make little skirts and stuff out of towels and other things. There's a sense of resourcefulness that comes from not being able to access traditional women's wear. You have to make whatever you have work.

What I saw in those photos was also a recollection for me that gay men, queer men, and transfeminine people built the modern women's fashion and beauty industries. And I just want to flip the script because I think we're told over and over again that we're trying to become cisgender women or are trying to look like cisgender women when actually we are not. They're often trying to look like us. We were the makeup artists, we were the designers, we taught them how to walk the runway, we taught them how to own femininity, we taught them how to pose. The difference is that our bodies were not allowed to make it onto the covers because people are so transmisogynist that they only understand femininity to be desirable when it's on a cis woman's body, not ours.

There was also a sense of sadness because this aesthetic genius and intelligence will be used and manipulated by an industry that will only prop up cis women and won't actually allow this person to be legitimated in their femininity.

Often when I've talked about fabulousness in certain circles I've gotten criticism along the lines of whether fabulousness is simply about gay men "doing" or "putting on" femininity, that this is primarily what fabulousness is all about.

And to that I would say, "You are a transmisogynist!" People need to actually understand that femininity does not belong to cis women. What you're doing is retreating into biological essentialism. It is a rhetoric and a discourse created by a fundamentally racist and misogynist state that has and continues to fund pseudo-science to legitimate the biological basis of race and gender. All of us who are committed to any type of social justice politic have to be deeply, deeply skeptical of biology because biology has been used in incredibly racist and colonial ways.

What you're doing is you're saying that because gay men do not have vaginas (which already erases the existence of gay trans men), then the only relationship they can have with femininity is mediated by the people who do have vaginas, that femininity belongs to people with vaginas, that the only way gay men can access femininity is parody. What you're not actually saying is that we live in a transmisogynistic binaristic world that teaches gay men that they're not entitled or allowed to be their own femininity, so they often have to go to the stage, have to sing Diana Ross, have to embody the femininity of cis women because they're not allowed to have it themselves. I think the more interesting conversation would be: How do we actually *end gender* so that we don't actually have to have such a reductive conversation of "gay man" "performing femininity" and instead have "person" "being transcendental"?

Old-school white cisgender feminists still believe in the importance and the significance of an essential womanhood, which I actually think is one of the most racist, colonial paradigms there ever was. Because actually, the category of "woman" is defined by the racist and patriarchal state. What you call "woman" is actually what you've been taught "woman" is by a medical, judicial, political, legal system that has always been colonial, racist, and sexist. What I call "femme" is actually not about biology. It's about power. It's about divinity. It's about witchcraft. It's about mysticism. It's about aesthetic genius.

One of the things I'm trying to point to is that fabulousness is actually a political-aesthetic practice, a queer embodied aesthetic that's illuminated largely by marginalized people and social outcasts. I believe it takes real aesthetic genius to create fabulousness, but I also believe that this genius is a response to the struggles, pressures, and traumas of living while marginalized.

We only legitimate political work that is associated with masculinity. We see screaming at a rally as political, but we don't see *dressing* as political. We undervalue the role of cultural work and art in shifting paradigms and doing revolutionary political work. Actually, for me to get dressed every day *is* part of my politics, is part of my protest work, because the images I'm conjuring and the anxieties I'm inducing and the dissonance I'm creating have done more for queer and trans progress than many of these pieces of policy or legislation. So many amazing trans women of color I know are never seen as "activists" because they're not speaking the correct language, because they don't have the "correct" (read: white, cis, masculine) self-posturing.

But the aesthetics they're creating are so political. What fabulousness allows us to do is to create reservoirs of confidence and hope and love for ourselves because we *don't* get that from the media, we don't get that from the gay community, we don't get that from the academy. We don't get that anywhere. So at some level we realized we had to devote ourselves to *ourselves*. We have to be in an emotional relationship with ourselves in order to get by. What aesthetic genius has allowed me to do is not make me so reliant on other people's validation and affirmation in order to survive. Now I can get ready in the morning, look at myself in the mirror, and be like, *Oh, my god!* And that energy and that relationship with myself is not about "vanity" or "narcissism." It's about survival.

The reason I do this is because I'm part of a tradition of warriors, and this is a part of my political resistance. This is not just some sort of aesthetic, vain project.

White Western culture has taught us that transfemininity is something superficial and artificial, whereas transfemininity in so many black people's and people of color's traditions is about resistance. What keeps me going is there's a long tradition of people doing this work, and it is *work*. It's not just getting ready. It's actual, political work. It's strategy, it's planning, it's PR, it's how we talk about it. Every walk I make is already a [protest] march. I'm already doing more visibility work than any of your boring-ass human rights campaign canvassers. To present outside of the gender binary is already an act of activism, and the fact that we don't understand that is really violent.

What does it feel like for you when you're putting a look together?

There are two different processes. There's a process for getting ready for walking around New York City, and then there's a process for getting ready for a performance. I have to think, what time am I coming home today? Do I know where I'm going? Am I ready psychologically to deal with potentially being assaulted? I think it's actually much more liberating for me to get dressed for performance because I don't have that same baggage when I look at my clothing, whereas when I'm just going around New York for the day I have so much baggage. I look at every article of my clothing and I remember when I got harassed in it and what people said and did to me. Those things become part of those pieces of clothing for me. It's not that they "trigger" me and I can't look at them anymore, it's just that it's a type of sadness where I remember looking *so good* in the mirror and then being made to feel like shit outside.

When I'm getting ready and dressed for the day, often I'm timid. And often I'm afraid, and often I'm *not* ready, and I wish that those could be just as much a part of our trans and queer narratives as the moments when we are fabulous. Often I feel utterly ashamed and not fabulous. It's ironic to me that I am forced to find safety and security in "men's" clothing, something that's been so violent in my life. But I know that if I just wear a T-shirt and some shorts, no one's going to shit on me. Some days I just can't take it so I wear that.

But for performance, every single time it's so full of joy. And because this world is so transmisogynist, it only allows people like me to exist on a stage and that means I can actually wear what I want to wear. Now I go shopping for my stage performance and that has allowed me to *really* expand my aesthetic genius where I'm wearing these six-inch platform heels, I'm wearing this *ridiculous* spandex, these *ridiculous* colors—and I just feel so free. But it's also heartbreaking because I feel so free and then the show ends. I don't think we have language to describe that sense of despair of being so high and free and wonderful for the past two hours but now I have to return back to this *boring* world with its relentless violence.

I always say let's add *boring* to our list of oppressor identities: cis, white, straight, *boring* men. The truth is I don't want to dress this way not just because I'm trans. It's because I don't want to be *boring!*

Fabulousness is almost certainly a rejection of boredom, and that brings me to your Instagram practice. Have you found that the selfies you upload are helpful to other queer people and people of trans experience who come across them? What has the feedback been?

People have told me that my Instagram images give permission for them to be themselves, and I think that's really important. A lot of people come up to me at my shows and say that seeing images of me helps them get through the day. And that's really great and important because as nonbinary, gender-nonconforming people, we have few templates of what we're allowed to look like. But—and it's a strong *but*—what I would ask is that we not conflate representation with social media. What happens is that we're locked in a digital glass ceiling where trans people of color are only allowed to exist on the Internet. It's this really weird trap where we say we have progress and victory for having media exposure, but social media exposure isn't the same thing as financial compensation.

Very few of us have actually been able to translate social media visibility into real institutional power. We're put into a digital zoo where you have a lot of people being able to scroll down our newsfeeds, look at us, and say, "Wow, so brave, so interesting," and then go on with their lives and not challenge anything. What I began to realize is that social media visibility of trans issues is part and parcel of a project of violence against us. They'll look at us and desire us on screens—but then do not show up for us in person. Where are you when we're being attacked? Social media has created a façade, an illusion of trans progress, trans visibility, trans acceptance that is not what the real situation is in person. All of these people "liking" my photos on Insta-gram make me think, where are you? Most trans people do not have any social media visibility at all. Why should we have to become a public figure to be protected from street harassment?

Speaking of street harassment, what's so com-pelling about the images you upload to Insta-gram is that they are each framed by complicated narratives you write that capture the experience of how people reacted to you that day as you moved around the city. These are narratives of harassment, transmisogyny, and struggle, and speak to the political nature of dressing while marginalized.

I started this project for many reasons. Like many transfemi-nine people of color, I have developed anxiety disorder for the amount of street harassment I've experienced. It doesn't just stop at the street—it continues to every avenue of our lives. We're constantly under surveillance, constantly picked apart. I needed a way to heal and cope. My art doesn't come from a place of wanting to be an artist but rather be-cause this is the only way I can feel whole. I've had to come up with my own language to describe what's happening to me. And often when I tell people about the things that have happened to me through those Instagram posts they say, "I had no idea this happened to you." And I ask them, "Why?" And then they begin to say, "Oh, you just look so confident." Or, "Oh, you just look so beautiful." But this is what I'm try-ing to get at. Transmisogyny would have you believe that my fabulousness comes from my confidence and not also from my struggle. I have to overcompensate because I am under attack and I have to get myself through it.

The way I get street-harassed is not only because I'm failing to be cis but because I'm failing to be trans. It's a double failure. I'm failing to be a nice, medicalized, beautiful woman, and I'm actually a failure as a man, as a woman, and a failure of this new media-constructed trans body. What that's done is that I only get to be a stage performer. The only frame of reference for me is as a stage performer. We are literally stuck onstage, in the photograph, or on the runway. We're not allowed to have an existence beyond being staged by other people.

I was having a really great conversation with Justin Tranter in LA and he had this really great point that when he moved to New York and would come home from the gym he'd be wearing basketball shorts and a tank and he would *still* get harassed. And then he realized if he's going to get harassed wearing that, *and* he's going to get harassed wearing heels and eye shadow, at *least* wear heels and eye shadow because that's his armor. And I realized that's so true. This is my armor. I just wish people would understand that. I dress this way because I'm going to get harassed inevitably, but at least I can get harassed fabulously.

Does that mean you would position fabulousness as an art practice/aesthetics of survival?

Absolutely. There's no way I would be alive if it wasn't for fabulousness. What I've had to do is give birth to myself because my family was bad at that and my culture was bad at that. They didn't give birth to me. They gave birth to an illusion of what they wanted me to be: a nice, good, Hindu upper-caste boy to keep up the family tradition of assimilation.

The irony of living in this country is that the American party line is that this is a place where you can be yourself, but those of us who actually are ourselves get punished for it. There can be no better case than trans people. We are out here, being ourselves in ways that no one wants, and what we realize is that the reason people hurt us is because they're jealous. It's not that they're afraid of me. They're afraid of the fact that they want me. It's much more complicated. I don't actually think people hate me or have prejudices against me. I think they want me and they're lonely and sad and I represent what they could have been and it's really tragic. Being trans for me has been so full of joy and pleasure and delight, and I feel like those narratives are completely lost because we are punished.

My friend Daisey Lopez—when I first moved to New York and she saw me she was like, "Do you know how to fight?" I said, "Excuse me?" And she said, "If you're going to dress like that in New York City, darling, you need to know how to fight." And she took me to the gym and she taught me how to fucking box with a pair of pink gloves and dramatic squeals to boot!

Part of the political thrust of fabulousness is that it emerges not from confidence or designer labels but from life-long periods of struggle, depression, self-loathing, and injury. All of these are forms of trauma that culture relentlessly thrusts upon brown, queer, and transfeminine people every day in nearly every aspect of our existence, from our work lives to our sex lives. In a new book of poetry called *Femme in Public*, Alok writes, "At 21 I put on a dress, and disappeared," a story that reflects the rampant misogyny gay men and transfeminine people face. Fabulous but lonely. Fabulous but undesirable. Fabulous but not masc. Fabulous but I won't date you or fight for you. Alok speaks beautifully and candidly about the political nature of clothing and dress as they note that getting dressed in the morning is political work, moving down the street is already a protest march, and that clothes are encoded with the memories of the violences thrown our way. How could I feel so bad when I looked so good?

To present outside of the gender binary, kept intact by patriarchal and capitalist systems, is in many ways a failure because gender-nonconforming bodies and other cultural renegades are punished for being themselves. How do we actually "end gender," Alok wonders, so that we no longer feel the need to rely on the "safety" of "men's" clothing just to walk down the street or make it to work? Why do we feel that "men's" clothing keeps us safe when "men" have precisely been the source of such intense anti-gay and transfeminine violence and erasure? How do we end gender so that marginalized people no longer feel that we can exist only on a stage, beyond a screen, in secret, and for entertainment purposes only? How do we actually "end gender" so that we no longer need to make the difficult choice between brilliant aesthetic expression and avoiding constant harassment, between being ourselves and getting beat up? Marred by trauma, fabulous people live in another dimension that skirts "gender" altogether, does away with it, and creates alternative, nonbinaristic ways of living in our bodies.

The complication and the paradox of fabulousness, though, is that despite the visibility and increased surveillance of transfeminine people, they are the most likely to disappear or be ignored. More visibility does not automatically lead to safety once and for all. At the time of writing Alok has nearly forty-seven thousand Instagram followers, many of whom leave comments on their photos about how "fabulous" they are, that they are such an inspiration. That is important work. But where are these forty-seven thousand people, Alok wonders, when they are being attacked and harassed on the streets? Where are these forty-seven thousand people when other transfeminine people are attacked? How can you look at a transfeminine or gender-nonbinary person, tell them they're fabulous, and not fight for them?

For all Alok's brilliance, one of the most important takeaways from their commentary is the politics of boredom, how the boredom-resistant flavor of fabulousness further highlights that this aesthetic genius is about a certain kind of agency and a seizing of the here and now. They emphasize that they don't do fabulousness simply because they want to but because they can't bear to be boring. When they say, "Let's add *boring* to our list of oppressor identities: cis, white, straight, *boring* men. The truth is I don't want to dress this way not just because I'm trans. It's because I don't want to be *boring!*" they highlight a politics of abundance, expression, and expansion that marginalized people embrace. This is ultimately what fabulousness is about: how people stand out and make a spectacle of themselves when it might be easier and safer, but no less toxic, to just fit in. If we're going to be harassed anyway, we might as well look fabulous.

2.
How to
Work
a Look

in september 2015, New York street fashion photographer Dusty Rebel shared an Instagram shot of the underground queer nightlife fashion icon Leo GuGu on his way from a Whole Foods Market on the Lower East Side on a day he was working a strong look. GuGu had on a green, orange, and hot-pink cheetah-print jacket with matching skinny pants. The whole look was iced with an orange sun hat and brown house slippers with teddy bears on top. It's "Dennis Rodman meets the joker . . . LOVE IT!" one Instagram commenter said about the look. "Werk," Dusty Rebel himself said. Even GuGu, who later reshared the photo to his own Instagram @gugueyes, said, "I sure love going to Whole Foods casual as fuck but still slaying shoppers in a look."[1] If fabulousness is about getting all dressed up and having somewhere to be, using fashion to get people thinking and looking, Leo GuGu certainly has a lot to say.

Here I tell the story of rogue, underground fashion-obsessed creatives like Leo GuGu who *work looks* in their everyday lives as a form of expressive resistance. Style is resistance—a way of rising up out of the ashes—and beauty, fashion, and getting dressed are political projects. It's difficult if not impossible to approach beauty, style, and fashion without also thinking about how they connect to race, class, gender, and queerness. I for one love to think of this expressive resistance as a form of critical mascara, a theory of the beautifully marginal as a form of cultural critique that happens to be pitched for the camera, the street, the catwalk, the blog, and the app. As media theorist Minh-Ha T. Pham shows in a fabulous article on the cultural power of selfies, much of the criticism against selfie culture, often led by white feminists, is about how it plays into the hands of extreme narcissism and the self-objectification of women, by no means a new blow against cultural or personal interest in the self. But what's so powerful about Pham's analysis is the way she links self-styled fashion images and politics—how she articulates that selfies are not necessarily vain or self-objectifying, especially when the person taking the photo is a marginalized or underrepresented person in the broader image economy. For Pham, the selfie is a "do-it-yourself technique of visibility," a "networked vanity" that forces social media image culture to showcase precisely the kinds of people who are regularly ex- 61 cluded from and indeed invisible in standard fashion, beauty, magazine, and other aesthetic image pools.[2]

Having great style isn't about following a system of fashion. It's about following an inner creative core, having an "eye." In *The Language of Fashion*, one of the first books to decode fashion as a system, cultural critic Roland Barthes wrote that being fashionable is about following what the fashion industry says is hot. "Blue is in fashion this year," for instance, and many of us may swear by that.[3] But today, and certainly in the age of Instagram and street fashion blogs, creative looks are less and less about following the fashion industry, editorial by editorial, trend for trend, and more about expressing an inner creative core. I'm calling this *working a look*, the labor of love that goes into eccentrically creating yourself anew again and again. *Working a look* is about turning yourself into a narrative, and it points to the labor that goes into how we style ourselves every day. What stories are we telling? What are we trying to reveal or, for that matter, conceal about ourselves? It's a concept that builds on the sartorial history of eighteenth- and nineteenth-century dandies such as Beau Brummell and Julius Soubise, figures who were committed to the art of using style to communicate a personalized aesthetic vision, or really a unique world, that focused on creativity, style, and the future.[4] Style, and learning to have our own effervescent sense of it, is how we create our own small utopias right here, right now. That's its gift. Through style we bring our versions of the world with us everywhere we go, offering more than simply aesthetics. This is aesthetics as a political gesture.

Think about the cool-looking girl minding her business but working a strong look, pumping down Bond Street in New York City. Maybe she threw on whatever was lying around the floor that morning, which I have definitely done before. Maybe she thought long and hard about her outfit, switching that pair of earrings for this pair, editing out the skinny jeans in favor of black harem pants, and instead of tying her hair back she teased it out—big and high and opulent. Someone rushes up to say how much they love her hair, where did she find her shoes, she looks fabulous, can I take your picture for my fashion blog? She is a vision of style,

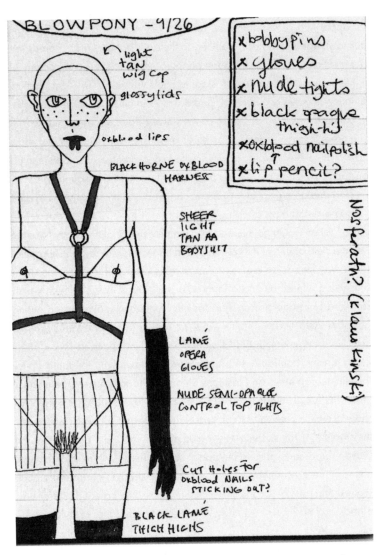

A sketch of how Faun Dae brings her looks to life, from ideas to the catwalk. (Courtesy of Faun Dae.)

an apparition of fabulousness, and her personhood and creativity get acknowledged by a flash, pointing to the art historian Krista Thompson's observation that black diasporic peoples turn to the "visual economy of light" in ways that are about "staging one's visibility."[5] This hypothetical situation is actually quite real, and it occurs in cities, in neighborhoods, in coffee shops, and on street corners every day, all around the world. The proof is in the street fashion blogs and Instagram accounts that show how style is seen, worn, photographed, documented, and commented on. Good style can't sit still. As political glitter, it needs to saunter around, coming and going, constantly being captured and narrated, seen and re-seen in order to have a lasting impact.

Leo GuGu got his start as a nightlife personality and stylist at the Patricia Field boutique in New York, and his Warholesque creative project is the way he has an endless treasure trove of looks for every occasion, presenting himself as an art form on a daily basis. Patricia Field, which ran as a brick-and-mortar shop for fifty years and moved to an online portal in 2016, was in many ways ground zero for a certain strand of creative strangeness. In 1984 *Details* described the space as "New York's living history 'boutique' and it never lets us down with the latest up-to-the-minute, fab items and fashions at fair, affordable prices. The jewelry case was full of things I couldn't even begin to describe, but when Pat showed me the plexi-mirror cuff bracelets that fasten with Velcro, I agreed they were *it*."[6] The stylists who worked at Patricia Field, like GuGu or the Queens-bred underground hip-pop artist Dai Burger, were often person-alities in the downtown nightlife, art, music, creative, and performance scenes, and usually ran their own club nights, fronted a band, were in art school, and had their own edgy, creatively strange sense of style.

When I first saw Dai Burger I noticed her immediately. She worked a shaved-at-the-sides-but-long-on-top candy-colored mohawk, an underground punk look dating from at least the 1980s that reached peak mainstream adaptation and commercial exposure when British "it" girl Alice Dellal, famous for the same style, was cast by Karl Lagerfeld in the spring 2012 Chanel ad campaign, a casting choice that gave Chanel an extra dose of subcultural punch. Edgy stylists like Dai Burger and Leo

GuGu are prime examples of what the sociologist Ashley Mears describes in her ethnography of the modeling industry as "walking billboards." In aesthetic markets like fashion retail or modeling, Mears writes, aesthetic labor is what happens when people who work in branded spaces start to *look* like they would work there, whether they are actually at work or not. To be a "walking billboard" means personifying the fantasy a brand wants to give you, offering up a seamless fit "between corporate brand identity and employee identity."[7] But not all walking billboards are created equal, and sometimes being one with the brand can lead to exclusionary hiring and visual media practices. Abercrombie & Fitch, which *Buzzfeed* succinctly described in 2013 as a preppy brand that has a "sex-meets-Ivy League aesthetic," has long come under fire for an in-store "look policy" that privileges whiteness and masculinity.[8] "We hire good-looking people in our stores," Abercrombie CEO Michael S. Jeffries told *Salon* in 2006, "because good-looking people attract other good-looking people, and we want to market to cool, good-looking people. We don't market to anyone other than that."[9] For Abercrombie & Fitch, "good-looking people," the "A&F Look," means white people, and a certain kind of heightened whiteness at that.

In 2004 former Abercrombie employees of color sued the brand and its look policy for this bald embrace of whiteness. The suit cited a "disproportionately white sales force," disproportionately white upper management, and disproportionately white editorial campaigns and visual media, slamming the way the brand typically regulated brown bodies to the stock room and overnight positions, strictly out of public view. The suit underscored how the "Abercrombie look" is an all-white image and exposed the company's racist, look-based hiring policies, where prospective applicants who do not fit the "Abercrombie look" are told that the company isn't hiring or are given applications that never get considered.[10] Here, Abercrombie is a strong example of a look policy or walking billboard gone wrong, where the discrimination is blatant, pervasive, and unapologetic. I remember what it was like being a black queer teenager in middle and high school in the late 1990s, and even in my first few years of college, during the height of Abercrombie's reign in popular culture.

Like Dwight McBride, whose *Why I Hate Abercrombie and Fitch* offers an excellent portrayal of race, sexuality, and desire in gay spaces, I also went to gay bars and was perplexed by the sea of white dudes in Abercrombie T-shirts, loose-fitting stonewashed jeans with the knees cut out, flip-flops, and blond tips—a look that was to my eyes as much a faux pas in 1999 as it will be in 2099.[11] But in certain gay spaces if you didn't have the "Abercrombie look" you weren't even desirable. Men in online gay spaces would proudly describe themselves as an "A&F Boy," whether they were black or white, and in all cases the word *Abercrombie* was used to convey whiteness and a certain kind of toxic masculinity. The power of the brand extended beyond its confines in suburban shopping malls, performances of coolness in AOL Instant Messenger screen names, and high school cafeterias across America.

The "Abercrombie look" highlights whiteness and being "normal," even as the A&F sense of "normal" is highly curated, edited, and produced. I want to be clear that the kind of "look" I find most inspiring celebrates the creatively strange, the nonnormative, the weirdos and the freaks, the people who make a spectacle of themselves when it would be so much easier to simply fit in. In queer circles it's called a *look* not because it blends in and disappears but because you have to look at it. You single it out. You want to look at it because it is interesting, so you look twice, three times, taking it in again and again, what Sianne Ngai describes as the practice of "returning us to the object for another look."[12] And as one London-based drag queen told me, "It's called a look, not a touch," highlighting even more the sense of the look as something that is visually stunning, tactile, opulent.

I suppose, in a sense, that a "look policy" or *working a look* is exclusionary in some way because there will always be people who care more about their style choices than others. But this is one of the critiques that nearly always plagues fashion discourse, as critics like Valerie Steele and Herbert Blau have shown. There will always be those who say they are styleless, that they don't give "a shit" about fashion, who scream loudly that they have no interest in fashion. But because we live in a visual economy, totally opting out of fashion is still a fashion choice, as Miranda

Priestly, editor in chief of the fictional *Runway* magazine, made clear in the 2006 film *The Devil Wears Prada*. No style is actually still style.

Before I moved to London I used to always go to Patricia Field when I wanted a bit of creative inspiration, especially if I needed to get a *look* together for a night out. I got to know GuGu by hanging out with him at the store and by going to the parties he hosted around the East Village at gay bars like Eastern Bloc. When we finally sat down to talk about his personal style our meeting was actually a theory of *working a look*. As walking billboards, to use Mears's term again, Patricia Field employees were usually in a *look* when they were on the clock, and for some reason I thought I would see GuGu in "regular" clothes because we met on one of his off days. On that spring afternoon I got out of the subway at Bleecker Street and looked around for him but he wasn't there. I waited for him, paranoid that maybe I'd missed our meeting. Then he approached me from behind, and when I turned around and saw him he was so fabulous I gasped. Picture it: he wore shiny parachute pants made out of what seemed like trash bag plastic, silver loafers covered in sequins with spikes coming out the top, an enormous fur coat with a high collar, a long, bone-straight black wig, and small, circular, John Lennon–style sunglasses with a skull hologram on each lens. He definitely "slayed me with a look," to use his own phrasing.

"Oh, *werk!*" I said the instant I saw him. As we made our way toward Bowery to sit down for coffee, another black gay male walked past and said, "Bitch, you better werk," a quick compliment that's relevant here because it reminds us that fabulousness is a kind of queer affirmation. It is a gift that can excite other people.

Working a look is a queer aesthetic and it is generally about getting dressed up to be consumed visually by strangers in dense, urban settings. Feminist film theorist Laura Mulvey famously wrote about the ways that women in film are there to connote "to-be-looked-at-ness" — their bodies are styled to be consumed visually both by the men on-screen and by the men watching them on-screen.[13] They are there to be looked at. In aesthetic worlds like fashion, where the primary good is an intangible aesthetic quality, a *look* is also a commodity. It's the thing that sells. There are three approaches to "looks" and the fashion world. First, models take the performance of gender, race, and class to the professional level and get paid to be an archetype. Second, in the modeling industry looks are a type of commodity that ties together personality and appearance but the look could change at any moment according to the whims of the market. And finally, a look relies on having the latest clothes.

But these approaches leave no room for the possibility of style as creative performance, style as a form of rising out of the ashes, and style as political glitter. For fabulous eccentrics, a motley crew of artists, singers, stylists, dancers, performers, and other creatives who are very often queer, of color, or both, *looks* are not about market forces or professionalized gender performance. They are a way of using aesthetics to unravel market forces or to end gender altogether and position themselves as works of art, works that emerge from struggle, trauma, depression, and violence. Portland-based designer RoRo Morales, known locally for his opulent caftans and chola earrings, told me that for him, fabulousness "is almost the truest form of art because it's using your body, your soul, and energy as the art form itself. You are the art and you are the art form." What drives him is a vision of fashion as one of the truest ways to see who someone is because you encounter what they *want* to look like, what they *want* you to see. These are the creative politics of fabulousness. "I dress the way I want to," he tells me. "I don't care what anyone else has to say about it. It's more about what makes me feel good and what I want to feel like that day. I'm always in a look. I don't even own sweats. I don't own white socks. I don't own white T-shirts. 'RoRo' has almost become an expectation, so when people see you they expect to see you in something. It becomes a brand and you have to continue that brand on a daily basis or else your brand won't be successful."[14]

Working a look is inherently queer. In an ethnography of the relationship between nightlife and queer world-making, Fiona Buckland writes about how dance clubs were "spaces to be fabulous." Because many queer bodies are "worldless"—disconnected from support networks of family or church—Buckland shows how fabulousness in the queer dance club gives partyers the chance to express themselves as well as their queerness. She calls this a "currency of fabulousness," a phrasing that has deep implications for queer self-imagining. This "currency of fabulousness" is about the process of getting ready to go out and putting outfits together from disparate materials and for as little coin as possible.[15] This is what I've been calling creative strangeness, an aesthetic that stands out because it pairs objects and situations that we think have no business together. Creative strangeness is a fashion editorial spread showing a guy standing in a trash can wearing a vintage wedding dress, shaved eyebrows, and rings on every finger, holding a fabulous snake, totally covered in oil, and posing for the gods. It doesn't make any sense—it's bizarre, interesting, forcing us to look over and over—but that's why it works. It's an exaggerated storyboard of the self, style as theater.

As a queer aesthetic, looks are ultimately short, theatrical vignettes that highlight the power of ideas, imagination, and creating a visual sensation, like Leo GuGu as he "slayed shoppers in a look" on the streets of New York. The day I met GuGu near Bleecker Street I asked him to describe his look to me: "Right now, I'm serving fashionista on her day off. I'm wearing these faux [Christian] Louboutins with the spikes. I'm wearing these trash bag harem pants—I got them at Goodwill. I feel like I'm in Milan right now, not in New York."[16] Fake Christian Louboutins, trash bag pants from Goodwill. Who cares whether the items are real or fake? It's the fantasy that counts. Working a look is not about expensive, designer goods, or about buying into an aesthetic that a fashion house has said is "in." It's about resourcefulness, self-couture, and knowing how to put together an arresting image, one that exposes an "inner theater that is costumed by choice in clothes," as cultural historian Anne Hollander describes. Working a look is about expressing a philosophy of creativity, about knowing how, through collage, to combine an array of materials into a full look, or story, giving "a visual aspect to consciousness" along the way.[17]

Ultimately, we're talking about style as utopia, a separate space where we get to play with ideas, creativity, and expression to create a whole new world, a stylish one at that, in the here and now. "It is my belief," José Muñoz writes beautifully in *Cruising Utopia,* a must-read for anyone interested in how art and beauty are created in duress, "that minoritarian subjects are cast as hopeless in a world without utopia." The pressures and anxieties, the violence and the depression of living while brown, of feeling constantly illegible within systems of normativity and white supremacy, even in queer spaces, create a situation in which brown people use art and performance to build an alternative, utopian possibility right here, right now. For Muñoz, utopia is a stage and it offers a separate way of being that is always in process, never fully finished. His point is not so much that utopian dreams are watershed moments that will make life perfect at last, but that for marginalized people utopian visions offer up a *should be* and a *could be* instead of the more forced, monolithic vision of what is and will always be.[18]

But is the dream of utopia enough? What good can come from utopian positive thinking? A romanticized vision of possibility? A castle in the sky? Critiques about a utopian vision don't denigrate the dream of a better future, nor do they assert that dreams are pointless. The problem people often have with notions of utopia is that thinking about an elsewhere does not put food on the table, so to speak, nor does it do much to topple the systems that oppress us every day. We don't need utopia. We need *results.* Imagining an elsewhere is not enough when we should be working tirelessly to create real social change right now. You can't pay your rent in utopia and you can't eat utopia for dinner. Utopia won't be there to save us when we're confronted with violence and oppression. And that's fair enough. Too much theory, not enough action.

But I think the reach for utopia, or even a separate dimension, is just as important as the long walk we take to get there. I dream of a world where I'm not called faggot or where I don't fear for my life because I'm in a pair of heels. I dream of a world where I can walk down the street in whatever I want without being ridiculed, harassed, stopped, and verbally or physically assaulted. I want a world where gay guys stop saying they are "masc 4 masc" or that some of us are "a bit feminine." I want a place where trans women and transfeminine people are able to express themselves freely every day and live in their bodies exactly the way they want to without being a moving target. Until that day comes, fabulousness as queer utopia is about living in the present but carrying an alternative possibility, a certain future, and yanking it into the here and now. This vision of living both now and in the future echoes queer theorist Carolyn Dinshaw's innovative thinking about how queer people have always imagined relationships with the past as a way of creating community. For Dinshaw, queer histories consist of affective relations that make the "past and present touch." She is broadly interested in how queer people reach back into the past, across time, in order to make sense of contemporary life. This gesture of reaching back toward the past "is queerly historical," she writes, "because it creates a relation across time that has an affective or an erotic component."[19] I'm suggesting that fabulousness ups the ante by doing the opposite. Instead of reaching back into time and imagining a relationship to the past, fabulousness imagines what life could be like in the future and yanks that vision to the present. To the now.

   Style affords us the potential dream, to inhabit another world, not "in theory" but in practice. This is what Chicago-based black queer rapper Mister Wallace meant when he told me that fabulousness "exists in queer communities because we can see a better and healthier way to view the world." Mister Wallace sees fabulousness as "a radicalized view of a modern world," and that better or healthier world is expressed through style.[20] There's a way of applying theoretical concepts to performance practices to make those practices fit a mold and to bring them into certain kinds of theoretical conversations. Fabulousness, though, is theory from the streets. It's a theory that's not limited to high-end academic discourse. It's urgent. It's a theory of the everyday that is happening right now, a theory of survival, a theory that's alive, a theory we can look at, a theory we can experience, call "faggot," and share on Instagram. When Leo GuGu works the streets of New York he is not an abstract concept, a thought experiment, or a proposition. He is *actually happening*. Fabulous eccentrics use individual style to show us that they live in their own individual, small utopias where it is normal, not weird, for them to be in their bodies the way they are and to style themselves the way they do.

   But living in the dream world of fabulous eccentricity means clashing with people who follow norms and who somehow feel the power to police nonconforming bodies. Sometimes we even police ourselves in the name of safety or desirability. Maybe we select a more masculine profile photo for Grindr because we know more guys will message us then, a sad but unfortunate reality for many, and maybe we identify as femme but are immediately harassed the moment we leave our front door to grab a sandwich or to go to work. "What feminine part of yourself did you have to destroy in order to survive in this world?" the multimedia artist Alok Vaid-Menon tweeted on April 17, 2016, and I can say for certain that there are "feminine" aspects of myself I've had to suppress or water down in my everyday life in order to make it through. In *Femme in Public*, a book of poetry by Vaid-Menon, they ask a series of questions that get at the heart of the precariousness and risk of living while fabulous:

> **what would it look like to leave the house and not be afraid of being bashed? what would it mean to leave the house and not be bashed? what would it mean to leave the house and not be harassed? what would it mean to leave the house and not be objectified? what would it mean to leave the house and not be gendered? what would it mean to no longer be forced to do the work of gender? what would it mean to own my own body? what would it mean to have a self beyond my body? what would it mean to log online and not being told to die? what would it mean to have people say "I'm sorry" instead of "you're fabulous?" what would it mean to no longer have to be fabulous to survive?**

For Vaid-Menon, fabulousness is complicated because it offers a rich space of creative expression as well as a declaration of personhood and self, but it is not always good news. Why do brown and trans bodies matter only when they're fabulous or on a stage? What if instead of telling the brown or trans person, "Wow, you're fabulous," you fought for them? What if you stood up for us in real life when someone calls us a faggot or physically harasses us on the street? Vaid-Menon wants us to interrogate this intersection between great style and politics. We look amazing—thank you—but why aren't you fighting for us?

A number of contemporary black queer and trans artists use digital portals like Instagram to reflect on exactly this type of sociocultural torture. Performance artist Travis Alabanza, @travisalabanza, posted an image on Instagram that would have looked like an ordinary selfie had it not been contextualized in the caption by the kinds of hate they received while simply walking down the street, getting in trouble for being themselves:

> **As soon as I walked outside yesterday I was harassed. I say this not for any reason other than to say it. . . . I was harassed every single day since the last time I posted. Either verbally, with unanimous stares, or by the violent ways in which gender policing harasses trans bodies every single day. . . . I did what so many trans femmes do— go inside quickly to a bathroom and change. I put on some trousers. Took off my makeup. And walked out. Still shaken, Sad, Smaller . . . but in my eyes, safer.**

Alabanza describes how a new friend, the artist Yunique Yunique, encouraged them to get back into the look while they took photos, smiled, laughed, and ate pizza. The point was to keep body fascism, policing, and surveillance from ruining a great outfit. When you are brown, queer, and marginalized, fabulousness is not simply about being beautiful and opulent but about seizing visual space on your own terms as an act of resistance, right now and in real time, even if that visibility is risky business. If no one gives you the space you need to thrive, make your own. If you can't see yourself represented in traditional media sources, do your own pictures, an idea the art historian Krista Thompson calls "the right to be seen."[21]

If there's still doubt about the political nature of beauty, style, and self-fashioning, about fabulousness as the politics of creativity and the creativity of politics, think of the blogger Blaqueer, who describes himself online as "fat, black, queer." In "The Fat Boi Diaries: Why Selfies?" a blog post from March 2013, Blaqueer poignantly describes why taking selfies matters to him:

> **I take my selfies because I am that guy who, unless he takes the picture or suggests it, doesn't get his picture taken. . . . I live in a world where I didn't hear someone romantically call me beautiful and desirable till I was 26. I live in a world where either body privilege or race privilege is always against me. So I point my camera at my face, most often when I am alone, and possibly bored, and I click; I upload it to instagram, and I hold my breath because the world is cruel and I am what some would call ugly, but I don't see it. At first I clicked so I could see what others saw, but I don't. So now I click and post and breathe, waiting for others to see what I see: beautiful dark skin, Afrika's son, a dream un-deferred, pretty eyes, and nice lips, and a nose that fits my face; I want them, you, to see that I am human, and there is a reason why I got to this size, but I owe you no explanation or justification for any part of my existence. . . . I owe you no explanation or justification for my smile or my swag or my selfie. . . . I owe you nothing, but I owe myself everything.[22]**

There's almost always a turning point with fabulousness, something like a caterpillar transforming into a butterfly, to borrow the cliché, and it starts as a conscious shift from a previously unhappy, norm-obeying self to one that essentially screams, without a doubt and to the hillside, "Fuck it!" Fuck it, let me put on a pair of pumps. Fuck it, I'm going to dress this way and move through public space, risking danger, attack, or scrutiny. The shift is about realizing the failures of normativity and giving up on them. When we say "Fuck it" and leave our past self behind and move into fabulousness, we give up on the rules of appearance and gender presentation, we give up on toxic masculinity, and we give up on suppressing what makes us different.

Choosing fabulousness means arming ourselves *through* and *with* style, what the cultural critic Chaédria LaBouvier calls "weaponized glamour" because it highlights the "tremendous confidence in facing a hostile world with a good outfit."[23] "Weaponized glamour" shows how aesthetics offer both a proclamation of the self and a protection of the self—great style as a tool to subvert dehumanizing experiences of the marginalized. Amy Cakes Danky Dank, a fashion design student from Parsons School of Design, told me, "I normally don't notice people looking at me for what I'm wearing, but every now and then I'll be like, 'Stop fucking staring at me. I'm a human being! If I were staring at you like that you would punch me in the face.'" As a rogue group of creative outcasts, fabulous eccentrics choose the harder path of making a spectacle of themselves when it would be so much easier to just fit in. "I've had moments where I think maybe I should dress down," Amy said, "but then I'm like, no—I wouldn't be being true to myself. It's not like I'm dressing for attention. I'm really dressing for how I feel on the inside on the outside. It is inherently part of myself."[24]

Take a look at a map of the New York City subway system and you see a tangled circuit of orange and red and green snaking through and connecting Manhattan, Brooklyn, and Queens. The black dots are for the local trains, subway lines that makes all the stops. The white ones are for express trains, those that stop only at the white spots on the map—the dreaded Weekend Schedule permitting. Step out of the N train at 23rd Street and grab a burger at the original Shake Shack in Madison Square Park. Head to 59th Street on the 1 and walk along the southern edge of Central Park. The subway system is the heart of the city. It's what gets people moving around from place to place, from work to play and back again. Known the world over, the iconic New York City subway system is part of the hustle and bustle, and it plays a role in the global myth of New York as a relentless twenty-four-hour beast that never sleeps. But the map's slithering patterns of brightly colored arteries and black and white dots aren't just destination points, tourist hot spots, or places to get out and sightsee. They're more like style nodes and they show how and what kinds of styles travel throughout the streets of the city, up and down, east and west, local and express.

These style nodes show us that personal fashion choices are public information. A fact. Style needs to be seen on the streets, moving and activated, to fully come to life. In "Publics and Counterpublics" Michael Warner shows that publics are invented as soon as they're addressed; a public can't exist until it is sculpted, however loosely, into a "concrete audience." "Public discourse craves attention like a child," Warner writes, zeroing in on the allure of selfie culture. "Texts clamor at us. Images solicit our gaze. *Look here! Listen! Yo!*"—and in the case of the fabulous eccentric, I might add, *werk!*[25]

But clothes mean virtually nothing, cultural historian Anne Hollander reminds us, when they're on their own or sitting in a pile in the dirty clothes hamper. Clothes must plug into a specific social or embodied context to have meaning. On its own, a leather jacket is simply a leather jacket. It comes to life the moment we put the jacket on. Only then does it show our consciousness and level of taste, and that's when the leather jacket becomes an expression of ourselves.[26] Style is often about taking a thing that already exists (like a safety pin) out of one use context and translating it into a brand-new one. Possibly the most compelling thing about style, what draws me to it, is not that it's seen, worn, or borrowed but that it has to *travel.* Style needs to be on the move, going, vibrantly darting around the city streets, minding its own business. The little dots on the subway map are not simply sites of coming, going, and missed connections. They're style points—arteries—that show us how fashion travels through and around the urban environment. Streets get us where we need to be, but they also form a style network, a place to tune in to the sudden flashes of individual creativity and expression that zip past when we least expect. This is how fabulousness goes public: it's performed in the streets, at the club, on blogs, and in social media. And it's this publicness that makes the fabulous compelling as a site of utopian vision. Fabulousness uses personal style every day to imagine and actually live in a different kind of world—"Put on a show, and see who shows up" to your world.[27] Through style, fabulousness allows us to wear that version of the world and to bring this world with us everywhere we go, proposing it, offering it, already living in it.

Call me a style queen, someone who loves seeing big, opulent, ridiculous displays of creative personal style on the streets. It's what I love about nightlife and it's also why I love fashion-focused television shows and movies like B*A*P*S, Sex and the City, The Devil Wears Prada, and let's not forget about Dynasty, where the clothes are just as much a part of the story as the storyline itself. Fashion and the city are deeply intertwined, and one of my favorite fashion and the city movies is the 1995 Parker Posey–led film Party Girl, an underground cult film in certain queer, fashion-obsessed circles. Party Girl stars Mary, a free-spirited "it" girl who slowly stops partying to work as a librarian so she can afford to pay her godmother back for bailing her out of jail. The film offers a not-so-veiled critique of queer club kid party culture in 1990s New York, and much of the film's humor lies in how Mary, the party girl who knows all the trends before they strike, can deal with the assumed seriousness of working in a library. For all its fun and campiness, Party Girl has a moral tone, and the lesson is that working looks to go partying is fun, but being a librarian takes real brainwork. Over the course of the movie Mary detaches herself from her party world and becomes more and more professional, culminating in the movie's final scene where her friends throw a surprise party she doesn't want. Mary shows up dressed professionally but her friends can't tell if she's serious or joking. "Well, *you're* working a new look," her gay male friend says with a tinge of sarcasm.

In a memorable moment from the film Mary pumps down the sidewalk in a colorful, creatively strange look that tells you she has a wild personality. Hear her roar (in fabulous fabric). Against the gritty urban backdrop, Mary works a pair of tiny sunglasses matched with a leopard-print jacket effortlessly thrown over a blue blazer, not to mention pink striped stockings and pointy purple pumps. She carries a purse shaped like a tub of Neapolitan ice cream and the tone of her walk is "I am absolutely *it*." The shot is so wide that the camera captures her full look as well as the street all at once, a whole seventeen seconds, and in it the camera flies back in pace with her walk so it looks like she's actually chasing it, running after the edge of the frame.

This is an image of "street style" and it is not unlike the Instagram shot of Leo GuGu pumping across Bowery in New York City "slaying shoppers in a look." Street style images, known by the way they capture how "real" people dress on the street, what I call the urban catwalk, are some of the largest contributors to the visual economy in the twenty-first century. Popular street fashion blogs like *Street Pepper, The Sartorialist,* and *Street Etiquette* have exploded in recent years, but contemporary culture has long been interested in the way other people dress, and personal style is one of the most documented aspects of visual, media, and literary culture. Since at least the rise of industrialization in the nineteenth century, when, as the French poet Baudelaire described, the city streets felt as comfortable as a living room to the socially plugged in, well-dressed flâneur, images and literary descriptions about other people's clothes have been a major storytelling device.

Take a look at John Sloan's painting *Sunday Afternoon in Union Square* (1912). On the surface the image tells the story of two fabulous women making a splash through Union Square in New York City. They sashay through the busy park, passing men, some of whom are reading newspapers while others are keeled over drunk. Many of the men and women in the frame look at the pair with fascination. Who are these fabulous divas? These two ladies are really working it, and I see this as a painting about the effervescence of style in urban space. As the two women go through the park they know they're fabulous, they know they're being looked at by everyone. The daring woman in purple works a pink parasol above her head; she is the only woman wearing pink or purple in the entire image. All the other women in the story are wearing white—even her well-dressed companion. Sloan is telling us that she is wearing the latest fashion of the day. Her parasol is hot off the press, and she holds it high, elevating its status as an accessory. Not to be outdone, her female companion carries a simple white handbag that she dangles out and away from the body just so in an unnatural way, highlighting its status as pure accessory.

Sunday Afternoon in Union Square is an excellent example of looking and being looked at, what the art historian Rebecca Zurier has described as "urban visuality." In an echo of John Berger's theories of vision, for Zurier urban visuality describes what happens when we live in an urban environment and know that we can see things but also that other people can see us too. The notion of taking in visual information and of ourselves being visual information is a key point of entry to Sloan's journalistic style of painting because he throws the viewer straight into the urban landscape. In Sunday Afternoon we're at eye level with the rest of the characters in the park, and just as we can see the action we must assume that we can also be seen. This dual experience of vision frames life in big cities like New York.[28] Urban visuality reminds us that the city is a place to see—advertisements, people, daily life, buildings, shop windows—but that the dressed body is also a sight to see, talk about, and document.

Over the past few decades cultural interest in "street style" has exploded into the popular sphere. In 1994 the Victoria & Albert Museum in London produced the exhibition Streetstyle: From Sidewalk to Catwalk, 1940 to Tomorrow, and in 2010 New York Times fashion photographer Bill Cunningham released Bill Cunningham New York, a documentary portrait of the photographer and his street images. Fresh Dressed, a 2015 film about the rise of contemporary black street style and hip-hop culture, uses the black colloquialism *freshness,* a throwback term meaning "cool" in the 1990s hip-hop circuit, to make a case for the power of black sartorial expression. "Fresh is more important than having money," Kanye West says in the film. "No money! Might have had 50 cents between us, but we were *fresh,*" Christopher "Kid" Reid from 1990s hip-hop duo Kid 'n Play remembers.[29] Freshness was a 1990s-era black dandyism, even though we may not talk about black style as "fresh" today. The art historian Richard Powell prefers the term *sharp,* which he uses to describe an ostentatiously stylish black person. "Many fashionable people have a precise and exacting edge," he writes, "a sense of how to look, of how, figuratively speaking, to 'stand out' and be 'a cut above' the dull and commonplace."[30] This sense of having an edge is about demanding presence for overlooked and underrepresented bodies. In *Slaves to Fashion: Black Dandyism and the Styling of Diasporic Identity,* a must-read for anyone interested in the history of radical black style, Monica Miller celebrates the black dandy, then and now, as an articulation of black personhood. Style not as fluff but as the stuff that makes us human. Dandies turn to style to flip the script and overturn degrading images of blackness. As blacks moved to the North and achieved freedom for the first time, Miller notes, they seized the opportunity to recast and reimagine themselves in a segregated, racist urban environment. Expressing oneself through style demonstrated the power of self-confidence as well as the value of self-worth, in particular in the face of stereotypes and marginalization. All told, black style is always about how black people have transformed themselves "from slaves to selves."[31]

Today, street style works as a synonym for subcultural identity; daily fashion choices are more about a poetics of the self than what look or designer the fashion industry says is hot. Street style excites the eye because it is anti-fashion, an expression of identity, a going against the grain of social norms and the marketplace. Fashion theorists Agnès Rocamora and Alistair O'Neil tell us it is an "apparent disregard of dominant fashion codes"; we create our own looks despite what the market says is hot. Street style ultimately comes from and is "celebrated in the streets rather than in the rarefied spaces in which fashion" is typically found.[32]

Ted Polhemus, an anthropologist who has written extensively on street style, shows that historically clothes were used in a Veblenian sense to say, "I am rich, or, I am powerful," whereas nowadays with street style the tune becomes "I am authentic."[33] Authenticity means showing off that sense of creative strangeness, fabulousness linked more to imagination than the marketplace.

Fashion is usually about change, and not simply because the shifts in seasons require different kinds of fabric. This is what the sociologist Georg Simmel meant when he described fashion as a system of imitation and differentiation. Simmel felt that fashion was about keeping the boundaries between classes intact by constantly changing where that boundary is located. The teal jumper you just bought? So last season. *How can you be seen in public wearing it?* Street style, on the other hand, is much more about bricolage and "talking back" to the dominant culture, even though it is true that styles that start on the street or underground almost always end up on the high street, at the mall, and on MTV.[34] Markets always want to keep their fingers on the pulse, but no matter how hard they try the most exciting creative innovations in style will almost always come from the street, not necessarily the boutique.[35]

Thinking about street style helps us build a philosophy of creativity that highlights what fabulousness does as a form of subcultural resistance.[36] Style snatches ordinary objects from one use context and puts them into a new context as "style" within subculture. Who says AA Duracell batteries can't also make for *fabulous* earrings? Style, then, poses an imminent threat to culture, and that's why it is seen as a "talking back." Dominant culture says to dress this way, but style allows us to say no, to resist, though not without suffering the consequences. Rogue style poses a cultural threat that gets photographed and put up on street style blogs, called "faggot" or other derogatory names as it moves around the city. The real value of subcultural style lies in how it goes "against nature" and hurls a metaphorical brick into the process of normalization at the same time as it calls the bluff of any kind of consensus.[37] The irony is that this "brick"—the brick of street style—eventually gets swallowed up by market forces and repackaged as "hot," making emblems of street cool available for purchase by anyone who shops in the right stores or reads the latest fashion magazines.

In a world that still devalues the impact of visibility, fashioned images of the self prove that creative expression is political, what Minh-Ha T. Pham calls a "do-it-yourself technique of visibility." It turns out that selfies are political, a way of framing opulent images of marginalized people who would otherwise be kept outside of the image sphere. The difference with participatory media, as Pham sees it, is that the relationship of power between the photographer and the person photographed is much more dynamic. In a selfie, you are the author of your own image. You control your own representation—an agency that's expressed the second you approve the image, press "send," and share it with the world. "It is precisely this shift in the visual relations of participatory media," Pham writes, "that make practices of networked vanity potentially so powerful for minoritized groups who have historically [borne] the greater burden of the dominating gaze."[38] Because people forced to the margins now have a say when their images hit the Internet as well as what they will look like, the game of representation and visibility is increasingly complex, with marginalized bodies exhibiting more control and self-authorship than ever before.

Amy Cakes moved to New York and quickly found herself in the city's fashion, party, and club scene. "I would go to a 99-cent store after class and just grab a bunch of weird shit and build an outfit out of it," she remembers. "So it was this ritual of what I did on Fridays." For Amy Cakes, fabulousness is an extension of her art practice, but even beyond that, the unique sense of self-authorship that fabulousness allows taught her to embrace her body type. "Being a big girl," she told me, "means I can walk into a store and find something really cool but they might not have it in my size." Instead of taking a hardship at face value she learned how to make lemonade: "What I really like to do when I'm shopping is go to a store like Top Shop and go through the sales racks. There's almost always some really weird item that I *know* nobody else is going to buy—it's in a really big size or something like that. So then I'm like, well, I'm going to buy this and it's like $5, and I'm going to turn it into something fabulous."[39] For Amy Cakes, fabulousness is about embracing her body the way it is while also exhibiting a degree of creative control. You can't have fabulousness without also relying on confidence, self-affirmation, and a strong, indefatigable sense of self, a self that carries with it the scars of public scrutiny, marginalization, body shaming, racism, and misogyny, and other forms of PTSD. There's nothing vain about wanting to look good, especially when you feel like a black queer error, like I used to feel and still struggle with from time to time.

Our "tendency to dismiss practices of sartorial display and extravagance as mere vanity," Pham tells us, "risks ignoring the lived experience of minoritized people for whom the right to be seen on their own terms and the right to take pleasure in their bodies and self-images has never been a given."[40] This is ultimately about how fashion offers a utopian vision, and I think of a retail outlet like KlubKidVintage, the edgy online secondhand shop run by the LA-based artist Ramdasha Bikceem. KlubKidVintage is an affordable boutique that specializes in unusual, eye-popping fashion gems—statement pieces—from the 1980s and 1990s, many of which have been spiced up or *werked* by Ramdasha herself, a queer woman of color. At the time of writing, a standout piece from the collection is a blue, vintage wool beret that's been studded by hand. "Instant Fabulousness!" the description promises.[41]

What you notice right away about KlubKidVintage is not just the pieces themselves or the way they have been werked but the edgy, editorial images that portray a utopian vision of people of color. The style has a specificity. Ramdasha's models pop right off the screen, fiercely, leaping out of the images themselves. One model compellingly captures the camera's gaze with purple lipstick and an explosive head of blue hair. A long, pink, chandelier-like earring with seven tassels cascades down her neck—if you listen closely you can hear it chime—and the look is topped off with a blue, pink, green, and black sequined jacket. It's a fabulous number, but not just because it looks great. It's fabulous because it shows a woman of color confidently holding our gaze as she embraces fashion, opulence, and joy. It's a powerful image because we are not looking at *her*. She is looking at *us*. KlubKidVintage trades on a queer punk aesthetic and typically shows only models of color in an urban environment, mostly women, and the store's brand unapologetically ties queerness, brownness, the street, and the unusual into a joyous, affirming, effervescent package of creativity, politics, and expression. KlubKidVintage offers up a world, a utopian vision of female-identified style warriors who live in their own vision of the here, the now, and the future.

When I'm out and about on a Saturday afternoon in Hackney, East London, rolling through the graffitied streets of Shoreditch, or walking around the grown-up urban cool of Broadway Market, I love seeing people dressed up as their best versions of themselves. I remember once passing a gender-nonconforming young black male who lovingly wore one single chunky gold triangle-shaped earring, a clear play off the androgyny and stylistic asymmetry of Prince, a backward snapback, a short neon pink skirt over a pair of dark skinny jeans, a white tank top, and white high-top sneakers. "Ooooh . . . yes," I said under my breath as he floated past, though I'm not sure he heard me. We exchanged a silent glance as if to acknowledge each other's opulence. Where was he going? I wondered. What was his story?

Each time I see a person with a unique sense of style I'm reminded of the poetic cultural theory of Wayne Koestenbaum, who wrote with love about paparazzi photographs of icon Jackie Onassis. He was fascinated by these images because he liked the way she always seemed to be on the move, in transit, going somewhere. These images showed her at the edge of the picture frame, always moving—on her way but not there yet. For Koestenbaum, Jackie O. was a figure of transportation. "Photographs of Jackie," he wrote, always "catch her *en passant*, moving quickly from one site to another." She was "a woman in a hurry."[42] Somehow, though, fabulous people almost always seem en passant. They almost always seem like they're going somewhere better than where you cross them on the street—late, pressed to get to the venue. This sense of movement, of queer motion, suggests the ways queer people "slaying us in a look" can't be contained. Drenched in their own versions of the world, the fabulous are flashes of queer utopia who are not at all bothered by the slow, dull pace of the here and now. They chase the edge of the picture frame, constantly in motion, headed into unknown territory, a place without GPS coordinates, not even on the map. Fabulousness is a flight from a stable identity to an eccentric, unknown somewhere else, and that means street style photographs capture fabulous people in transit. On their way there we experience the fabulous as an event, a happening that burns itself into the camera's lens and into our retinas too. I don't need permission from heteronormative society or gay misogyny, queer style says, to wear glitter all over my face; I will do it if I want to. Queer people use style on the street to make declarative statements about *their* versions of the world. Of course, not every queer person is a fabulous eccentric, not every queer person should be, and not every queer person relies on style as a medium of politics or personal expression. I didn't write this book as some kind of instruction manual or a reprimand—"Get it together!"—for people who don't want to make themselves stand out. But because all style is visible, immediate, and personal, it does seem that when style is on the table, people who don't give "a shit" about it feel judged under a microscope.[43]

Mister Wallace, a Chicago-based hip-hop artist who is part of the hip-hop collective Banjee Report, and who also works looks day in and day out, loves using the street to express his unique sense of style. "Sometimes I'll wear these long braids or a caftan or a muumuu on a Tuesday, just going to get coffee," he told me. "People seem to lose their minds seeing someone that's not the norm." The difficulty in being this fabulous, though, is when people on the street easily overlook your art practice and think you're wearing a costume, that you're some kind of clown, a bad joke without a punch line. "When I was in Provincetown," Wallace told me, "it's very New England and everybody's walking up and down the street and the whole place is giving you theme park. And then *I'm* walking around with braids down to my ass and wearing a white dress and people are stopping left and right to take photos of me with their children. I'm not a clown. I'm just a person getting my coffee, working on my performance." His story captures the confrontational nature of queer street style, of being creatively strange, because as exciting as fabulous street style can be, and as much as it can and does inspire other people to reject the norms watching over them, queer street fashion is about exposure in the broadest sense. You're exposed because more people can see you, whether that's on the street or on the fashion blog, and greater exposure means you're more subject to public scrutiny or harm. "This is my life," Wallace says. "I'm not a clown and this is not a costume. I get that all the time—'I love your costume!' It's not a costume. It's *fashion!*"[44]

Amy Cakes, too, spoke about moments where people thought her look was just a costume. "There was one time in high school," she told me, "where my best friend and I put on wigs and weird hats. We were just hanging out. Someone came up and they were like, 'Oh, are you in a play or something?' I was like, 'No, it's Saturday. It's just another day.' I still love doing that to people sometimes where they're like, 'Oh! What are you dressed as?' I'm like, 'Yeah. It's a Wednesday. This is me.'"

What is it about working looks that begs to be stopped, commented on, photographed and posed with? How does a photographer know when to stop a person with a unique sense of style? "A lot of it is their confidence and their energy and conviction," Katya Moorman, a New York–based fashion photographer, said. "They have to have a good look—it's like porn. You know it when you see it." Working a look is about how a great outfit bursts with energy, an energy that soaks up particles of attention from every direction. Joseph Roach coined the phrase *ambulant architecture* to describe the way Mardi Gras suits coast down the street during a parade. These looks protrude up and out and away from the body and ultimately take up actual physical space along the parade path.[45] I daydreamed about ambulant architecture while I stared in awe at a Zulu queen suit in the Mardi Gras Museum in New Orleans. The thing radiated opulence—tall, full, with sequins covering nearly every inch of visual space. An enormous neckpiece radiated high and up and out and away from the body. Here was ambulant architecture, style on the loose. But what struck me about the look was how much space it took up behind the glass it was held in, barely contained, threatening to run off without a moment's notice. The suit was a theory of fabulous eccentricity. Fabulous queers and queens working looks do not always take up this much physical space as works of ambulant architecture, but they do take up just as much if not more visual, mental, and digital storage space, centering themselves in the narrative of fabulousness, taking up the bandwidth instead of asking for permission to exist. In this way, ambulant architecture is about style that coasts down the street on autopilot as it seizes attention, space, excitement, and the camera's lens.

"A hairstyle is about something," queer theorist David Halperin writes in his polemical text *How to Be Gay.* "It has to be about something. If it is not about anything, it's not a hairstyle—it's just hair."[46] This, to my eyes, underscores the content of style, that styles do have social content. More than unbridled narcissism, fabulousness as style shows how creativity intersects with politics, where style is the political content. It's what happens when marginalized people take their own selfies, slay shoppers in a look, and post themselves to Instagram—a firm response to the processes of marginalization, though this exposure does not come without a cost. In the end, fabulousness is urgent. It's about snatching space not later but *right now*—seizing it—instead of taking a number and waiting patiently for permission. Why wait for permission, why wait at all, when you can do it right now and on your terms?

When I dream about how marginalized people use style and creativity to take up space and assert themselves, I think not only of voguing and ballroom culture, I think not only of pumping down the catwalk at a ball, and I think not only of Diahann Carroll on every episode of *Dynasty* she appeared in—I also think of the dazzling mixed-media paintings of the contemporary artist Mickalene Thomas, which offer their own theory of fabulousness. *Portrait of Din #2* from 2011, for instance, is a colorful portrait of a black woman who seems ready to hit the town. She looks stunning, cropped from the breasts up, wearing a black-and-white-patterned top that goes well with her beaded necklace and oversized earrings. She stares the viewer in the eyes: firmly, elegantly, opulently. But look closely and you notice that all the color—the pops of purple eye shadow, the statement red highlights in her hair, her deep red lips—is done with rhinestones. At sixty inches by forty-eight inches, she *is* opulence: the contours of her chin, ears, and nose, the whole of her body framed by decadent black rhinestones. Mixing rhinestones with traditional elements of painting, photography, and collage is part of Thomas's style, an effect you can just barely grasp in a reproduction but which has an awesome effect when you see her work in a gallery, blackness glistening, singing around the room.

Portrait of Din #2 is just one example of what Krista Thompson calls the "surface of the surface," the way light bounces off reflective, blinged-up exteriors, these shiny surfaces acting as the primary chosen representational mode for marginalized people.[47] The marginalized choose bling and light as a way to bring themselves into visibility, to be recognized, seen and noticed. I don't need a camera to notice me if I can be my own flash. Maybe that's why I've always loved sequins and shiny reflective surfaces. Sequins will never go out of style, no way, and maybe that explains why I love going to thrift stores—because there are always fabulous sequins no one wants anymore. I suppose I get that from my grandmother, who always worked something shiny when we went to church on Sundays. It was the Lord's day, she reminded us, so we needed to be our best selves. When I look at Mickalene Thomas's paintings, drenched as they are in rhinestones, I see my own love of sequins and I see my grandmother getting dressed for church on Sunday. This painting is about the reclamation of black beauty, and it is about the power of rhinestones not only to put black women in a white-washed space such as a commercial art gallery but to let them hold the room.

There's more to bling than just the OED definitions "ostentatious jewellery" and "conspicuous consumption." Bling is also about how marginalized people use light and reflective surfaces to spotlight their own visibility. In Shine: The Visual Economy of Light in African Diasporic Aesthetic Practice by Thompson, a must-read for anyone interested in the history of bling, light is positioned as part of the "everyday aspirational practices of black urban communities, who make do and more with what they have, creating prestige through the resources at hand." The secret to this visual economy of light, however, is that instead of celebrating conspicuous consumption and materialism, bling privileges "not things but their visual effects." Bling is not about ostentatious jewelry but the light that dances off it. Who cares if the jewelry is real as long as it sparkles? Thompson makes this point clear when she tells the story of a famous Bahamian prom entrance in 2004; a young woman hired fake paparazzi to take pictures of her on the red carpet, a practice that falls into pop culture's fascination with paparazzi and celebrity culture. While services like Celeb-4-a-Day have allowed posers to hire paparazzi to follow them around so that they look famous, at this Bahamian prom, there were paparazzi but they took no pictures. All the young woman needed was the flash. "She did not hire the photographers to produce photographs," Thompson writes, "but instead to highlight her own visibility and representability."[48] Werk!

"I'm almost ready, anyway," Edie Sedgwick tells her friend Chuck Wein, the male off-camera presence who waits for her to finish an extensive ritual of dressing for nightlife. The year is 1965. "Tonight's the Night" by the Shirelles plays loudly in the background while Sedgwick sits at her vanity, wearing only black patent leather boots and black tights with matching lace lingerie. Despite the inappropriateness of public displays of undergarments, she thinks about wearing the lingerie and an open leopard-print coat to the party. "Why *can't* I go like this?" she protests to Wein. As the two talk about what else she should wear to the function, Sedgwick cakes on more and more makeup, and the camera delicately zooms in on her face to show how dramatic it looks. When Sedgwick turns to her closet and continues to try out a variety of *looks*, Chuck Wein throws her a white jacket, remarking, "*That* would be a show-stopper." She tries the jacket on but, for one reason or another, it's not the look she wants to serve. "Well, what else could you wear?" Wein asks. "Why don't you wear a large hat? If you're going to appear, you might as well *appear*."[49]

     Nearly every Saturday, for a number of years, my grandmother played dress-up. During the week she drove the city bus around Saint

Louis, Missouri, but Saturday was her night off, and getting dressed for the scene of the casino slots was how she spent it. As a young boy I was fascinated by the intricate way she dressed, captivated both by what she wore and by how she actually prepared. Her pieces may not have been as expensive as those of the millionaire socialite Edie Sedgwick, but nevertheless her small mirrored closet exploded with brightly colored sequined jackets, dresses, and skirts. High heels and pumps in daring colors clustered at the bottom of the closet floor. On the top shelf, a wide variety of brown wigs—bobbed wigs or shorter ones with tight curls— lived next to a pink jewelry box that overflowed with fabulous costume jewelry. Pearls, rubies, broaches, and diamonds of all sorts. With music playing in the background, she adorned herself. How could I ever forget her peculiar ritual of dressing to go out, and the peculiar fragrance of perfume, makeup, and lipstick that floated out of the bedroom? As I think about the meaning of fabulousness and the value it has as a way of creating space for the people who do it, I wonder what alternative worlds these appearances produce. Why did my grandmother get dressed this way? What's the difference between her modest approach to fabulous eccentricity fashion and that of a rich heiress who could afford anything at any moment?

Andy Warhol's 1965 film *Poor Little Rich Girl* follows Edie Sedgwick's life as a socialite and member of what the social economist Thorstein Veblen termed the "leisure class." The first half hour of the hour-long documentary portrait shows Sedgwick wasting time by sleeping and talking on the phone, while the second, more telling portion documents her process of emergence and the intentionality of spectacular appearance, or what I think of as the ritual of preparing the body to be consumed visually and socially. Warhol met Sedgwick for the first time on January 15, 1965, on the occasion of a party at television producer Lester Persky's penthouse on 59th Street in Manhattan. The artist had long been fascinated by celebrities and the allure of glamour, an intellectual obsession that was turned outward via his many silkscreen paintings of Marilyn Monroe and Elvis Presley, among other American cultural icons. Warhol was particularly interested in how celebrity functioned as an expressive medium in American culture. Stunned by how Sedgwick's presence authoritatively claimed the space of the party—the way she "appeared"—Warhol turned to his friend the photographer Nat Finkelstein when he saw her and said, "Oh she's so fa-bu-lous."[50]

But my grandmother is fabulous too and, like Edie Sedgwick, she took an enormous interest and care not simply in getting dressed but in using social occasions and her creativity to assert a sense of self. In *Poor Little Rich Girl,* when Chuck Wein says, "If you're going to appear, you might as well *appear,*" the stakes of "appearing" for Sedgwick, as for my grandmother, are not merely to show up, to arrive, or to be present in the room. "Appearing" is to visually and physically demand space, attention, and to announce oneself through the creative labor of self-expression. "Appearing" is a rush of visual and sensorial intensification into normative social space.

The one question that plagues most of us when we're getting ready for a social occasion like a party, a date, or cocktails with friends is "What am I going to wear?" But it's the most fun question we ask too. There's a certain joy in getting ready to go out into the social world. We stand in front of our closets, or the pile of clothes on the floor, faced with a choice of images. Sequins or leather? Button-down or polo? Harem pants or leggings? Colorful socks or black ones? We stare blankly, reaching for a shirt we bought three years ago but have never really worn, and we realize that the shirt we really want to wear is funky—maybe with enough deodorant it will be okay. This process of getting dressed to go out shows how we step into a very special, ready-for-the-club self.

When it comes to getting dressed for the night, most of us have a ritual, an exacting process of putting ourselves together to create the impression we want to give, to look the way we want to look. In *On the Make: The Hustle of Urban Nightlife,* a fascinating study of how students in the Philadelphia area experience nightlife, sociologist David Grazian describes the intricate ways young people get dressed for a night on the town. One of his students, Abigail, describes her process this way:

I undergo the usual one-hour getting-ready ritual of showering, ironing my hair, and applying my makeup, which all takes a combined thirty minutes. The rest of my time is spent pondering over the most important question of the evening: "What am I going to wear?" After trying on about five pairs of jeans, all Sevens and Diesels but varying slightly in shades of washed-out-ness and having rips in slightly different places, I finally decide on my lightest Sevens. Then I spend the rest of the time accessorizing the outfit with a hot pink belt and fun earrings. . . . After frantically running around my room collecting my belongings for the evening, I'm finally ready to go. "Oh shit, what jacket should I take?" I throw about six jackets off my coat rack, [my boyfriend] grabs my long, black, puffy one, and we're out the door.[51]

Notice the routine nature of it all—first the shower, then the hair, then the makeup—and note how hard it is for her to pin down a look for the night, tearing through five pairs of jeans before making a final decision, not to mention the time it takes to edit the outfit once it has all been put together. Haven't we all been there? Abigail's story narrates the way she sifts through her closet, like many of us do, trying on a variety of looks and combinations of looks before deciding on the one that expresses the kind of personality she hopes to capture, the impression she aims to make. For Abigail, as for the rest of us, getting dressed to go out is an arduous, time-consuming feat. Time is invested in ironing her hair, applying her makeup, choosing the jeans, finalizing the accessories. But I question whether hers is the process of creative emergence—of *working a look*—or if it is more likely about stepping into an idealized heteronormative version of femininity.

Men too, gay and straight, also have intense rituals of getting ready for nightlife. I remember being in college and living in a frat house surrounded by straight boys who shaved, showered, and caked on terrible cologne before going out. Certain of my gay male friends even go to the gym just before going clubbing so they can be that much more buff on the dance floor, something I don't identify with at all. "When I go out," Tyler says, "I love meeting new people, especially those of the opposite sex. With this in mind, I take pride in getting ready before I go out. . . . This process includes taking a shower, putting on deodorant, aftershave lotion, cologne, and my 'clubbing clothes,' which are comprised of jeans and a dark collared shirt. The process of getting ready usually takes anywhere between ten and twenty-five minutes." Tyler turns to his "clubbing clothes" for the chase of women. They allow him to become more competitive for female attention in the largely anonymous space of the nightclub. But what I find most revealing is that Tyler has a secret set of "clubbing clothes" that he wears only when he goes out. "If you know where to go," Tyler says, then "you also know what to wear, right?"[52]

We can all relate to the stories Grazian tells because they show that most of us have a process of getting ready for nightlife, even if it's as simple as spraying on cologne. Fashion at nighttime gives us the opportunity to create heightened, idealized versions of ourselves, and who doesn't want the chance to be their best self? The problem that clouds his analysis, though, is that certain idealized versions of ourselves play into the hands of archetypical gender roles. It's no surprise that I'm less interested in nightlife fashion that plays by the rules because, as we have seen, the rules are about keeping gender and identity intact. I want aesthetic choices that break the rules—nightlife fashion that questions normativity, and I want a spectacle that creates visual damage.

In the July 1991 issue of *Interview* magazine, nightlife personality Susanne Bartsch details her intricate process of getting ready for a party. The story illustrates how Bartsch makes the transition from her day look, which she confesses is still very visual, to her night look. There's a picture for each stage in her process. Readers go with her step by step as she puts on her look—or "regalia" as the queer New York performer Michael T. calls it— which includes fake fingernails, a black wig, glitter, and dramatic eye makeup. At the end Bartsch wears fishnet stockings, thigh-high boots, a corset, and a giant plume. She concludes, "You know, darling, getting dressed is easy. Planning what to wear is what takes time."[53]

Bartsch's story highlights the ritualistic ways we prepare ourselves to hit the club, the casino, or the church. What we choose to wear could be as casual as a T-shirt and jeans, or maybe now is the time to put on our favorite pair of shoes, those spiked shoulder pads we found in a thrift store in Silver Lake—or maybe it's the right time to try out a whole new look. Answering the question of what to wear at night, which occupies a unit of time Jack Halberstam sees as "the perverse turn away," a space associated with freedom, community, experimentation, and desire, allows us to be our best version of ourselves.[54] When we go out at night we put on a special body, what Grazian calls a "nocturnal self," that distinguishes our nighttime self from our daytime self, the latter always subject to intense daylight scrutiny. For Grazian this nocturnal self is ultimately about how we create whole new identities for ourselves at night.[55] We fabricate a special night body so we can feel the difference between what we have to do during the day and what we choose to do at night, ultimately the difference between work and play.

Nighttime is a different kind of temporal unit that not only separates light from dark but also shapes how we dress. On Saturday night we typically dress in a style that's freer and less "professional," more revealing, and which highlights our individuality, sexuality, and availability. A number of stories in the fashion advice industry teach us how to transform ourselves from day to night without having to go home from work to change. Pull this string and poof!—now you're ready for the club! This transition from "day" to "night" is as canonical a fashion story as they come. Magazines like *Cosmopolitan, Marie Claire, Vogue,* and *Page Six* have all published stories on dressing for day and night in one look. With an easy transition from day to night we can take a single look from the office straight to the club. "The era of lugging a sequined dress to work and slinking out of a skirt suit in the office bathroom at 6 P.M. is over," *Harper's Bazaar* tells us. "It's a function of economy and creativity—

today's best party looks are a clever twist on the workaday outfit that transcends the time stamp."[56]

Nightlife fashion is exciting because it's the one space where we are encouraged to experiment with identity. There are those who get dressed at night to stabilize their identity, stepping into an idealized, hyper femininity or masculinity, and there are others who *work a look*—people who are more interested in creating characters for each night. By and large, fabulous people are invested in the instability of identity. You could tell one history of nightlife, for instance, by focusing only on the subcultural groups that used fashion to talk back to oppressive ideals of self-presentation and respectability. I'm thinking of the "flapper" of the 1920s, a woman like Lois Long, the first nightlife columnist at the *New Yorker*, who wrote openly about men, drinking, and partying—and wore sexy, free-flowing flapper dresses to match her attitude. As the historian Kathy Peiss has shown, the "putting on of style" was one of the freedoms that new women of nightlife enjoyed. As dance halls, theaters, and social clubs rose to prominence, women could "put on style" as a way to play with identity. Marrying fashion and nightlife meant creating a space where women could spit in the face of the workaday world, dressing to soften the harsh realities of everyday life. For Peiss, fashion allowed women the opportunity to play with identity and to assert a distinct kind of presence.[57]

There is a party in London called Gloria's, an over-the-top, forward-thinking queer dance party that celebrates the culture of working a look. The party abides by a "Big Look, Zero Pay" door policy—"Don your heels and ready your weaves!"—meaning that if you pump to the venue in a strong, creative look, you'll be let in for free. (Regular admission clocks in at £15 on the door.) Such an incentivized approach to creative nightlife dressing creates a space that is visually rich for partygoers: the room overflows with hair and beads and jewels and feathers. It's a participatory event—partygoers as set decoration. But that's just it: based on the call for fashion, partygoers who do turn up to the party in a full look are not necessarily doing it for themselves. It turns out they're working *for* the party, whether they know it or not, by adding to the brand, the party's fantasy. It's one thing if you turn up in a look because you feel like it, or because it's you or, for that matter, because you're being paid. In New York City queer club worlds, for instance, it's common to have a number of "hosts" at a party, people who are simply paid to be there, bring their friends, and look fabulous, helping to set the tone for the party. When I hosted a party with Amanda Lepore at Santos Party House in New York City, part of the goal was to use hosts to attract diverse audiences. Party hosts are like brand names, and when a particular name is splashed on the face of a flyer or attached to the party in some way, that alone says a great deal about what kind of function it's going to be. Every party host is plugged into a different set of subcultural universes. This particular party listed Andrew WK as the "Master of Ceremonies," but it also listed performances by Cherie Lily, Amanda Lepore, and Cazwell, three icons in the New York gay scene. It also showed that Vjuan Allure, one of the biggest DJ names in the house/ballroom circuit, would be spinning. In curating the names on the flyer for our party, we essentially sent signals to a number of subcultures at once.

In 1993, five fabulous party hosts named Michael Alig, James St. James, Amanda Lepore, Leigh Bowery, and Ernie Glam appeared on *The Joan Rivers Show* to talk about their fabulous nocturnal selves. Rivers introduced the group to the audience as "five simple people with a dream . . . and a wardrobe from hell." When she asked why they dress the way they do, Leigh Bowery, wearing a curly blond wig covering his entire face, pointed to the power of shock value: "It's more about expressing our sort of ideas and having fantasies and making them all happen, and also looking different and being a bit subversive. And I think we deliberately try to shock people as well."[58] In his history of club kid culture Frank Owen describes the quintessential club kid look: "Hats made out of Oreo boxes, dresses made out of Tide detergent containers, shirts made of Saran Wrap, and Fruit Loops earrings were among the bright pop-art influenced fashions Alig and his cohorts modeled."[59] This was a kind of fabulousness that was specifically about creative strangeness, not necessarily about embracing gender, doing femininity, or showcasing high-end

labels. These club kids, known for being "fabulous," were featured prominently in popular culture from the late 1980s through the early 2000s. In
a memorable line from the 2003 film *Party Monster,* an eager, wide-eyed
Michael Alig says to James St. James, then queen of New York nightlife,
"I want you to teach me how to be *fabulous!*"[60] The club kids appeared
on *The Joan Rivers Show* and *Geraldo* as well as on the covers of *Life,*
People, and *New York* magazines, and they were a primary inspiration
for the early bizarre looks of Lady Gaga, as the cultural historian Victor P.
Corona shows in his new book *Night Class.*

Alig was born in South Bend, Indiana. He came to New York
City to study at the Fashion Institute of Technology. He always said he
dropped out of fashion school because there was no way he "could stay
home and write a paper knowing that Andy Warhol and Boy George
were partying at Danceteria."[61] Before he was convicted for the murder
of fellow club kid Angel Martinez over drug money he owed, a story that
was retold by club kid James St. James in his best-selling 1999 memoir
Disco Bloodbath: A Fabulous but True Tale of Murder in Clubland and
in the movie *Party Monster,* Alig was known in the late 1980s and early
1990s for throwing transgressive parties that blurred cultural boundaries.
These spectacular costume parties included the infamous Disco 2000 at
the Limelight, a church cum nightclub, Peter Gatien's answer to Studio
54 that opened in 1983 with a huge crowd at the door. Alig's events
also included the concentrated energy of "outlaw" or "pop-up" parties
that took back urban space. Vito Bruno, an architect who wanted to re-
invigorate the city's unused urban spaces by throwing illegal parties in
them, first imagined outlaw parties. In November 1985, an outlaw party
brought 3,142 people to a deserted amphitheater in Corlears Hook Park
in Lower Manhattan, which one lawyer described as "giving parties political confrontation."[62] Alig's own outlaw parties brought back Bruno's original idea, and these costumed confrontations happened in places like the
back of a tractor-trailer—the so-called Disco Truck—or the Union Square
subway platform, and even at a Burger King in Times Square. These
parties completely usurped or "poached" everyday spaces and gave
them a brand-new meaning. Outlaw or pop-up parties not only allowed

nightlife to move outside the increasing corporatization of the nightclub, they also paved the way for increased stimulation by giving clubgoers a new, unexpected experience.

In my own experience as a lover of nightlife, I have always been drawn to the kinds of excessive parties where straight people, gay people, and anybody in between can inhabit the same space. In 2009 I visited a collection of fashion archives at UCLA and found myself hanging out in Echo Park in my downtime. One afternoon I peeked into the now-closed Echo Park Independent Co-op, a fashion boutique that carried only clothes by local designers. I told the shop owner that I had come to LA in search of fabulousness. Her face instantly lit up. "You *have* to go to Rhonda," she told me, and she couldn't have been more thrilled to let me in on this secret. When I asked what Rhonda was, she said that it was the stomping ground for LA club kids, that it was "a fashion party. Very Studio 54. Gay, straight, anything goes." Her words. I was so excited. When I got to Rhonda, which was held at the El Cid restaurant on Sunset Boulevard, the queue stretched down the block. The party was full of people from varying ethnic backgrounds and sexualities, some dressed casually, others working serious looks. The door person was a drag queen, but it was not a gay party. It was a space of convergence where people from a variety of backgrounds came together.

"Rhonda is, I don't know, the home of hedonism in L.A.," Gregory Alexander, one of the founders of Rhonda, told me. "It's the place where gay, straight, fashion and music people that just want to hook up, people that just want to dance, people that want to be seen, people that want to hear really good music come and cohabitate together."[63] A Club Called Rhonda, which *Paper* has described as LA's "kookiest dance party," is the brainchild of Gregory Alexander and Loren Granic.[64] The party came together out of frustration that there were no parties with good house music in a proper venue in Los Angeles. There was house music, to be sure, but it was mostly heard in spaces like the Avalon, where it cost an arm and a leg for parking, entry, and drinks. "I would never go to those venues because I didn't want to drive and pay $10 for parking and then $25 to get into the space, and then another $25 just for one drink," Gregory told me.[65]

Rhonda is not a person but a character, a deity, an eternal club kid rendered brilliantly in the party's own branding as a pair of encircled legs, lately reimagined as a set of disco legs, mirror ball style. "Rhonda, the person, she's this playgirl from all time, basically," Gregory tells me. "She's had her hand in every dance moment in history, whether it's sleeping with somebody who made *the* dance hit of 1980, or whether it's coaching the future promoter of whatever party. She was at Paradise Garage, Studio 54, and Fabric in London. She was at *everything*."[66] Using a fictional club kid who has seen it all as the face of a party is excellent branding, but so is Gregory Alexander's own unique sense of dress, how he works a look. Rhonda might be the name of the party, but for all intents and purposes Gregory Alexander is the queer, transgressive face of it. Though he doesn't identify as a female impersonator or a drag queen, he does use fashion to play with gender roles, Janet Jackson style. Chest hair or beard on full display, and almost never any pants, Gregory turns to heels, fur, and sometimes even opulent statement eye pieces, leading by example in a queer universe where play with gender and fashion is part of creative expression.

Aside from a stellar music policy, what makes Rhonda special is the way the party celebrates the culture of working looks. "A look is basically just an outfit," Gregory tells me, "but it takes into account the hair, makeup, and attitude choices. It's a full head-to-toe vision. It's all perfectly coordinated, like a look right off the runway or from a movie."[67] Every Rhonda event culminates in a post-party gallery of images, easily viewable on Facebook or Instagram, showcasing the party's unique look, feel, and ethos. It's by no means the first party to rely on party photos, an entire genre of nightlife journalism that would lead us back to the earliest issues of *Interview* magazine, the society photos of New York–based photographer Patrick McMullan, the photos from the Misshapes party, the style photos from the AfroPunk Festival, and the party photos featured in *Purple* magazine. The point of party photos, in many ways, is to show the extent to which nightlife is a separate world. It's to show that nightlife is about a politics of joy.

One of the things fabulous eccentricity pushes up against is boredom—and we can all relate to wanting to alleviate boredom when it pops up. The harsh anonymity of the urban environment turns us into a bland, mass phantasmagoria of "things." We become boring. As the cultural critic Georg Simmel wrote in his 1903 "The Metropolis and Mental Life," "Man is a creature whose existence is dependent on differences, i.e. his mind is stimulated by the difference between present impressions and those which have preceded." For Simmel, we need perception to tell the difference between our surroundings and ourselves. The problem is that fast-paced, urban environments inundate us with much more stimuli than we can handle, stretching our nerves so thin that we lose the ability to react to anything. Simmel calls this "the blasé metropolitan attitude," or a burned-out incapacity to respond to new stimuli. Things "appear to the blasé person in a homogeneous, flat and grey color with no one of them worthy of being preferred to another."[68] What a dull, depressing vision of urban living. Fabulousness rejuvenates us and pulls us past this urban blasé sentiment with sudden brilliant acts of astonishment.

Fabulousness is style that's constantly performing in and with the city. It's style we can see on Instagram and it's style we go to the party with. In my mind's eye, a daring *look* is a Barthesian "punctum," or puncture wound, and it shoots out at us like an arrow. As mobile one-act shows, looks are endless performances that continue as long as we stay in public space and as long as we can be seen and reseen, shared and liked. Fabulousness is confrontational because as long as my look can be seen it can also be commented on, positively or negatively, and it can be critiqued, photographed, smiled or smirked at every time I walk into a new room, take a different bus, pass a different group of people—every time I can be seen again.

With fabulousness, dreams and theories of stylish utopias are yanked from the future and brought to the present. Any suggestion other-wise regulates queer people and queer people of color to a life of waiting, taking a number, and holding on for better times. I think of the late José Muñoz, who felt that "there is something black about waiting. And there is something queer, Latino, and transgender about waiting."[69] Not waiting—that is, doing it now, loudly and in the streets and at the club—is precisely the magic of fabulousness. As a queer aesthetic, fabulousness is not about waiting for permission or holding on long enough for social, cultural, governmental, or legal conditions to change. It's about creating a unique world for yourself according to your own terms, a world you can inhabit right now.

"I Create My Own Space" A Conversation about Fierceness

STYLE IS POLITICAL. The way we dress shapes how strangers react to us as we walk down the street, and it alters the dynamics of a room the moment we walk through the door. More than just looking good and showing off, style is also about conceptualizing a unique version of the world—a separate dimension, a portal—and bringing that world/portal/dimension with us everywhere we go. *Fierce*—a word that indicates the potential violence of style—highlights what aesthetic visions do: they create chaos. In this interview I discuss the power and chaos of fierceness, eccentricity, and radical styling with an untenured black female scholar who has been told more than once, and by more than one institution, to tone down her look, an unsubtle suggestion that blackness, wherever it appears, always presents a surplus, an excess that needs to be tamed. But instead of allowing that excess to be suppressed and placed under punitive surveillance, she has used it to create space for herself on her own terms.

> Fierceness is a term that I think captures the political heft of what eccentricity is and how style impacts people in the here and now. It's a violent word—FIERCE!—but I'd like to think of that violence as creative and aesthetic rather than puni-

103

tive or harmful. There's an urgency, an immediacy with fierceness. Instead of asking for permission to exist, fierceness seizes that permission and places a lien on it. And in the process it creates space. I'm wondering how practicing fierceness in everyday life has impacted you personally, creatively, and professionally.

When I hear that term it makes me think of a James Baldwin quote from his 1962 article in the *New Yorker* titled "Letter from a Region in My Mind," which is: "To be sensual, I think, is to respect and rejoice in the force of life, of life itself, and to be present in all that one does." I feel like sensuality and being present in your body—to me *fierce* is being present and occupying that space. You're saying, *this* is my space. It is uniquely mine, and by uniquely mine I don't mean this sort of rugged individualism, but uniquely mine as this intersection of categories, realities, and aesthetics that come together in this body. That's what fierceness is—that flatfooted grandma stance. "Take it. Do what you will with it, but take it." For me, that's fierce. Just standing in one's own space.

You have such a great sense of style, but even in the twenty-first century there are folks out there who think that having style or being expressive automatically means you're empty intellectually or that all you care about is the surface. Have you faced any style-induced struggles or policing, especially as a black female scholar working in a largely white university context?

There are so many challenges at so many times to my authority as a scholar, my authority as an intellect, my legitimacy as a scholar, the rigor of my work based on my positionality, so for me, when I give that job talk or that conference paper, it's about saying, "I'm here. I'm standing in this space and I'm representing everybody who came before me." And it's my armor. It's me saying: "I'm going to be myself and that's going to be expressed in my work, in my dress, in the way I move, in the way I talk." I express myself in my gesture, in my look for the day, in my shoe choice, in my earrings. And I just feel like all of that allows me one more level of exclusion, and it kind of sets the tone for me to say, "This is me. This is my work. This is what I do." I feel like I use fierceness to put people on notice.

I had pushback in grad school. Professors who looked out for me, who really believed in me, who said: "You look like you spend so much time and money on your outward appearance that you don't seem serious. That can be a hindrance for you." But if I'm going to be in this space, I'm going to be *me*. To borrow a phrase from [the rapper] Fabolous, you can *get down* or you can *lay down*. I'm coming! So I think my clothes help me do that. My look helps me do that. It's me expressing myself in this space where I'm not supposed to be.

When I look at my grandmother and the women who came before me, they occupied an even more contested space. It's always about being subservient. So my grandmother would be walking into those homes while she was cleaning them, while she was earning her master's degree, in her fiercest coat with the full collar and saying, "You may think that this work defines me, but I define myself. Here's how I signify that to you—in my look."

Whenever I hear folks say that fashion and style aren't political, or that fashion shouldn't matter, I think about the people out there who feel compelled to turn down their outward appearance

just so they can walk down the street and get a sandwich or because they want to be loved. More people should realize how dehumanizing it is to feel pressure to renounce yourself just so you can walk down the street, be taken seriously, or keep your job.

I think when one of my advisors said to me, "I know where you spend all of your stipend," it made me . . . I already felt like I was in a space where I don't belong, so that signaled that I need to signal to people that I'm serious, so that they'll take me seriously. So, let me tone down my earrings, let me tone down my bangles, let me put on my flat shoes and give them what they need to feel comfortable. But it just made me feel even less like myself and even less like I belonged there. Because in truth, I realize that I don't belong anywhere. *I create my own space.* And I do that by being myself. So I put *back* on my bangles, I put *back* on my wedges and my four-inch heels. Everybody else can walk in flats, if that's your space: *work.* I love a ballet flat. It's just not my thing. So I've gone back to what makes me comfortable, and I've found that I'm a better professor, I'm a better teacher, I'm better when I'm in my own space. I'm not uncomfortable, I'm not resentful. When you surrender parts of yourself, you become incredibly bitter and incredibly resentful. So I'm not a good mentor when I'm trying to fit into someone else's model, I'm not a good scholar. It's no small thing to be yourself. If I have to do it somebody else's way, I'm not going to do it.

You're talking about inhabiting your own space and not waiting to be given permission. I know it sounds very utopian, which I don't think is a bad thing, but it's clear that the forces that oppress us—capitalism, racism, misogyny, patriarchy, sys-

temic inequality—are not going to collapse or disappear in our lifetimes. Are we all supposed to wait until we have achieved equality for everyone once and for all? I don't think so, because that day may never come. And that's why I think it's so important to express ourselves immediately, right now, and to hell with people who don't get it.

When I think about fierceness I equate it with what I heard growing up in the church. And it's this spirit of excellence. You step out, you come for everybody. If you're going to do it, do it all the way. And those church ladies with their big hats, they are like . . . *what!* And all for the glory of god. I love that. It's just like everything to the fullest. Some people—even though they admire a fierce person, they kind of shy away from it, thinking either they can't be like that or it's a performance. And I think everything is a performance in some way, but it's not a performance in the way that people think. It is the fullest expression. Encouraging people to bring more of themselves to a space is something I encourage students to do all the time, because the space needs you.

Fierce is the highest level of expression, the deepest form of engagement. Fierce is not just a look. You know, RuPaul is fierce. Nobody comes for RuPaul. And it's not because he has the face that's beat, it's because he will read you. Don't come for him. *Don't.* He's not just a pretty face. He can tell you about any number of topics. When you come across somebody that's fierce, you're not just looking at a look. You're looking at someone who owns the space. Of course that's a tool for success, because it's about an incredible look, a high level of skill, and the ability to present it all in one. That's what makes people amazing.

How do you think fabulous eccentricity impacts people in their everyday lives?

When I see fabulous people I feel like I can be more of myself. When I see RuPaul I'm like, "That cheek is *killing me.* I'm going to do mine just like that." It draws you in to say . . . there's more. There's more of me to express, there's more joy, there's more beauty. There's something joyous about fierceness. Fabulousness makes people want to be more themselves. And we let them have it. It's an armor. It readies you for battle. It's my way of saying, "I'm myself," it sets my energy and it sets my tone, but when I'm dressed, I feel my grandmother with me, I feel like I'm not alone.

Probably the most difficult thing about choosing to stand out is that it so closely courts risk and danger. By being yourself and living your own fantasy, you're also subject to surveillance and policing and you become a potential target for any level of violence. What's so compelling, I find, is that folks take the risk anyway.

People won't be comfortable. There are people out there who aren't comfortable with me now, and they wouldn't be comfortable with me if I was any less extra. Out of the history from which fierce comes, these are people that are already marginalized, so it's not like the spaces we're occupying are welcome to us in the first place. Walking into the space as I am lets them know that I'm comfortable with this body that they're not comfortable with. And that's a risk, because people don't want you to be comfortable and confident if *they're* not comfortable with who you are. But we do live in the social world, so what are we supposed to do? Wear one bangle instead of twenty? It's tough, because we do have workspaces and we do have to feed our families and we do have to walk down the street. Sometimes you have to fold into the pressure, but you know, I'm always like . . . let me put on something *extra* underneath! You know, to sort of be myself. I think you always have to have a reserve. The self has to be expressed. It does. People need to know that you can carve out a space for yourself where you don't have to surrender at all.

Fierceness, fabulousness, and all other visions of spectacular appearance are about imagining space and carving it out for yourself in the here and now, not waiting for the right time to do so in the future. This is important because brown people live in an ecosystem that is constantly on the attack, one that steadily reminds us that we are "too much," "over the top," and that we ought to "tone it down" or suffer the consequences. "Renounce yourself," the philosopher Michel Foucault once wrote, "or suffer the penalty of being suppressed; do not appear if you do not want to disappear. Your existence will be maintained only at the cost of your nullification."[1] What he's saying is that society wants weirdos, outcasts, and eccentrics to be suppressed, and it will systematically penalize anyone who steps too far out of the box. The only way to stay alive and safe, Foucault says, is to participate in the fantasy of a bland, normative group consciousness.

But fabulousness resonates and has value, I think, when we decide not to cave in to this oppressive ecosystem but to confront it with our versions of the world. At some point we do cave to the demands—we take off our bangles and we take off our wedged heels, so to speak—but soon enough the things we do to feel "safe" don't necessarily feel safe anymore. They produce just as much anxiety as the fear and reality of being reprimanded verbally, physically, and professionally. So when we say, "This is my space," we're creating the tiniest utopia and asserting ourselves in a world we're not supposed to inhabit, and that is a beautiful gesture.

There are folks we will make uncomfortable whether or not we're fully expressing ourselves. They don't like us, so why should we walk around looking so fabulous and free? But how does the way we inhabit our bodies have anything to do with anybody else? Why do you feel so threatened by how comfortable we are with ourselves? How does the way we dress have anything to do with the way we teach, the art we make, the kind of friend or lover we are, the food we make, the intellectual work we do, or any of our other talents and contributions? We know that the more visible we are, the more we are also subject to surveillance. But we shouldn't let oppressive systems zap all our joy and vibrancy. The second they do—the second we throw in the towel and renounce ourselves, as Foucault put it—the system wins.

3.
Up in
the Club

i'm waiting in line at Berghain, a stunning, cathedral-like techno club housed in an old power plant on an industrial plot of land in the former East Berlin neighborhood of Friedrichshain.[1] Born in 2004, Berghain is, at its heart, a straight-friendly gay club and cultural center with roots in the underground sexually liberated queer, leather, fetish, and sex party scene of Berlin. There is a gay sex club, the Lab.oratory, in the club's basement in addition to dark rooms, and many of the flyers for the sex parties held in the Lab were designed by the German photographer Wolfgang Tillmans.[2] The club's name—berg-hain—comes from a stringing together of the former West Berlin neighborhood of Kreuz*berg*, just over the river Spree, and its current location in Friedrichs*hain*, symbolizing a unified Berlin after the fall of the wall in 1989. It's my first time in Berlin, and I came to the club because a friend of mine from New York, who knows how much I love gritty club culture, told me, "You *must* go to Berghain. I tried when I was there but I didn't get in." Another friend, also a scholar of club culture, promised me, "It's the shit." I was sold.

But getting into Berghain is "tough," as nearly every item written in Facebook statuses, online forums, blogs, on Instagram, newspaper and magazine articles, and really any conversation about the club highlights. One eager clubgoer, who tried to get in five times, to no avail, finally asked the Reddit community for emergency assistance: "Hello dear friends, i am staying in Berlin for 1 week, going for culture, food and party. Since 2013, i have tried to get into Berghain 5 times, i got into an afterhour in the garden once, but not inside. If there is any regular seeing this post, plz help us getting in, i'd love to see Dinky on Saturday."[3]

In 2015 *Vice* published "How to Get into Berghain. Maybe. Hopefully," a piece focused on hard style and behavioral tips to help people get into the club.[4] That article was followed by "Photos of People Who Didn't Get into Berghain," a photo gallery shot by the photographers Benedikt Brandhofer and Leif Marcus, whom *Vice* asked to document what people were wearing when they were rejected by the club. The piece tells the story of people like Pierre from Berlin, who "is about to go to sleep and come back after breakfast on Sunday morning to give it another shot," and Lievwkje, who "wonders why she didn't get in and

A sunny exterior shot of Berghain/Panorama Bar/Säule, often cited as the best club in the world at the time of writing.

is determined to try again next time. Being turned away has only stoked her curiosity about Berghain."[5] There's even a website—getintoberghain. com—run by Max Wunderbar that offers a $49 step-by-step "Get into Berghain Tonight" guide. "I am convinced that my product will get you inside Berghain. I have no doubt about it," he promises.[6] There's a money-back guarantee if you get turned away.

What is now known as Berghain is actually the new home of the old Ostgut, a difficult to get to underground gay club where partyers danced in a faceless gray building built to repair trains that opened in 1998 but closed in January 2003 to make way for what is now the Mercedes Benz Arena.[7] Daniel Wang, a queer Berlin-based DJ, remembered the old Ostgut this way:

> **Ostgut was the epicenter of Berlin nightlife starting late 1998, and was not only a place to hang out from Friday night until Sunday evening—often non-stop—*it was a world unto itself.* The old Ostgut was built inside an abandoned factory next to the Ostbahnhof railways, and there were not even street lamps anywhere near the entrance. In fact, officially, Ostgut was not on any street at all. (On a city map, there is only an empty space there.) One could reach it from Muehlenstrasse, where a long section of the Berlin Wall still remains; but we always preferred to walk down from the bridge over Warschauer Strasse station. We'd climb down a precarious and illegal metal staircase, and then walk, on raw concrete, through absolute darkness for a few minutes, until we could see the bouncers and the clubbers in their boots and bomber jackets waiting at the door.[8]**

Berghain/Panorama Bar opened on Friday, October 15, 2004. The new venue had already created a reputation for itself before it even opened, without any advertisement or advance publicity. "Seven or eight of us who live nearby, plus three friends visiting from Paris," Wang remembered,

are taking two huge taxis to the opening party. We arrive at 11:15 pm, and discover that about 80 other people have already arrived earlier than we did; but we also can't help but be excited by this fact—the weather has been freezing cold for the past week, and if anyone can imagine a major club opening nowadays in a big city, which could attract over 500 people at the door an hour before opening, without ANY advertisement at all—this would have to be a very special club indeed. . . . As the bouncer slowly opened the door, everyone rushed forward, and I vaguely feared being trampled over by all these people who simply wanted IN.[9]

I show up at the club on a warm Saturday night at about 1:30 a.m., which is early for me. In New York I would normally go out a bit later than that, and also I'm aware that the party at Berghain goes from Saturday until sometime Monday morning. I expected the line to be long, but I thought that getting here early by New York standards would mean there wouldn't be much of a wait. But even at 1 a.m., only an hour after the club opened for the weekend, the line was already two hundred people deep, packed with easyJet clubbers who have come here from all around Europe. If I'd known, I could have used the Is There a Line at Berghain? app, a simple crowdsourced smartphone program that tells you what its name implies.[10] As the journalist Tobias Rapp wrote in a recent history of the Berlin club scene and what he calls the "Easy Jet set," "It's as if these people are

A German concert ticket service lures customers by telling them, "You're not getting into Berghain anyway."

queuing to get into another country. And in a sense, they are."[11] So I wait, taking in the crowd, and as I do I'm reminded of Baudelaire, who wrote in 1855 that "it is not given to every man to take a bath of multitude; enjoying a crowd is an art."[12] The most compelling thing about the wait is listening to people's conversations. They talk about the line itself, how long they think it will take to get to the door, how much they've heard about Berghain, what they'll do if they don't get in, what other clubs they could go to, how they've heard you're supposed to act at the door. The line alone is an etude in human behavior.

A number of clubs I know in New York have tight door policies, places like Le Bain, the Boom Boom Room, the Box, Beatrice Inn, or Le Baron, where getting in often means being rich, powerful, and connected—that or wearing expensive labels, being a celebrity, fabulous, or a friend of the doorman. In *Night Class: A Downtown Memoir*, a luscious story of self-transformation, creativity, and nightlife, sociologist Victor P. Corona describes how he transformed from drab to fab, though not overnight, of course. He opens the book with a tale about how hard it was for him and a group of friends to get into a hot New York nightclub. "Clearly that night's dreary version of me, pathetically pleading with the doorman, would not fly in clubland. Of course his rejections hurt," he writes, "but it also pushed me to become a better version of myself." Much of nightlife is about getting into club spaces, by having an ID (real or fake), the right or wrong look, and often by being the wrong race. "To some," Corona writes, "it all might just expose nightlife as a snobbish, sadomasochistic practice. But as I often tell my students, if they let just anyone into this school, your diplomas wouldn't mean anything. It's the filter, the gatekeeping, the conscious curation of a community inside that creates value."[13]

The tighter the door, the hotter the club, where "hotness" is what the sociologist David Grazian describes as the will to suffer long lines just to go to the most fashionable clubs, "the epicenters of cool."[14] This sense of hot and cool, the major form of currency in the club industry, is what Sarah Thornton sees as subcultural capital, a form of hipness that's about being "in the know."[15] It's hard to tell what value subcultural capital has my first time waiting to get into Berghain. People dressed in expensive clothes are being turned away, and people wearing all black are being turned away, even though a number of blogs tell their followers that wearing all black is the key to getting into Berghain. Sven Marquardt, the head of security at Berghain as well as the face of the club's door, wears mostly dark colors and has a dark, minimalist appearance, a well-curated goth aesthetic with tattoos covering his face and rings on each finger. "My colleagues tease me about it," Marquardt said in an interview published in *GQ*. "Like, hey, Sven, why don't you dress more colorfully so the guests will stop wearing all black? Last weekend I actually wore all white at the door, to mess with everybody."[16] There's a subcultural flavor to the crowd at Berghain, but people with tattoos and nose piercings are being turned away too. "Whether you're a queen or a farmer," Rapp wrote, getting rejected at Berghain's door can really "happen to anyone."[17] This knowledge only creates even more anxiety in the line because no one can figure out why certain people are being rejected, leading some to scrutinize those who didn't get in and come up with their own conspiracy theories about what they did wrong.

In general, doors are usually the last stage of access in nightlife settings to ensure a party has the vibe it wants. Most people who go clubbing have a story to tell about something that happened to them at the door, like my friend Chad, a Berlin-based student who has been going to Berghain for years, who sent me a frantic Facebook message the first time he didn't get in. In *Club Cultures: Music, Media, and Subcultural Capital,* Sarah Thornton points out that club audiences are nearly always preselected. We have already seen the flyers and selected the venues we want to go to before we even show up at the door. Even Wolfgang Tillmans, whose art is prominently featured at Berghain upstairs in Panorama Bar, knows that "people take significant pain and trouble to get there in the first place and then get in."[18] With preselection and "tight" door policies, where paying to get into a club is not the only thing it takes to get in—where, in fact, being chosen means the privilege to pay the entrance fee—clubs become social worlds based on a unified taste in a certain style of fashion, music, or other aesthetic. And that means that most people already know where to go at night before they even leave the house. "The door policies which sometimes restrict entry," Thornton writes, "are simply a last measure. If access to information about the club and taste in music fail to segregate the crowd, the bouncers will ensure the semi-private nature of these public spaces by refusing admission to 'those who don't belong.'"[19] But clubs with tight doors are often less about refusing admission and denying entry than they are about actually creating special worlds that are much removed from the humdrum of everyday life. Clubs with tight door policies don't want to let anyone in who will destroy the unique fantasy the venue has staged.

Aside from its top-notch music program, unparalleled sound system, and unique architectural space, part of the appeal of Berghain is that it's a special world that, as the artist Sarah Schönfeld sees it, is "beyond image technology." You can't take pictures inside and there are no mirrors or reflective surfaces anywhere in the venue—not even in the bathroom. For Schönfeld, being beyond image technology means that "the space is also beyond narrative." It can't be represented in images; the special world the club has created can be represented only in metaphors.[20] This special world is one of hedonism, sexual permissiveness, and experimentation. It is a place where you can essentially do what you want. "You could get completely lost in little Purgatories as well," Wang remembered, "the long stairwells and various dark rooms, complete with chains, slings and urinals with tubes leading who-knows-where, and corners in which men and men, and men and women, discovered parts of their sexuality which they had not explored before."[21] Tillmans, who has been associated with the club since its opening, believes that the sexual permissiveness and the special hedonistic world that Berghain has created are "not just about the darkrooms in themselves, but instead about the possibilities that they embody and symbolize."[22] You don't *have* to use the dark rooms for sex, he suggests, but you *could*. And that sense of exploration or potential is what makes nightlife exciting.

When you get to the front of the line at Berghain, a bright white spotlight splashes on you so the doormen can get a good look. The closer we get to the front, the less people talk. The conspiracy theories have stopped. The advice on getting in has stopped. We snake through the end of the line and we all stand and observe the door theater being enacted in front of us. Some go in; most do not. I am nervous, nauseous even. The more I watch people in front of me get turned away and the more I hear the beats pour out of the Panorama Bar upstairs—I'm already dancing, feeling the fantasy—the more I just want *in*.

There's something deeply human about the thrill of being *in* hot nightclubs, and this frames how we have partied for the last hundred years and beyond. Through nightlife we seek transgression; we're pressing up against cultural restrictions and norms, and we're creating experience. In *Steppin' Out: New York Nightlife and the Transformation of American Culture, 1890–1930,* one of the first books devoted to night-life culture in New York, Lewis Erenberg observed that "the night is a time for dreaming," an idea that is as relevant now as it was in the time frame of Erenberg's study. "Fantasies and hidden desires," he wrote, "seek realization in an urban world whose very anonymity permits them."[23] Now as then, party people use the club to distance themselves from the grind of daily life and they pursue hidden desires and transgressive fantasies all while cloaked in a pool of anonymity.

Through nightlife, we transition out of our domestic, private selves and go in search of a "wider life." Erenberg shows how during the first forty years of the long twentieth century, the heightened experience that nightlife institutions engendered managed to make broad social changes to American culture. One of the most important was a fierce challenge to stodgy Victorian ideals of family and domesticity. Life during the Victorian era was centered on the parallel notions of a healthy domestic environment, refinement, and a genteel style that "produced a stifling domesticity and social formality." You're supposed to be at home, not at the club. By the 1890s, when nocturnal amusements had exploded as a new cultural fad, and certainly through the age of the cabaret in the 1920s, Erenberg observes, this nightlife appealed to both sexes as they sought a life outside of the home and up in the club.[24]

In 1915, a young party-going New York heiress by the name of Eugenia Kelly found herself in internationally publicized trouble. Frustrated by Eugenia's drinking habits and insouciant ways, her mother was determined to save her "incorrigible" party girl by having her daughter arrested to stop her from going out. Think about that for a moment: a parent who has their child arrested because they party too much. At Mrs. Kelly's request, the young Eugenia was snatched at Pennsylvania Station and served an arrest warrant. According to testimony, Mrs. Kelly worried because her daughter regularly stayed out until 3:00 or 4:00 in the morning.[25] I can only imagine what Mrs. Kelly would have to say to me when I come home after eighteen hours of partying or going to the club during the day.

But what are the implications of staying out until 4:00 in the morning or later? If staying out beyond the translucence and surveillance of daytime produces anxiety, then going out under the cloak of darkness shows us the extent to which nightlife perhaps always facilitates transgression. To criticize those staying out late when many people are home is to underscore the condescending distance between work and productivity and pleasure and leisure. In 1926, New York mayor Jimmy Walker attempted to curb late-night revelry by installing a 3:00 a.m. curfew because, according to one testimony, being out until the wee hours of the morning "gave a bad impression to the poor working man, on his way to honest labor at dawn, to see groups of tipsy people in evening clothes coming out of night clubs."[26]

At her trial Eugenia Kelly responded in bewilderment to the charges against her: "Why, if I didn't go to at least six cabarets a night I would lose my social standing." Being able to stay out as late as she wanted, enjoying as many cabarets as possible, suggests that for Eugenia Kelly, in concert with what historians of nightlife have argued, the cabaret was a space for transgressive freedom, anonymity, and escape from the patterns of restrictive Victorian etiquette. But it is also a testament to the power of going out to be seen. Yet the more Miss Kelly went out, it seems, the more insubordinate she became. Her mother once slapped her in the middle of Hotel Gotham, a posh Fifth Avenue hotel, for a snide remark she made.[27]

Eugenia Kelly, who sought freedom in the darkness of the nightclub, shows us the growing pull that the new nightlife exerted on an old, established social order. Indeed, conversations about nightlife during this period—what it was and why it needed to be controlled—were particularly rich. By the early twentieth century, then the peak of nightlife amusements, women broke free from the responsibilities of the home and explored the night, like the New Yorker nightlife columnist Lois Long who, beginning in 1925, wrote columns about her drinking, dancing, and sex life under the pseudonym Lipstick, often going straight from the bar to the office.

Nightclubs are portals to another dimension. They are not necessarily safe spaces, nor are they utopian in nature, but they do offer a vision of life on the other side. And that means that doors are thresholds, abstract regulation points that carry us from one state of being to another as soon as we cross them. "It starts with the doormen," the artist Sarah Schönfeld said about Berghain, "who are something like guardians of the temple. You have to get past them, but whether you get in or not is unclear every time. If you succeed, then you virtually have a blessing for the evening: today you're ready for it, now you're allowed. This authority that's imparted to a person, the fact that you are welcome today and allowed to pass through the barrier is very important."[28] Doors do the visual and psychological work of setting these special, protected spaces up to begin with. In cartoons, fantasy movies, fairytales, and films like *Harry Potter* or *Maleficent*, doors are protected by guards—or sometimes accessible only by getting over the bridge to the other side of the moat—to keep the bad guys out. During Prohibition, the doors to speakeasies were hidden and difficult to access for fear of police raids by undercover agents. And at military checkpoints, international borders, airports, fancy corporate offices, and college dorms, as well as at nightclubs, we are asked to prove we are who we say we are before we are allowed to come in.

My interest in doors to nightclubs has to do with how, on the one hand, they are gateways to a special fantasy world that is protected by doormen, and how, on the other, they facilitate identity. Think again of the first time the young Rastignac appeared at the home of Madame de Restaud, pretending to be a person of note. The doorman barely let him into the house! Style plays a key role in fabricating identity, and often working a look is a key part of showing you belong. In the best-selling tell-all of his life as a doorman to some of New York City's most sought-after nightspots, Thomas Onorato is emphatic that the most important thing you can do to get into a "hot" club is to "work a look! Don't look like you've just been hit by a Banana Republic delivery truck. Whether that look is a plastic lobster and a baguette tied to your head or just a cute skirt and a vintage tee, if you want to get past the door bitch work it, boys and girls, work it."[29] All told, doors are checkpoints of identity, and in this way getting through them is a performance of belonging. Onorato's warning echoes performance theorist Richard Schechner's key point about performance: any successful performance means that "a certain definite threshold is crossed. And if it isn't, the performance fails."[30] Like performance, gaining access to nightclubs with tight doors—or really, getting past any guarded door—is about successfully performing identity in a way that allows us to pass over the threshold and enter the protected world on the other side, whatever that protected world may be. We need to convince the doormen not that we are not bad people but that we are not the kind of people who will jam the specific fantasy the club imagines it provides. If we can't get our foot through the door, so to speak, then our performance fails.

Luis-Manuel Garcia, one of the leading scholars of the Berlin electronic music scene, calls what we do to get into certain nightclubs a performance of "subcultural integration." Here, getting in means you are already "an insider; but if one is not already inside this scene, then one can at least perform 'insiderness' and hope that the doorperson will read this performance as a positive indicator of one's likelihood to integrate successfully into the scene." I've been going to Berghain regularly now since July 2013, and over the years there have been many times I've been waiting in line at the club and an eager clubgoer, often a straight guy who may only know about Berghain because he heard about it on a music blog or saw it spoofed on *Conan*, reads my outfit and assumes I'm going to get in (I never assume I'm getting in) and latches onto me for dear life. He does this because he thinks that being with me can help him get in. But I always feel a pressure to distance myself from people who seem like they are "failing" at being a part of the scene—not because I think I'm too cool for school (I don't) but because I suspect they have come to Berghain to treat it as a zoo: to gawk at all the crazy nightlife animals in their natural habitat, which ruins the fantasy for everybody else. As Garcia describes, and we should take his word for it, "The lesson is clear:

to get (socially) inside, one must act like one is already (culturally) inside." Tourists at the door to nightclubs in Berlin are read closely for their cultural fluency and subcultural knowledge, all of which is reflected in language, dress, and attitude.[31]

Most popular conversations about nightclubs with tight doors are about the policies that discriminate and keep people out based on race alone. Doormen to hot nightclubs often act as agents of social control who regularly deny minorities, working-class people, and other seemingly "unfit" clubbers.[32] In 2012 Murat, a young German-Turkish student, was denied entry to Agostea, a big club in Hanover, and when he asked why the bouncer allegedly told him, "The boss doesn't want any foreigners to come in." He later sued the venue and the Hanover District Court awarded him 1,000 euros.[33] In London, Jermain Jackson, the 2014 winner of the reality singing competition *The Voice*, was denied entry to his own party after a performance on the show. One of the bouncers said to him, rather ridiculously, "We don't know your haircut, it might be a gang-affiliated type of haircut."[34] Berghain's own door policy has been described as xenophobic, racist, and sexist in online forums. In February 2015 Felix Da Housecat was denied entry to the club and turned to Twitter to share his frustration with his 120,000 followers. "Yo I love Berghain for turning my Black beautiful ass away . . . u jus pissed on Frankie knuckles and Larry Levan u hitler racist," he tweeted.[35]

Certain clubs post visible signage at the door, a warning to patrons about the kinds of things they can't wear inside, a call always rooted in racism. I was waiting in line at a queer punk rock club I used to go to in Tribeca, standing behind a group of four white men who didn't seem all that queer. Instead of turning them away the bouncer lied and told them the cover was $30 that night, even though it was only $10, and the boys turned away on their own. Another time I walked past a club in the Shockoe Bottom neighborhood of Richmond, Virginia, that had posted a sign outside: "No Sneakers, Do-Rags, Hoodies, Tank Tops or Sportswear," so what they were really saying is no young black men. Observing the door to a Midtown Manhattan nightclub, I saw a young black man get thrown out of the line because he was wearing tennis shoes and baggy jeans. Why were his clothes so inappropriate for the venue? What did they signal to the doorman? The prohibition of certain kinds of styles shows that tight doors are problematic because they can and do reinforce cultural anxieties and stereotypes.[36]

At the height of the popularity of Studio 54, the New York night-club that commercialized black, brown, and queer disco and slapped a white face on it, publicity around its tight door led the head of the New York State Liquor Authority to caution club owners that their admission policies might infringe on individual constitutional rights. It argued that any club "barring admission is a violation of Rule 36 (d) of the rules of the State Liquor Authority, and could result in license revocation proceed-ings."[37] Unless these stiff policies were relaxed, the commissioner warned, a club could be shut down.

Part of the problem with door policies, of any kind, is that they rely on and even help circulate structures of racism and classism in con-temporary society. It is very unlikely you will ever go to a club and see a sign that says, "No boat shoes, no kitten heels, no polo shirts, no seer-sucker pants, no blond highlights" and other stereotypes of whiteness in the same way you will see clubs reject and profile people based on stereotypes of blackness. White folks are not very likely to be denied entry to a club in the same way people of color are every weekend in venues around the world. In 2014 an African American ex-Stanford ath-lete went to New York hot spot 1OAK with two friends, one white and one black. They were ready for a great night on the town. But the doorman waved her white friend in and snatched the velvet rope shut right in front of the two black women, telling them, "Sorry, ladies. Not gonna hap-pen tonight."[38] A few blocks over, at a new Chelsea destination gay spot called Rebar that opened in 2017, stories of anti-black racism at the door dampened what was supposed to be a celebratory opening of a new gay bar.[39] White gays only?

Many clubs in cities around the world *do* have door policies that use race to keep people out. But there are other parties and venues that welcome folks who don't play into narratives of wealth, whiteness, mas-culinity, and heterosexuality. These kinds of spaces value a subcultural clientele, clubs like ://aboutblank, a left-leaning Berlin nightclub with a "commitment" to social justice. A tight or difficult door, in this kind of subcultural context, is about curation more than anything else. Doormen essentially curate the crowd for the night. Outside of Berlin and Amsterdam, the techno world—my musical love—can sometimes feel hostile to folks who are not straight white men even though, truth tea, brown people and queers invented this music. I've been to techno parties in London without door policies, for instance, where I've often wished there were more sissies, more women, more artsy people, and a tight door policy does much to create that ambiance. Although, to be fair, so would more targeted marketing. Self-selection plays a big role in where we choose to go at night. We don't want to go to this club because it's too far, and we don't want to go to that one because there's too much attitude. We don't go to this club because we don't like the music, and we avoid that one because there aren't enough people like us in the room. Clubs fail us, I think, when they try too hard to be everything to everyone. Being everything to everyone is without a doubt about cold hard cash—making money, hoarding and often times overcrowding bodies in a venue to make as much money as possible on door fees, the coat check, and especially at the bar. Being everything to everyone is about high cost with very little payoff for the partygoer. Clubs keep us coming back again and again when they can offer a focused, one-of-a-kind experience that is as specific as it is diverse.

In a profile of doormen published by the *New York Times* in 1979, Charles Yancy, the door person at the Xenon, a popular off-Broadway club that popped up in the shadow of Studio 54, remarked that every night he would "look around and see what I created—every night it's different."[40] Here, curating an audience for the party has to do with the art of the mixture, and that means ensuring that people from a range of backgrounds are on the dance floor. As Sarah Thornton describes, club cultures create, or curate, the right environment by relying on tools of targeted promotion, including flyers, telecommunications, promoters, and finally door policy, which she sees as the last resort to ensure that the club is speaking to the right people. For Thornton, the club audience is already preselected and presorted, and door policy is just a final measure to segregate the crowd, separating those who "belong" or fit the mix from those who do not.[41]

Nightlife is a space where identities are created, tested, questioned, confirmed, and rehearsed, and sometimes the most difficult thing about going out is actually getting in. By thinking about the role nightclubs play in identity formation, not to mention the kinds of things people do or say at the door to get inside a club, we uncover the power of social ambition in the modern city. The artist duo Elmgreen and Dragset, famous for their *Prada Marfa* installation twenty-two miles from the U.S./Mexico border, may have had a number of party people in mind, from Bret Easton Ellis's fictional Victor Ward to the real-life Lois Long, when they created a sculpture titled *But I'm on the Guest List*.[42] Poking fun at the impact of the door on modern club life, the work is basically a white, stand-alone door floating outside with the letters "VIP" engraved on the front.[43] As both physical and psychological barriers, doors can be hype-inducing, and they create an insatiable need to know what lies beyond them. But that's the humor of Elmgreen and Dragset's sculpture. Despite our need to know what this VIP door hides, it's obvious the thing opens to nowhere in particular.

There are a number of things to notice about Elmgreen and Dragset's sculpture and its relationship to access in what cultural critics Celeste Fraser Delgado and José Muñoz have called "every night life."[44] We could wonder, for instance, why the artists made a VIP door in an art context. Is this white door about how high-flying status has increasingly penetrated the global contemporary art market, which has become an endless parade of parties, art fairs, galas, receptions, and VIP booths, none of which has anything to do with the art itself? *But I'm on the Guest List* could also be the story of contemporary art's obsessive relationship to status, money, and luxury consumption.[45] Or we could see it as about exposing exclusivity. We could say that when some people approach a door and are turned away, this alone is an instance of exclusion and rejection that preserves the boundaries between social groups. But actually, where clubs are concerned, the relationship between venues and partygoers

ColorPlates

Amadéus Leopold, the violin virtuoso with a definite flair for spectacle, leopard print, and sixty-fourth notes. Leopold, who studied with the legendary Itzhak Perlman at Juilliard, often says the classical music world is taking a nap. He's here to wake it up. (Anne Cusack/Los Angeles Times/Contour by Getty Images.)

Facing Page: Madaew Fashionista, the viral fashion star who became famous for making haute couture out of things that have little or nothing to do with fashion. This look, for instance, in which Madaew stands atop a ladder in his family's garden in Khon Kaen, Thailand, is made from mosquito netting—solid proof that you don't need a ton of money to look great. All you need is creativity. Do try this at home. (Photo by Taylor Weidman/Getty Images.)

This Page: Pepper Pepper, a Portland-based performance artist, punk rock drag queen, and the brains behind Critical Mascara: A Post-Realness Drag Ball, which for five years took place at the Portland Institute for Contemporary Art. Pepper's show D.I.V.A. Practice investigates *fabulous* as a verb and as a critical practice. (Courtesy of Pepper Pepper and Sean Johnson. Photography by Sean M. Johnson, 2016 Portland, Oregon, www.seanMjohnson.com.)

This Page: Saturday, September 9, 2017, was the final edition of Critical Mascara: A Post-Realness Drag Ball, which has been part of the Time-Based Art Festival at the Portland Institute for Contemporary Art for the past five years. For the last hurrah, mistress of ceremonies Pepper Pepper invited me to DJ and moderate a panel on ballroom culture with brown, queer, and transfeminine folks from the Pacific Northwest. Here, a glimpse of what I wore to the function next to a limited-edition Critical Mascara screen print.

Facing Page: RoRo Morales, original NYC club kid and winner of the Food Network cooking competition series *Chopped Champions*, serving a strong black-and-white-printed look. Note the fab hoop earrings, a staple in my wardrobe. (Courtesy of RoRo Morales.)

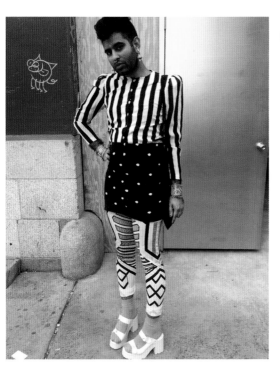

alokvmenon   Follow

2,190 likes   14w

alokvmenon really wanting to wear a dress today but i can't because i am back at home with family. so i am looking at old photos of myself to remember that i am real and contain multitudes and that there people and spaces in the world where i can have control of my body and what i look like. thinking today of all of my queer & trans babes out there who are having to camouflage themselves today and all days. as always -- dreaming of a world where we can reclaim our joy from their fear. love you.

view all 51 comments

p.skelly 🖤🖤🖤

kiminoa_seattle 🖤🙏🏿🖤

archive_boutique love the socks!! #sockgame #onpoint

isaidyuu #icon

70bellababe You look beautiful in this picture. I'm so sorry that you have to hide at

Log in to like or comment.   ○ ○ ○

Facing Page: Professor Carolyn Cooper, a scholar of Caribbean aesthetics, in a look created for her by the Jamaican designer Elaine Witter. The look moves away from static conceptions of African fabric. Belying Valerie Steele's quip that academics may be the worst dressed occupational group in America, Cooper calls out the seeming incompatibility between being a serious scholar and having serious style. (Courtesy of Carolyn Cooper and Peter Ferguson.)

This Page: Alok Vaid-Menon, a transfeminine performance artist whose practice destabilizes gender, white supremacy, and patriarchal norms. Alok regularly posts images of themselves on Instagram, and what's urgent about their Instagram practice is the way they seemingly participate in selfie culture by documenting their outfits while simultaneously drawing attention to the transphobic violences hurled at them in the urban environment. Their art practice shows that we live in a society where simply moving safely from Point A to Point B in public space is one of the major daily struggles for transfeminine people, who are terrorized on the street and risk physical and verbal violence by simply minding their own business. How can you feel so bad when you remember looking so good, Alok wonders. (Courtesy of Alok Vaid-Menon.)

Leo GuGu, photographed by Katya Moorman.
This look captures the drama of fabulousness. It
seizes the camera's gaze, taking up physical,
digital, and emotional space in the process.
(Katya Moorman, photographer. See more
of her work at karenandkatya.com or on
Instagram at @mynycnight.)

French DJ, producer, and performer Kiddy Smile working the streets of Barcelona, moments before his ballroom-flavored set at Sónar 2017. The look is made from scratch and shows an impeccable eye for drama and detail in fashion. (Courtesy of Kiddy Smile.)

Previous Spread: A "photograph" taken of Berghain's "interior." Photos are very strictly prohibited inside the club, and though this image was physically taken inside Berghain, it purposefully doesn't show or reveal anything about the club. Before you're allowed inside, a colorful dot is placed over your smartphone's camera lens. The dot is a way of reminding you to stay in the party and not on your phone. The stickers also become a recognizable part of the club's brand as well as a keepsake.

This Page: One hazy morning at the Ostbahnhof train station near Berghain I saw six neon-yellow stickers a group of friends must have peeled off their phones and stuck to a metal bench while they waited for the train to come. It really made me smile.

Artist Victoria Sin, long fascinated by New York nightlife icon Amanda Lepore, who herself is inspired by Jessica Rabbit and Marilyn Monroe, uses drag to interrogate, dismantle, and critique the construction of femininity. In their art practice, which brilliantly combines artifice and moving image, femininity is a source of power. Their drag also de-centers the notion that cisgendered men are the only (or best) kind of drag queens. (Courtesy of Ronan McKenzie.)

Facing Page: Amy Cakes, a New York City–based artist and designer who jumped feet first into the club scene the moment she arrived in the city to study at Parsons School of Design. (Photograph by Ian Scott Stoner.)

This Page: Katya Moorman, a New York City–based photographer and longtime *chroniqueuse* of street and club fashion. (Katya Moorman, photographer. See more of her work at karenandkatya.com or on Instagram at @mynycnight.)

Cherie Lily, a fitness enthusiast, club kid, and performer who is a staple in the underground queer club scene in New York. (Courtesy of Daniel D'Ottavio.)

Randal Jacobs, a stylist and image maker with a one-of-a-kind approach to style. (Randal Jacobs, shot by Timothy Lee, Harlem, NY, 2017.)

Portrait of Din #2 by the artist Mickalene Thomas fully captures how aesthetics and style are used to create space for yourself. (Courtesy of Mickalene Thomas, Susanne Vielmetter Los Angeles Projects, and Artists Rights Society (ARS), New York.)

Shaun J. Wright, a Chicago-bred DJ and vocalist known for his mind-bending sets and effervescent mixing style. (Courtesy of Frederic Aranda, www.fredericaranda.com.)

A still of DJ/producer Vjuan Allure in the middle of the beat at the 2016 Berlin Voguing Out Festival. (HomardPayette/Berlin Voguing Out.)

A still of Lasseindra Ninja doing a dip at the 2016 Berlin Voguing Out Festival. (HomardPayette/Berlin Voguing Out.)

An illustration of Stephane Mizrahi, of the House of Mizrahi, in the midst of a classic Old Way voguing move, posing with his legendary fan. (© Ben Chu/www.benchuart.com.)

hinges on the fact that in order to be successful, clubs need to distinguish themselves from every other venue to offer a unique experience. With so many choices of where to go after sunset, people align themselves with the kinds of clubs and parties they identify with most and that offer the particular experience they want. "Club cultures are taste cultures," Sarah Thornton says, meaning we already choose the right environments for ourselves well before we even show up at the door.[46]

Clubs with tight door policies aren't a new phenomenon in the twenty-first century. In 1920s Harlem the fashionable black socialite A'Lelia Walker, daughter of Madame C. J. Walker, the first black millionaire, who invented new ways for black women to care for their hair, held wild parties in her townhouse that were known to be piping hot. "Unless you went early," Langston Hughes remembered, "there was no possible way of getting in. Her parties were as crowded as the New York subway at the rush hour—entrance, lobby, steps, hallway, and apartment a milling crush of guests, with everybody seeming to enjoy the crowding." Once a Scandinavian prince heard about Walker's parties and showed up at the door, but the place was so crowded he wasn't let in. But Walker didn't want to be rude, so she offered to send a batch of refreshments out to him while he sat in his car, defeated.[47]

The irony of the tight door is that somehow, the tighter the door, the more people want to get past it. In 1931 the comedian Jimmy Durante told a story about the door scene of a brand-new all-black revue at the Plantation Club in New York starring the cabaret singer Florence Mills. Mills's performance was conceptualized by the Broadway producer Lew Leslie, who had the novel idea to create an impossible door to drum up public interest, even though Mills was already a headlining talent in New York and Paris. When excited fans approached the door to the Plantation Club, they heard live music pouring out of the venue, but imposing red velvet curtains were drawn over the club door and a big bouncer stood outside explaining he could not let anyone in. Does this sound familiar? Shattered, concertgoers asked if they could come back tomorrow, but the bouncer told them the reservation list was full then too. But there was no reservation list and no one was even inside the club during the performance. This door scene reportedly went on for weeks before the door-man finally started to let people in. The revue was a runaway success. As Durante wrote of the spectacle, there is a certain "New York manner of flocking only to places where it's hard to get in."[48]

Or if there's a line outside.

The first exclusive nightlife venues in New York were not caba-rets or nightclubs; they emerged in the Gilded Age as exclusive restau-rants and hotels. Even earlier in the nineteenth century, the upper classes viewed dining out as a social occasion, in particular at a place like Del-monico's, which in the mid-1800s became a sophisticated culinary insti-tution known for serving elaborate European dishes.[49] One of the earliest spaces for nightlife in New York debuted during the Gilded Age: the Wal-dorf Astoria Hotel. Opened in 1893 "in celebration of the 400th anniver-sary of the discovery of this continent by Columbus," the original Waldorf, the first big hotel in America, was received with much fanfare.[50] With a prime address on Fifth Avenue between 33rd and 34th Streets, the loca-tion of the Empire State Building, the original Waldorf was a theater of luxury and a monument of elegance for the city's most moneyed families, the kind of conspicuous space that brought Veblen to launch his scath-ing critique of the leisure class.[51] The hotel opened on March 14, 1893, on the occasion of a charity concert for St. Mary's Free Hospital for Chil-dren, and Mrs. William K. Vanderbilt donated the services of the New York Symphony Orchestra. More than fifteen hundred people attended the opening celebration.

The Waldorf became synonymous with opulence and luxury, but soon the hotel outgrew its own designer footprint. In a crunch for space, hotelier George Boldt persuaded John Jacob Astor, whose mansion was adjacent to the Waldorf, to demolish his house to pave the way for a new hotel that would be combined with the original Waldorf. Four years later, on November 1, 1897, the Waldorf Astoria opened, causing an even bigger sensation than the original. This new combined hotel contained a thousand rooms and stood seventeen stories high, all of it "the last word, if not the Ultima Thule, in luxurious living."[52] In New York City historian Lloyd Morris's words, the Waldorf Astoria was "a vast, glittering, iridescent fantasy that had been conjured up to infect millions of plain Americans with a new ideal—the aspiration to lead an expensive, gregarious life as publicly as possible." As the Waldorf introduced looks and fashionable exclusivity and social life to the masses, so too the hotel became one of the first institutions of democratized glamour. It essentially dared anyone who could afford even the cheapest meal to go there to be seen, or perhaps mis-seen, by others as someone with big money. Come enjoy the same amenities, cuisine, and décor as millionaires do, the hotel seemed to suggest.[53]

With its imposing, opulent architecture, grand ballrooms, and private banquet halls, here was a palace where people could see and be seen in an appropriately splendid environment, a theater where the actors were also the audience. The splendid Waldorf Astoria was so popular that often tables in its Palm Garden restaurant were booked weeks in advance. And in what might be the birth of exclusive door culture, anyone who showed up at the restaurant after 7:00 was met with a taut velvet rope, a signal that unless you were of the highest prestige (or on the list), you should make plans to dine elsewhere.[54] You're not getting in.

By 1915, opportunities for nightlife in New York City were endless, stretching from Greenwich Village to the Broadway theater district and into Harlem. Cabarets, speakeasies, vaudeville shows, lobster palaces, rent parties, pansy and burlesque shows, and the newly formed "nightclub" offered unique opportunities for nighttime amusement. These forms of nightlife were captured by a range of films and novels that emerged between the 1920s and the 1940s that focused on or were set in nightclubs, including literary works by F. Scott Fitzgerald. In the 1920s the term *nightlife* referred specifically to elaborate spaces for dining, drinking, and socializing.[55] The capital of fabulous nightlife during the 1920s was Harlem, the center of black cultural production. White New Yorkers flocked to Harlem hot spots like the Cotton Club and Connie's Inn to witness the spectacle of blackness firsthand. Jimmy Durante described the feel of Harlem this way: "Harlem! Fifteen minutes on the subway and you were right in the middle of Broadway, where all the big shots played the bazoo. . . . Yes, sir, on my way! There were cabarets and cafes down there that were the talk of the world. That's where I wanted to go."[56] Novelists like Carl Van Vechten, a patron of the Harlem Renaissance, fictionalized and further promoted the Harlem party scene in his works *Nigger Heaven* (1926) and *Parties* (1930). Van Vechten once even held a "gossip party" where attendees went around the room and said the worst things about each other.[57]

The paradox about this hot Harlem party scene, however, was that it was largely unfrequented by African Americans. Langston Hughes remembered that "white people began to come to Harlem in droves. For several years they packed the expensive Cotton Club on Lenox Avenue." But the black audience did not take kindly to "the growing influx of whites toward Harlem after sundown, flooding the little cabarets and bars where formerly only colored people laughed and sang, and where now these strangers were given the best ringside tables to sit and stare at the Negro customers—like amusing animals in a zoo."[58] Hughes's phrase "ringside tables" conjures up the image of a circus, highlighting how the cabaret space, for a white audience, was an unfiltered point of the gaze.[59]

If black audiences were not going out in the fashionable Harlem nightclub circuit, then where did they go? Saturday nights in Harlem were filled with excitement, but it was the invitation-only, secret rent parties where the black population celebrated the night. A rent party was essentially a house party where guests paid a small entrance fee of around 50 cents, money that went toward the apartment's monthly rent. One of the most interesting aspects of the rent party was the way it was promoted. Admission to the fete was by secret invitation only, and the only way to get through the door was to present the business card–sized "flyer" you'd received with your invitation. An early example of these whimsical, poetic, and well-thought-out tokens, from a rent party held on September 14, 1929, told guests: "Some wear pajamas, some wear pants, what does it matter just so you can dance." Another, this one from March 18, 1955, illustrated nightlife as the time when anything goes because no one is watching: "You can wake up the Devil, raise all the Hell; No one will be there to go home and tell." As proof that these playful tag lines were not taken lightly—that they were carefully constructed—there is a draft from

May 9, 1929, perhaps written by Hughes himself, that was scribbled in pencil on a large sheet of thin white paper: "I ain't Mae West. My man ain't Jack the Bear—But when I'm going to a Party, You better be there."[60]

Once inside the rent party guests enjoyed live jazz, bootleg whiskey, and dancing with the opposite sex in "a miasma of smoke, booze, collard greens, and hot music" until dawn.[61] Many, like Hughes, found the rent parties more stimulating than any nightclub. He remembered, "Almost every Saturday night when I was in Harlem I went to a house-rent party. . . . I met ladies' maids and truck drivers, laundry workers and shoe shine boys, seamstresses and porters. I can still hear their laughter in my ears, hear the soft slow music, and feel the floor shaking as the dancers danced."[62] The rent parties show how nightlife creates another world, separated only by a tight door or a secret invitation, a place of heightened experience where people from a wide variety of backgrounds come together under the trance of music, freedom, action, and dancing. The allure of a secret invitation, much like a tight door policy, protects the special nature and otherworldliness that nightlife offers.

One of the first nightclubs, or discotheques, to specifically use tight door theater was Chez Régine's, which opened in Paris in 1958.[63] When the club opened it did not admit anyone for an entire month, in what we should now see as a familiar, even favored PR stunt. A "Disco Full" sign was posted on the outside of the club, refusing entrance to all, even as music blared to the outside. Twenty-seven years later, in 1975, Régine Zylberberg packed two hundred pounds of Louis Vuitton luggage and eight hundred pairs of shoes and moved from Paris to New York City, where she opened a Régine's on the bottom floor of the Delmonico Hotel.[64] There were only two ways to get into the New York Régine's. One, you were subjected to intense scrutiny through the peephole of a door without a handle to the outside, an admissions process exclusive enough that the New York State Liquor Authority leveraged a suit against the club for discrimination. Another New York restaurateur even sued Régine's for $2 million in damages because he and his wife were barred entry.[65] Two, if you couldn't get past the peephole, you could pay a flat fee of $600 to become a permanent member of the club. Membership came with a personalized gold card tucked into a Cartier case, and it guaranteed free admission for up to eight guests.[66]

On January 22, 1981, Régine sent a permanent member card to Andy Warhol as a token of their friendship, even though he did not necessarily need the card to get into the club. Warhol, who was so into parties he once said he'd go to the opening of an envelope, frequently described the scene at Régine's during the late 1970s in *The Andy Warhol Diaries*. For instance, on Monday, January 31, 1977: "Worked until 7:30. Went to Regine's. Warren Beatty was there looking a little older and heavier. Jack Nicholson was there looking a little older and heavier. Anjelica Huston and Apollonia the model were there. I like Apollonia now, she's really sweet. And Catherine Deneuve was there, who the party was for. Warren was dating Iman, the black model. Barbara Allen and her beau Philip Niarchos were there and James Brady and the *Women's Wear Daily* guy, Coady."[67] Celebrities are branded people, and for Warhol this was ultimately an extension of pop art. In his diary entry Warhol's obsession with celebrity is clear. The entry is virtually empty of meaning, merely listing who was there without telling us what they were doing. It is a list of bold-faced brand names that uses the language and style of the high-society gossip page to ground Régine's cultural relevance while at the same time displaying the pull of celebrity culture in America. Régine's hotness was due in large part to who was there—and who couldn't get in.

Nightlife is about storytelling, tales about who was at which club, what they did there, and who they took home. The day after a big night out we are eager to jot down or tell our friends stories about what happened last night. But the backdrop to the stories we tell, the thing that actually enables them, is darkness. Darkness opens us up to create new, unexpected narratives. As Bryan Palmer observes in a fascinating history of darkness, the night is different because it is marked by both darkness and danger, offering an escape from the "routines that define humanity in specific duties, obligations, and tasks." How can we tell exciting stories about new things we've done and lose ourselves in the fantasy of nightlife if we are hemmed in by the watchful eye of light? If you've ever been to a party, then you know that when the lights come on the party's over, and that's usually around the same time the DJ plays "Don't Stop Believing" by Journey. You could write a whole book on the last songs played at parties and club nights in venues around the world. The last song frames the end of the club experience at the same time it also marks a return to everyday life. Nightlife allows us to transgress because whatever we do in the club stays there—these are activities that happen away from the surveillance of daylight hours. The last song is a reminder that we are about to be launched back into the brightness of day. Removal from surveillance leads us to acts of liberated storytelling and allows what Palmer calls "the deviant, the dissident, the different" to test limitations and break away from rules, regulations, and restrictions.[68] And that's where storytelling comes in. Because nightlife is experienced as a different kind of time that's shrouded in darkness, danger, and the pursuit of illicit pleasures, it is always already an ideal site for stories and tall tales about what happened last night.

Dealing with door culture is as much a fact of going out as it is a topic explored in literature, fictionalized and sensationalized in novels and magazines about the worlds of fashion and nightlife by authors such as Tom Wolfe, Jay McInerney, and Bret Easton Ellis. Victor Ward, the hip, A-list protagonist of Bret Easton Ellis's novel *Glamorama*, is the type of fellow who lives in society columns and party photos, gets in everywhere, and easily coasts from one grand bash to the next—in the backseat of a chauffeured black car, no less. Set in the mid-1990s deep in the throes of the so-called Supermodel Era, *Glamorama* is a somewhat rambling novel, an international "glamour thriller" that satirizes the glitz and wickedness of fashion, nightlife, and celebrity culture. Along the way, the novel manages to critique popular culture's dependence on surface and artifice even though it does not propose an antidote to it, nor does the novel see the creative value in the aesthetics of fabulousness. As Victor, a bisexual male model, works the never-ending catwalks through the New York glamour worlds, he finds himself involved with a ring of London-based terrorists, a plotline that would be more terrifying if it weren't for one little twist: the terrorists in question are all fashion models.

If writing a novel about model-terrorists doesn't create enough dissonance, this will: these unsuspicious-looking model-terrorists leave their bombs outside hotels, in airplanes, and on subways stashed inside Louis Vuitton, Hermès, and Prada bags. A frightening narrative of terrorism becomes a satirical commentary on the nature of conspicuous consumption and the false value of surface impressions. By turning consumer culture's most coveted and identity-defining items—"it" bags—into bombs detonated by models, and by implicating the luxury industry more specifically, Easton Ellis plays with perception and the psychology of appearances. Appearances *do* matter. He forces us to interrogate the notion that somehow a model couldn't be a terrorist, or that for some reason a Louis Vuitton suitcase would not have a bomb inside of it. The dissonance between models/terrorists and luxury goods/bombs unveils "the truth" behind appearances, a contemporary reimagining of the age-old idiom "You can't judge a book by its cover." People are quick to say that appearances don't matter, as I have shown, but the reality is that in almost every social situation—from job interviews to first dates, and especially in nightlife—appearances are valuable and communicate a great deal about social structures, what we value, who we think we are, and where we can go.

Glamorama is filled with a cast of models, partyers, photographers, and celebrities, but the most prescient observation about the role of appearances comes from Victor's personal mantra, "The better you look, the more you see," helpful because it crystallizes a theory of glamour as well as anchoring Ellis's overarching theme. The mantra highlights the kinds of doors that fling open for us once we learn to perform certain sociocultural roles.[69] Victor's phrase presents a beautiful, philosophical symmetry in the sense that "The better you look, the more you see" could mean the closer we look at a surface impression, the more Vaseline we wipe off the lens, the more likely we are to notice the imperfections, scars, acne, and calluses of glamour. But it could also mean the more we create ourselves through fashion and style, the better we look and the more we *work a look,* the more access we gain to roped-off or difficult to access areas of culture. That is, the more we actually get to see. Having *a look* becomes a key tool not only in gaining access but also in *performing* access—certainly not the only tool, but an important one in the supermarket of appearances.

As for Victor and his party-going ways, you could say his looks are choreographed so that whatever he does, and whoever he is with, appears on the gossip pages in time for the morning news cycle. If where we party at night is any indication of our social capital, take a good look at Victor, who once went to a club in London that was so fabulous "you can't get in even if you're *on* the guest list."[70] While this might seem like a bald critique of exclusivity, the more interesting aspect of the quip is the implication that people desire admission to places that are hard to get into in the first place. The more difficult it is to get in, the more it seems people actually want to be allowed in. Easton Ellis, who has made a literary career of astute yet painfully pessimistic observations about hipness, money, and youth, created a moral tale à la Balzac in *Glamorama*, a world of social climbers whose primary occupation is to be more fabulous today than they were yesterday—a satirical take on American popular culture's obsession with fashion, nightlife, and celebrity.

By the 1980s entire publications dedicated to nightlife as a cultural form emerged on the cultural scene. These magazines created literary narratives of nightlife as they documented the door scenes of certain clubs. One such publication was *Details,* the hip, downtown magazine launched in June 1982 that published many of the first creative contributions by fashion mainstays like André Leon Talley, Patrick McMullan, Michael Musto, and Bill Cunningham. Published until December 2016 by Condé Nast, the publisher of *Vogue, Details* shifted into a men's magazine with a primary focus on making style accessible for a younger, metrosexual male audience. But in its original incarnation, *Details* was the diary of cultural happenings and observations of the New York "downtown" creative scene. In New York City, "downtown" is a site-specific term that generally refers to the area below 14th Street in Manhattan. But according to New York City historian Marvin Taylor, "downtown" is conceptual as much as it is geographical. As opposed to the moneyed personality and uptightness found "uptown," "downtown" is a subversive aesthetic sensibility that emerged in the mid-1970s, one that, Taylor describes, "is synonymous with experimentation. Experimentation with art, sex, drugs, rock and roll."[71] For Michael Musto, downtown is "a state of mind so fabulous that, unless there's a guest list for public transportation too, all it needs to travel is a token."[72] This downtown sensibility was about a new attitude toward art making that unhinged the stern boundaries that existed between various kinds of art creation. "It was not a new aesthetic, not a new style, and not a unified movement, but rather an attitude toward the possibilities and production of art."[73] It was interdisciplinary and included performance, music, fashion, art, painting, and dance but also the spaces between them.

Details was perhaps the first magazine to document the dictatorship and scrutiny at the door to downtown nightclubs by assuring its audience that by virtue of reading Details, they were already "on the list." The subscription insert to the magazine itself was a guest list. As the first issue of the magazine tells readers: "Yes, you're on the list: In most of New York's private clubs, if you're on the list, you're in. Then you never know what to expect inside. The same applies here at Details: if you're on our list, you're in. In for surprises. We're a private publication. Our doorman is your mailman."[74] A subscription to Details allowed readers to buy into a sense of "downtown cool." In fact, Details was wholly dedicated to the idea of cool. It was normal for any page of the magazine to christen a person, a fashion item, or a nightclub as "it," a term theater historian Joseph Roach sees as a "certain quality, easy to perceive but hard to define, possessed by abnormally interesting people."[75] Downtown fashion designer and party promoter Dianne Brill, prominently featured throughout the early history of the magazine, was the "it" girl of downtown 1980s New York. At one point the magazine said her mere presence at an event meant that, "like it or not, the occasion happened. You made it."[76] The event happened because her presence there made the event reportable news—a "pseudo-event," in cultural critic Daniel Boorstin's phrasing—that would receive a kind of intensified visibility in the press.[77] Though Brill was only in her twenties at the time of her rise to downtown stardom, the magazine praised her connectedness when it wrote, "When she dies her list will surely go up for auction."[78]

The "list" has historically been a social tool that distinguished between various groups, as with Mrs. Astor's powerful List of 400. Even Andy Warhol was interested in "the list" as a form of social currency when he wrote humorously in *Exposures* that club promoter Carmen D'Alessio "has a list. Her list is worth a fortune. She has the names (spelled correctly), the addresses (summer, winter, city, and country), and the phone numbers (with area codes) of everyone beautiful, young, and loaded."[79] Being on "the list" is less about financial wealth and more about having a different kind of social wealth—or rather, being connected to certain kinds of social scenes.

Through its extensive profiles of clubs, art openings, and downtown party promoters, the magazine provided its readers snapshots of club happenings relevant to the tastes of the downtown New York creative scene. You could read the short "Deejay Vu" articles, for instance, if you were unsure about where to go on a given night. These snippets listed a group of known DJs, the venue where each was performing that night, and the two songs guaranteed to be played. You could go to Danceteria and hear Mark Kamins spinning "Holiday" by Madonna or "Where Is My Man" by Eartha Kitt. Over at the Peppermint Lounge, David Azarc would surely play "Looking for a Kiss" by the New York Dolls or "I Want You Back" by the Jackson 5.[80] Clubgoers could personalize their evening and choose where to go based purely on their individual music tastes. And as a testament to the rise of club culture across the United States during the 1980s, the backs of most issues of *Details* carried an advertisement for a single nightclub. Several high-profile clubs in other cities, like San Francisco's CLVB DV8, also advertised in *Details*. Taken together, these advertisements and DJ playlists illustrated the far reach of nightlife as a cultural form in the United States.

Details is an interesting cultural text because of the way its aesthetics and content captured the culture of the downtown nightlife scene in New York City. In one description of the Chelsea gay nightclub Phoenix that appeared in the December–January 1983–84 double issue, the venue was described as "seedy," with go-go boys dancing in shorts or a G string—"really performing." The description continued: "It's the place to be on Wednesday. But don't go, and don't tell anyone about it. If word gets out, it'll be ruined."[81] The article has an insider's perspective, one that gives readers an "exclusive" look at red-hot venues they may not have known about otherwise. *Details* provided readers with a sense of being where the magazine goes and therefore of being "cool." But don't go and don't tell anyone about it. Even as the article gives an insider's perspective when it tells readers, in a hush-hush fashion, "Don't go, and don't tell anyone about it," it highlights that its readers are not "in the know," that they don't have subcultural capital. If you are in the know or have subcultural capital and connectedness to a scene, you don't need a magazine to tell you where to be. You're there right now. "Whoever is not seen 'on the scene,'" the art theorist Pascal Gielen says, "does not belong to the scene."[82] If you don't know to be there, then you don't belong. While putting its readers on the A-list to popular nightclubs and spaces, *Details* used the language of exclusivity and hipness to commoditize and "sell" the special world of downtown nightlife.

The central feature of the early issues of *Details* was the nightlife column "Nocturnal Admissions" written by nightlife impresario and prominent club doorman Stephen Saban, a founding editor of the magazine. Saban's columns were specifically about door culture and the anxiety the door creates. In one column Saban described the scene at the opening of the Peppermint Lounge:

> **From my safe vantage point on the step, behind the ropes, it was truly a sea. The crowd bobbed and undulated, forming gentle breakers that lapped inevitably over the ropes, receded, and broke again. Fifth Avenue between 15th and 16th streets was awash with people, smiling, expectant, eager, as far as the eye could see. The all new Peppermint Lounge had invited them to its opening and they had the invitations to prove it. By 9:30, the sea had turned ugly. No longer calm,**

it crashed violently at the ropes, threatening to turn into the biggest storm in history. The ropes, once a mighty bulwark, seemed suddenly flimsy against the surge. I stepped back, fearing for my life, my tuxedo. You see, I held the list.[83]

The crowd festers because it knows it is on the verge of something, feeling something is coming that can't be missed, what the philosopher Brian Massumi called the "just-beginning-to-stir" or what we refer to nowadays as FOMO—fear of missing out. The audience realizes it is on the cusp. People are not waiting to go inside a nightclub or even to cross a threshold into a new sensorial experience. They're waiting for *something else*. Being at the door to a hot nightclub, experiencing the "just-beginning-to-stir," is about how space holds energy in an edgy anticipation of something that *might* happen.[84] The "just-beginning-to-stir" emphasizes the exciting possibility, even uncertainty, of something that can't be missed but that can't be talked about because it hasn't happened. This is akin to what we call nowadays the "fear of missing out."

There's a human drive to be where the line is, and somehow where there's a line there's also a party, as Jimmy Durante wrote about in 1931 and as Berghain made clear almost a century later. Tight door policies in nightclubs are often a process of *curation* that is almost always about protecting the subcultural capital of a space, the special world that exists on the other side of the door. This is particularly true of a venue that, for instance, started as a niche, underground space but that has suddenly become popular, or if the club wants to stay under the radar to avoid police raids.[85] "The most important question a doorman must ask himself," Stephen Saban wrote, is "would I want to hang out in a club with this person?" In one column Saban talks specifically about the kinds of people he didn't let in. They included: "1) roving gangs of teenagers; 2) children; 3) unescorted men dressed in denim; 4) known drug dealers, abusers, and agents; 5) drunks; 6) people who called us assholes; 7) known troublemakers; 8) tasteless dressers."[86] What these groups have in common is

141 Up in the Club

their perceived inappropriateness for the club environment, and this in-appropriateness is based primarily on legal status and the potentiality for igniting hostile situations.

When he decided not to let a person in, Saban used standard rejections that are actually deterrents meant to make the clubgoers frustrated and ready to leave on their own. Among the statements: "It's very crowded"; "No jeans, no sneakers"; and, most important, "Are you on the guest list?" But what I find interesting about the door as a site of control is how clubgoers will do and say anything to get inside. At the Peppermint Lounge, clubgoers got angry if they weren't allowed in. Some took it a step further by trying to lie or trick their way inside. Once a group approached a door pretending to be close friends of Stephen Saban, without realizing they were actually talking to Saban himself:

> **"We're friends of Stephen Saban,"** one of them says.
> **"He's not here right now,"** I tell them. **"It's ten each."**
> **"Could you get him?"**
> **"He's been fired."** I'll play the game.[87]

Such trickery is "the hustle" of urban nightlife, the way nightlife demands that partyers use a range of sly tactics to gain access to club settings. Going clubbing means forever being "on the make" and using the art of the hustle to get what you want, a hustle that "requires the smooth magician's skills of sleight of hard and deceptive trickery."[88] It's a Goffmanian process of learning how to gain access by trial and error, a performance of wit in which one person makes a proposition and the other person either accepts the proposition or ups the ante. This game of wits is often a crucial part of the nightlife experience.

From the tight door at Berghain to the secret, invitation-only parties of 1920s Harlem, and from the "Disco Full" sign at Régine's to the representation of the tight door in literature, nightlife relies on creating a special interior fantasy world that is often separated from the outside by a strict or tight door. A tight door policy means that having the money to get in is not enough; once you are selected from an anonymous crowd of hundreds, only then are you given the privilege to pay to be there. It is by nature a discriminatory practice, especially when the policies are blatantly racist, as evidenced by bans on certain styles of clothes. But it is also a curatorial one that tries to protect the ambiance a club thinks it offers.

Carmen D'Alessio, a Peruvian club promoter, told Christie's, the auction house, that "probably the most relevant experience that I have [had] in New York was the creation of Studio 54."[89] Partially, though not entirely, the brainchild of nightlife entrepreneurs Steve Rubell and Ian Schrager, Studio 54 flung its doors open for the first time on April 26, 1977, and between its opening and a police raid that occurred on December 14, 1978, just a year and a half later, Studio 54 would freeze in time to become one of the most gimmicky and commercial nightclubs in New York history, but also one of the most narrated. It was a commercial enterprise that whitewashed disco, which was originally brown and queer. Jim Fouratt, the manager of the 1980s New York nightclub Danceteria, once said that "looking fabulous was the only thing that got you past the door" at Studio 54.[90] "I think Studio 54 brought a glamor back to New York," Liza Minelli said, "that we haven't seen since the 60's. It's made New York get dressed up again."[91] My interest in Studio 54 is not about the club's position in the history of disco or gay culture because it represents a heightened, commercialized, whitened version of underground dance music culture. Studio 54 fascinates me because the club was one of the most visible in using the tight door to shape fabulousness as a theatrical performance. As Tim Lawrence shows in *Love Saves the Day: A History of American Dance Music Culture, 1970–1979*, the idea to make Studio 54 a theatrical experience was D'Alessio's. It was D'Alessio who hired all the designers. "The idea of having a discotheque in a theater was completely new and completely revolutionary and completely different. I saw that the space could be used in a very creative and artistic way. I envisioned movie shootings, television programs, and fashion shows."[92]

Perhaps more famous than the club itself are the well-publicized stories about who did not get in. John Kennedy Jr. and Warren Beatty at one point did not get in.[93] Andy Warhol remembers being nervous about not getting through the velvet ropes every time, and he was a regular.[94] Studio's dictator-like door policy was so infamous that even taxi drivers, those often overlooked yet key figures in the nightlife economy, played the role of doorman. One taxi driver confessed: "I tell people not to go there because I know they're not going to get in. I know which ones will get in. I try to tell them they just aren't dressed right."[95] Many artists and performers translated the frustration of not getting into the club to song. "Le Freak," the iconic single by Chic, was originally titled "Fuck Off" and was written on a snowy New Year's Eve in 1977 immediately after the group was denied admission to the club, despite a personal invitation from Grace Jones, who was already inside.[96] In 1979 Kid Creole and the Coconuts followed their lead and penned the song "Dario," whose chorus pleads, "Dario, Can you get me into Studio 54?" And in the late 1970s, fashion photographer Gordon Munro gave everyone a way into the club with a special line of Studio 54 jeans that had the club's logo on the back pocket. In the ad a naked man bends over as he pulls the jeans up, framed by the tongue-in-cheek line, "Now everybody can get into Studio 54."[97]

The building at 254 West 54th Street that held Studio 54 passed through many hands before it became a world-famous nightclub. The space was built in 1927 as an opera house for the San Gallo Opera Company. But three years later, in 1930, the opera house went bankrupt and the space soon became the New Yorker theater. The building changed hands again in 1937 when the Federal Theater Project leased the space and called it the Federal Music Theater. Columbia Broadcasting Company claimed the space five years later in 1942 and for thirty years used it as a soundstage for radio and television productions, including popular shows like *The Johnny Carson Show* and the *$64,000 Question*. As one CBS employee described, "All the studios had numbers. We had 52, 56, 57. Studio 43 was up on Vanderbilt Avenue. Studio 53 was this one. I know, because I was an associate director of Studio 53 back in the fifties."[98] When CBS moved its production to Los Angeles, the building sat vacant yet again before it became a nightclub.

French cultural theorist Roland Barthes, who was also a party boy, wrote about a Parisian club called Le Palace, an old seventeenth-century theater that was rehabilitated into a nightclub—the "Studio 54" of Paris. He described the space as a spectacle of lights, bodies, and dancing. It was "indeed a place devoted to seeing: you spend your time looking around the room, and, when you come back from dancing, you start looking again . . . you look at the lights, the shadows, the decor, but you also do something else at the same time (dance, talk, look at each other): a practice known in the ancient theater."[99] For Barthes it is no wonder that the spectacle of nightlife occurs in the reclaimed space of an old theater, which returns the building to its original intent as an environment devoted to different ways of seeing and being seen.

Though there were already hundreds of discotheques in New York City, Studio 54 was unique in that it deliberately framed nightlife as a spectacular extension of the theater and television. The space featured scenery and lighting by Broadway producers Jules Fisher and Paul Marantz, who created a variety of effects in the club, including snow-storms, a volcano, a solar system, and wind machines.[100] But this was not the first time a nightclub uncovered the deep ties between Hollywood, performance, and nightlife. As Burton Peretti has written, the Great Depression did much to curb the nightlife excesses of the 1920s, but it also created important frames for major nightlife innovations in the 1930s and 1940s. Among these was the Hollywood Restaurant, operated by Broadway producer Nils T. Granlund. The space neither charged a cover for entry nor served alcohol, but it was unique in that it used the style and themes of Hollywood as décor. Large posters of movie stars as well as other clichés of Hollywood interpretations of nightclub design—tuxedos and streamlined staircases in particular—were lifted from film and placed into a real setting, giving nightclubs a touch of movie magic.[101]

But while the nightclubs fictionalized in films such as *Queen of the Night Clubs* brought nightlife to the movies, Studio 54, on the other hand, cast the partygoer in the production. In the April 1977 issue of *Interview* magazine, Carmen D'Alessio, who was hired to promote the new venue, offered readers a preview of the new discotheque set to open at the end of the month:

> **You walk in under a big marquee. I would say that the opening night will be like going to a premier more than going to a discotheque. Then you walk into this enormous hall with very, very high ceilings and Art Deco mirrors and crystal chandeliers and then into this enormous, enormous room where there are like 85-foot ceilings—it's like five stories. *It's the backstage of a television set* with the wires and the cords and you know the place where the cameraman sits? Even that is there, too. The dance floor is 11,000 square feet. It's very, very large. Then upstairs is a theater with a seating arrangement.**[102]

In her preview of the club D'Alessio shows that it will offer a unique theatrical experience. But most important is her discussion of the architecture of the club as the backstage of a television studio. This is key because Studio 54 emerged as media saturation and celebrity culture reached a peak. In 1969 Andy Warhol launched *Interview,* then a magazine of unedited interviews with celebrities. According to Warhol, at that time "everyone, absolutely everyone, was tape-recording everyone else. Machinery had already taken over people's sex lives—dildos and all kinds of vibrators—and now it was taking over their social lives, too, with tape recorders and Polaroids." Realizing the potential of this new fad, Warhol discovered that tapes introduced new possibilities for interviews with celebrities. "Since we were a long time between movies lately," Warhol said, "I began to think about starting a magazine of nothing but taped interviews. Then John Wilcock dropped by one day and asked me if I would start a newspaper with him. Together we brought out the first issue of *Interview* magazine in the fall of '69."[103]

At first, *Interview* was a rag devoted to underground film stars, but by the 1970s it would shift its emphasis toward colorful, hand-drawn covers and unedited interviews with celebrities from the cultural arenas of art, fashion, music, film, and nightlife. The magazine published interviews exactly as they were recorded. This was the "mainstreaming of Warhol's sensibility," one that loved crossing the boundaries between the arts and pop culture.[104] But it was also the explosion of gossip as news. In 1973 Bob Colacello, then editor in chief of the magazine, devoted sizable space to nightlife in a monthly society column called "Out." *People* magazine launched in 1974, and gossip columnist Liz Smith's society column in the *Daily News* began in 1976.[105] All three publications continued the media coverage of celebrity culture, gossip, and society life as a source of news.

Studio 54 facilitated the relationship between celebrity culture, paparazzi culture, Hollywood, disco, and liberated (white) gay culture. It was a multi-sensory media spectacle that brought nightlife to the level of cinematic experience. Joanne Horowitz, a secretary at Universal Pictures, reportedly promised Steve Rubell she would invite celebrities. "Listen! I know where the celebrities are. Give me the invitations and I'll invite them to the opening."[106] In archival footage of the door scene at Studio 54 filmed in 1979, hundreds of well-dressed people on narrow 54th Street are herded behind a plush velvet rope, their arms held high in the air. They are working to get the attention of Marc Benecke, the doorman at Studio 54 and the last word on who could enter the space. Commenting on how he selects people to enter, Benecke said that he "would just zero in on somebody I knew was going to get in and frankly pretty much ignore people who I knew weren't going to get in. And the funny thing was when I did change tactics and say to people, 'I'm really sorry. You really don't have a chance. Maybe you should come back another night' they would just stand there for two or three hours anyway. It was amazing to me that anyone would do that. But there was such a fervor. Such a need to be inside."[107] Benecke is perched on top of a standpipe, peering over the crowd, combing through it with his eyes, pointing to and waving forward those he wants to admit. As the audience fights for his attention what we see is that this door scene reveals in-the-middle-of-something-ness, the excitement around something that is about to happen. In this way there were two scenes at Studio 54—the activity on the inside of the club, driven by heightened sensory experiences that drugs, music, and dancing facilitate, and then the spectacle of street theater on the outside of the club, where audiences wait in anticipation.

If there's a line or a crowd of people outside of a club then there's got to be something to see, right? A scene at the door to a nightclub is almost always about hype, buzz—a marketing gimmick. How many times have I been to a nightclub with a long line outside only to find out that there is no one inside? Seasoned clubbers know this experience all too well. Keeping people outside is almost always a question of hype building. The Oxford English Dictionary lists the earliest usage of the word hype as 1924. At the time the term was used primarily as slang for drug addicts because it described the hypodermic needle or syringe used for injection.[108] Hype. This tells us that the hype surrounding a scene correlates directly to how that scene is also able to create a culture of addicts. Village Voice columnist Michael Musto remembered that he "would just stand outside [of Studio 54] for hours and hours, and that would be a full night's entertainment, just watching the celebrities' limousines pull up, and see who would come out of them. We didn't even try to get in."[109] For Musto, staying out and watching the crowd, not going in, was the real event.

Any nightclub with a tight door and a long line outside is doing three things: marketing itself, curating a world, and casting people to put in that world. As one door person remarked in 1979, "I feel like I'm casting a show every night."[110] In many ways nightlife is about community, and door culture is a way of preserving that sense of closeness. Because clubs are often sealed off from the outside in darkness, where darkness animates all kinds of illegal and other transgressive activities, doors are used to keep people out who would otherwise police the freedom within the space. Writing in 1933, New York Herald Tribune editor Stanley Walker narrated the creative tricks bar owners and partyers used to drink alcohol during Prohibition—and to avoid the police in the process. Prohibition agents targeted any establishment suspected of serving liquor—that is, if they could find the speakeasies where people were consuming *and* if they could persuade the door person to let them inside. The speakeasy was a clandestine bar "where customers were admitted after undergoing scrutiny through a peep-hole," which is not at all dissimilar to the scrutiny we are up against as we try to get admitted to nightclubs with tight or exclusive doors.[111] This rite of passage based on appearance had to do with proving you were not a Prohibition agent intending to blow up the joint and invade the privateness, illegality, and transgressive nature of the space.

Nightlife, and queer nightlife especially, is in many ways about time: the time it takes to get ready for a night out, the time it takes to find a taxi or get a bus, the time it takes to get into the club, the time you wait to put your coat in the coat check, and however long it takes you to get a drink or the nerve to talk to the cute guy in the corner. But once we get to the venue, once we've proved that we have the subcultural capital and belong on the inside, once we cross the threshold at last, then what? I'm with queer theorist Jack Halberstam, who argues for a logic of "queer time" and "queer space." As Halberstam sees it, "queer time" is a kind of time that goes against structures of productivity, family, reproduction, and heterosexuality, and focuses on the immediacy of the present, squeezing as much "time" as possible out of the here and now.[112]

But what happens if we think about queer nightlife not just as a kind of queer time or queer space but actually as a *portal,* a door or a teleportation to another universe that we slip through to access other sides of ourselves and other heightened states of being? Like those phone calls in *The Matrix,* nightlife portals suck you in and transport you to a different place, a fantasy, a whole set of new experiences. Through the portal you find yourself in a place where time doesn't even exist but actually turns off, stops. Once on the other side you can focus on joy, experience, relationships, and community, all of these counter-capitalist things that go against the impulse to be productive. Then, when the party is over—tick tock—you put your sunglasses on and cross *back* over to the other side, *back* through the portal, *back* into the harsh daylight hours, *back* into productivity, *back* into the homework you've put off all weekend, now faced with the difficulty of being productive when the hangover is so bad or the comedown so deep.

In their iconic text *Dialectic of Enlightenment,* Marxist critics Adorno and Horkheimer believed that the only reason culture has mass entertainment is so that we can distract ourselves from the fact that we have to go to work again in a few more hours. It's a pessimistic viewpoint, but I actually think they're right, and it's why I think part of the magic of the queer night is the promise of dropping through this portal. As the cultural theorist Jonathan Crary has observed, contemporary capitalism is focused on a twenty-four hours a day, seven days a week schedule, what he calls an "inscription of human life into duration without breaks." This is a life that exists beyond "clock time," where you are always reachable no matter the time of day.[113] For Crary, a 24/7 environment turns us all into machines, highlighting the way we now work without sleep, without limits—sleep being the thing that gets in the way of productivity. The kind of portal I'm proposing, though, is not necessarily tied to a certain day or time but is actually a physical structure, a door you pass through that promises a scenario just for you on the other side. The portal removes you from daylight's responsibilities and throws you into another dimension, and even if for just a moment you have the chance, at last, to opt out of notions of time and productivity.

One of the things I love about going clubbing is the moment you first walk up to the venue and can already hear the bass rumbling through the building, pouring outside. The club is a spaceship that's about to take off, a ride to a brand-new dimension. Depending on where you're going, you can hear bass even before you see any people. It's a helpful tool if you're lost and not quite sure where the venue is: just follow the low frequencies, like the time I went to a rave in a forest in Hackney Wick, a formerly industrial but now hip/gentrifying area of East London. It was one of those things where the invitation didn't have an address, just a set of Google Maps coordinates you had to follow. I got out of the bus, trying desperately to follow Google Maps into a dark forest. I couldn't see anything and I wasn't even sure I was going in the right direction, but then after a few minutes on the trail I started hearing the bass and knew I could stop looking at the map and follow the frequency.

The downside of portals, like the illegal rave I went to in Hackney Wick, is that they disappear, close up, and sometimes if you don't make it back in time you could be stuck, left behind. When portals close they leave an ephemeral trace, what José Muñoz thought of as "the remains, the things that are left, hanging in the air like a rumor."[114] For Muñoz, these ephemeral traces are what define queer acts, and you can find traces of portals that have disappeared in the nostalgic stories of the nightclubs and small bars that were once legendary but don't exist anymore.

One such space was TrouwAmsterdam, a nightclub, restaurant, and art space located just a few metro stops away from the Amsterdam Central Station. Though the club stayed open for five years, it was meant to be open only for two. It was always supposed to be a temporary project. "It's the only way," Trouw owner Olaf Boswijk told me when I asked about why he made his space temporary. "All the energy is going to that focal point on our side as the people running it. Suddenly we're doing all our most crazy ideas because we know we're going to end."[115] Today, Trouw doesn't even exist: the building has been completely razed to the ground.

I first learned about Trouw just a few months before going for the first time because I saw an image of the venue's iconic lighting design on a music blog. I was fascinated. Held in a former newspaper factory where a Dutch paper also called *Trouw* was printed, the main club room was a long rectangle, an effect that created an immediate point of visual interest toward the stage. In the image I saw the club was full of people, dark but flooded by a stream of twelve fluorescent yellow lights. Produced by Dutch light artist Meeus van Dis, the fluorescent light tubes dangled from the ceiling and traveled at a diagonal down the center of the room. What I didn't know until I got to the club itself was that there were even more strobes and light tubes hidden on the stage, behind the DJ booth, in the ceiling, and along the massive concrete walls that came on and off only at certain emotional highs on the dance floor, punctuating rhythm and heightened emotions brought on by the music. I'd never seen anything like it.

To get to Trouw, a nightclub in an old factory that had essentially remained untouched, you took the number 51 metro from Amsterdam Central Station and got out at Wibautstraat, an unremarkable area that felt a lot farther away from a big city than just two metro stops. As you approached the venue you weren't sure if it was a nightclub or an office building, and that, for me, was part of the allure. The way the bass rattled its way through the building created a sense of potentiality, the Massumian thing that is about to happen, so you knew you were in the right place. You made your way into the club, past the security guards, down two sets of metal stairs, through the portal—and suddenly you fell onto the booming, gritty edge of art, music, fashion, and performance.

"One of the philosophies behind this place," Trouw owner Olaf Boswijk told me when I asked about what made Trouw unique, "is to be a little city within the city. And that's why we have a restaurant, we have an arts program. It's a club, there's concerts, it's a 24-hour license, so there really shouldn't be any need to leave. That's the whole idea: there's always another experience around the corner in another room."[116] In designing Trouw the way he did, Boswijk understood the nature of nightlife as an alternative universe, a third dimension you slip through. He knew that nightlife was not necessarily about time but about *portals*—a unique, spectacular experience that is tied off from the everyday, a transformative experience enabled and protected by a physical door itself.

In club worlds there's a lot of talk about the comedown, the aftermath of taking stimulating recreational drugs which, along with the music, help transport us to a different emotional plane. As Joshua Javier Guzmán writes, "The comedown arrives when the high is over, depression kicks in, and it is time to return to reality and all the displeasures that were suspended, if only for a while."[117] The comedown is what happens when we must cross back through the portal and out into the real world. If nightlife is about the remains, the trace, when it's time to cross back through the portal, how are we changed? What if instead of asking what remains and struggling through a comedown, what if we thought about coming *back?* When we come back through the portal and into the real world, what do we bring with us?

A list of possibilities: an STI, a phone number, a bad hangover, a bad comedown, new ideas for your next DJ set, new ideas for your next outfit, a favorite track, a new friend or two, a new lover, an interesting thought, a memorable story—you just *had* to be there!—a club stamp, a drink ticket, a gig or other professional creative opportunity, and the list goes on and on.

Nightlife disappears when the sun comes up and clubs lose their cultural cachet, their licenses, or get razed to the ground. But nightlife always leaves a trace—a memory, a story, a bar stamp, a creative idea—and these traces can help us think about the kinds of things we bring back with us from our nightlife experiences. How are we changed once we cross back through the portal to the other side? The portal is the enabling device that creates the stories we tell and it helps us experience things we wouldn't normally see. Once on the other side we are opened up to new, unexpected narratives. We come down and we come back, but through the experience we are always changed in some way.

"I Was Born a Queen, I've Always Been a Queen" A Conversation with Shaun J. Wright

SHAUN J. WRIGHT IS A DJ, vocalist, producer, and former member of the group Hercules & Love Affair. Born and raised in west suburban Chicagoland, Shaun spent most of his teen years immersed in the sounds of house music. His love for dance music expanded throughout his high school years as he participated in the underground dance scene now globally known as juke. While an undergrad at Morehouse College in Atlanta, he developed his skills as a dancer/voguer in professional dance companies and the ballroom scene. Beyond his impressive creative talents, which bring other fabulous black divas like Sylvester to mind, what drew me to Shaun is the way he is the total picture of fabulousness: brown, queer, talented.

> **For me, your uniqueness as an artist, DJ, thinker, and a critically black queen is inseparable from the fact that you grew up in an impoverished suburb of Chicago, a city that has a definitive connection to black gay club culture and to house music in particular.**

155

I don't think I could exist as I am without being born and raised here. I say this because I was born in the 1980s, raised in the '80s and '90s, and I came of age in the '90s before YouTube. At the time the only way to experience other music cultures was to go to that place, or maybe having the music sent to you, maybe some VHS tapes, which is a whole different way of conceptualizing the world. When I moved to Atlanta I realized my experience was unique, that I was born and raised in Chicago, exposed to a lot of early disco classics, a lot of early New York garage, a lot of Chicago house. I was going to ghetto house parties. I was sneaking into the Generator when I was fifteen, sixteen, I was sneaking into the Prop House, these black gay clubs that play house music.

It sounds like you grew up in the clubs, but did you always want to be a singer? Did you always want to do house music?

I was telling this story to a friend the other day. The first time I started singing in public was at Roosevelt Elementary School in Broadview, Illinois. I was in eighth grade and I don't know who overheard me sing but my teacher demanded I sing for her after class one day. And when I did, she told me, "You're going to be in the black history program." So I gathered about four friends and they did my background, and the song I sang was this revisiting of "Day by Day" by Dajae, who at that time was the biggest influence on me musically. She was a prominent artist on Cashmere Records in Chicago. It was this underground house music song that I'm sure no one in the audience knew, even though I was in the Chicago suburbs. The song's about struggling through the mundane and I thought it was appropriate for a black history program. But I never considered a career as a professional singer until I met Andy Butler from Hercules & Love Affair. There were always people pushing me to sing but I never felt confident about my voice until I met Andy.

How did you get connected with Andy? Did you send in a demo?

I did send him a demo but I didn't have demos waiting around. I whipped up this really quick song on Fruity Loops and sent it to him and it kind of went from there. But I wasn't thinking about singing at the time, I honestly wasn't.

Do you remember how you two met?

I remember the day exactly. It was August 8, 2008, the year after I moved to New York to the day. I moved to New York to be a fashion curator and worked as an adjunct professor at LIM College teaching visual merchandising and fashion show production. Long story short, my friend Omar and I went to the Hercules show—I dragged him there—and I was just really intrigued by what they were doing. They seemed pretty special. I was done that day. I don't think I've been that done since that day—it was a special night. At the show this girl in front of us was like, "Are you going to the after-party?" We were like, sure. So we snuck into the after-party—we were not on the list, but we were on the list that night, if you know what I mean. We slid upstairs and Andy was there at some point and I congratulated him on the show and the work they'd been doing. And then he said, "I noticed you all night at the show. You reminded me a lot of Sylvester [the legendary black queer disco singer]." And at the time I had dreadlocks and I was wearing them in a fringe bang at the front and long at the back, very Rick James. So you couldn't tell me nothing. Everywhere I went was a show, a spectacle.

I said, "Oh, well, if I remind you of Sylvester I can

sing like him too," and he told me to send him something. So I sent him my demo via Myspace and then I saw him again at another party and then again at another and we exchanged numbers and started working together after that. But it was weird because I didn't go to the show with that intention. I wasn't looking for a career. But there was something about the music that drew me. And at the end I was like, "I'm going to be in Hercules & Love Affair." It was one of those things that you *know,* and it changed the trajectory of my life.

I was spending a lot of time doing things I was passionate about but I wasn't really following my true desires. I was intimidated by music. Music scales and music theory always seemed so difficult to grasp—always so esoteric. And that was just insecurity. I always envisioned I would be involved with music in some way but I always did everything around it. I worked with fashion, dance, visual communication, but music was the one I wouldn't touch. In a way it works because I'm approaching music from all these other disciplines. There's an effort to make it four-dimensional.

I'm less interested in articulating a sense of fabulousness as a look or a specific item or any specific thing and am more captivated by what fabulousness does, what it allows, and what it opens up for folks.

When I think about fabulous people I think about people who approach life in a way that is singular to them. You won't confuse them with anyone else. When I think of someone who is fabulous, they have a certain presence that calls your attention. And it makes you feel like you're special in the room with them. If you can impact the room in such a way that everyone wants to be freer, everyone feels like more of themselves or a better version of themselves, that's the ultimate fabulousness.

Exactly. When someone is fabulous it changes the dynamics of a room. It brings the room *up*. Conversely, it also reminds people that they too can turn it up a notch. If Grace Jones pumps into a room and she's giving you Grace Jones, you're reminded how normal everything else is. You want to match her rhythm in some way.

Yeah! You want to step it up. I think it's a gift to be fabulous, I think it's an anointing. It's something you have to utilize not just to your advantage but to the advantage of others, and it feeds that spirit and causes you to grow. If you're at the center of all the things you do, that's not fabulous. That's narcissism. And it's in line with American consumption culture. A fabulous expression of life is about giving. It's an offering.

And as a thing that has aesthetic properties, fabulousness is also about possibilities, it's about separate dimensions, about imagining a different world or set of things. I'm always confused when people say things like, "Oh, I wish I could wear that." And I'm thinking, "Well, who says you *can't* wear it? Who is actually saying you can't wear this sequined jacket? I mean it: *who?*"

The whole world tells you you can't, in its own way. But I'm sure all of us at some point saw somebody who gave us the notion that there was a possibility. And that's fabulousness. Prince was that for me. Michael Jackson. Artists have always been good at this. Queen Latifah. Bea Arthur. My mom, she used to wear sequins all the time—in Maywood! She was a performer and I would see her and take it in. My mom was the first fabulous person I ever saw. She had short hair and a bang, just one blond bang, and she would curl it, put on her sequined nails, get her sequined dress. And I would just watch the procedure of her getting ready. It was so captivating, not knowing that I would be doing something so similar.

Fabulousness is an aesthetic thing, a world produced by people who are marginalized in some way and who have created their own version of the world here and now. It's utopian. Instead of waiting for things to get better, instead of waiting for rights or for laws to be passed, fabulous people imagine an alternative universe right now, and that's why it's so important to articulate fabulousness as a queer aesthetic.

Absolutely. We're always looking for presence. Fabulousness means you can be seen without even trying. And then we go to the club and no matter where we turn we are literally the most different people in the room. And we're different from one another. It's recognizable, nobody can deny it. Bringing it. *Bringing* it. That's what's so diverse about the ballroom scene. You had to bring something, and if you wanted to make a real statement, then you had to bring something of yourself, a newness, to get any kind of grace. I don't see that in mass culture. In normative culture there's just a redundancy: we just keep regurgitating the same old tired tropes. But in ballroom, authenticity is key. Because if you copy too much, you're going to get *read* and *chopped*. When you're fabulous you're not trying to bring the mundane or the mediocre or the good enough. You've got to take it to the highest level you can take it.

You and I have been to Berghain together a number of times, and I have to say that the times I've been there with you have been the most magical. Not to add any more hype but it's the best club I've ever been to. What do you think it is that makes Berghain such a unique place?

There's not one key thing, it's just a combination of everything. I think about it being at the intersection of the old and new for the city itself. Berlin has always been a safe space for creatives and the outcast, that and being at the intersection of two different neighborhoods with two different histories. Being a power plant, with the myth of magnets underneath it. Apparently there are magnets underneath the surface of the building, so maybe even the magnetic energies in the rooms are different. A place that can be mythologized already lends itself to its own magic because you go in there with expectations.

It's an exhausting place because it allows you to pursue fun and dancing; unlike any other place you can endure it without trying to go somewhere else. There's always a new crevice, or a new secret cubby or sitting area to find every single time. I've been going there six years, and every single time I see a new part of the club that I'd never seen before. There's always something they can open and close that can make the clubbing experience very different than the last time.

There's the time I was there for fifteen hours and I was telling my friend back in the States about it, and he was like, "What did you do in there for fifteen hours?" and I told him, "I don't even know. I don't know!"

I was just telling someone this! The longest I've ever gone is twelve hours, and most of the time all I can recall is running around. Sometimes there are songs that just hit the right chord in my body, and they epitomize my experience in the club. Downstairs in Berghain there's always the chance of walking down the stairs as that beat is hitting . . .

Girl . . .

. . . You know that back gated area and you're hitting that runway, and that beat is *boom boom boom boom boom!* And every part of that song just tears me up. Or I'm coming up the steps and the beat is greeting me, and I see the bodies in cathartic movements, just gyrating. Visually it's so arresting. That *feels* fabulous. It's the music meets the bodies meets the people going past me, and it just forms these moments where it's my own personal movie.

The first time I was in Berlin I was performing in Berghain with Hercules. So it was a very different experience because it was a concert night during the week. I was impressed by the space right away. Seeing this building that looked liked a prison, so aggressively built. It's high design without the fluff.

I'd love to know what it's like for you to perform there. You've played Panorama Bar many times now. I'm wondering what it was like the first time you played.

Transcendent. It really was transcendent, the most transcendent experience I've ever had DJing. I'm already so hyped about the space, so in love with the possibilities there, the way that people are primed. You can tell that people come there to give the party. They're so excited to have gotten past those doors. You have to prep yourself for that club, it is a ritual. You know how we peeled off our pants in the corner one winter to put on our poom poom shorts? We spotted people bringing in blueberries and bananas. So you come *ready* like you're about to run a marathon. You come ready to have fun. So in turn, it is! When I played there I knew what would indicate that I was doing an okay job. For me, it was the raising of the shutters. The bartenders and the staff were the real gauge for me, even more than the crowd, because they hear it *all*. And they opened the shutters three times?!

Can you tell us what it means that they opened the shutters during your performance?

It means that the energy of the performance is reaching such a level that it's peaking. When the sun pours in people raise their hands and scream, "Yes!" and then they close them real fast.

So during the daylight the shutters are closed and then during high emotional moments they open them as a theatrical effect.

It's a theatrical effect. And it's a church effect, like the sun coming in through the stained glass windows. I know I can get away with a lot there as a performer.

In many ways you've made it. You perform regularly at Panorama Bar and other nightclubs around the world, you run a Chicago-based label called Twirl, you were in Hercules & Love Affair, you travel constantly, and in general everywhere you go people are enamored. What would you say you want as an artist?

Autonomy. I'm working toward a platform that will get the music I make to as many listeners as possible. I want to be a possibility. That's what fabulousness is. You are the embodiment of new possibilities. That's fabulous. The highest honor as an artist is to be the possibility for someone else to follow and do better than. I was born a queen, I've always been a queen. And if we were at the club dancing, I was going to do the most feminine moves I could do because that was what called me. So as an artist, I want other artists who come after me, in this space—as a black queen from the west suburbs of Chicago, a pretty impoverished, gang-ridden area—for just another little black queen to see themselves and think, "Oh, I can do that too," or "I want to do that." That's what I want.

Brown people have to wait for things in a way that white folks don't necessarily have to. We wait for people to swipe right on us on Tinder and we wait to get booked for gigs or to get noticed for our creative talents. We wait to get paid, we wait for rights and we wait for justice, and we take a deep breath because the next micro-aggression is right around the corner. But waiting gets so damn exhausting, like sitting in a doctor's office reading an issue of *Redbook,* waiting for your name to be called, looking up with thirsty anticipation every time the nurse steps into the room. Is it my turn yet? No, it isn't, and it's never going to be our turn. So instead of waiting, waiting, and more waiting, marginalized folks seize space and create opportunities for ourselves right now and on our own terms. This is about bringing something of yourself—about knowing you're good, knowing you're talented, knowing you bring something to the table, and being confident in that. From there, you use style and creativity to take space for yourself instead of waiting for it to be handed over to you for free. When have marginalized people ever been handed anything?

Fabulous eccentricity is about living a life that's singular to you and doing so on your own terms without regard to norms, systems, and institutions that want nothing more than to keep you hemmed in. It allows folks to imagine another way, a different possibility, and for Shaun, those alternative blueprints were people like Queen Latifah, Michael Jackson, and Prince, a figure who forever escaped categorization and labels. Even Shaun's mother was an example of what could be possible, a template for how to bring something of yourself to the table. That's why one of the most important aspects of fabulousness might be the sense of living as a possibility, particularly when marginalized folks have long been told to wait our turn. But despite it all, we exist strongly, flamboyantly, and fiercely even though nearly every aspect of contemporary life reminds us we shouldn't be here. But we are here, and we're out here in the vogue ball, honing our creative talents and dancing at the club for hours on end.

Will fabulousness pay the rent? Will fabulousness protect us from getting beaten up or harassed on the street? Will fabulous find us love or get us laid? Will fabulousness land us an office job? Will fabulousness overthrow the systems that oppress us—all of us—every single day? No, it won't. But when we cave to the negativity and the cultural, social, and emotional poverty that oppressive systems force onto us, we're actually letting the system win. They win. We should be angry and we should be fighting, but we should also remember that joy, friendship, clubbing, music, creativity, and community are just as important as the fight for a brand-new day.

4.
What's Queer about the Catwalk?

in november 2016 a friend of mine shared a video on Facebook of Leiomy Maldonado, the so-called Wonder Woman of Vogue, slithering through a crowd and voguing from here to eternity. The video wasn't necessarily that surprising because Leiomy is known internationally for her precise, decadent, jaw-dropping approach to vogue femme, and her performances nearly always slay. Filmed on November 26, 2016, at Vogue Knights in New York City and uploaded to the YouTube channel BRTB TV (Ballroom Throwbacks TV), the clip shows Leiomy floating out of the crowd to an edit of "Work This Pussy," an iconic track in the ballroom scene that really brings the girls to the floor. She wears a long-sleeved black and white leotard with knee-high black stiletto boots, and the look is sickening. As she comes out of the crowd and onto the dance floor, she violently prances, splits, slides, seduces us, and drops to the floor, all while being cheered on by an audience of brown, queer, and trans people. Leiomy's drops are mesmerizing, and they are indeed her signature, but what made the clip that much more poignant was that the friend who shared it on Facebook captioned it: "Storming into Trump's America like . . ."

Sharing articles, links, and videos on Facebook is a fascinating phenomenon because we think we're sharing a story that will interest the folks in our online bubbles, but what we're actually doing is revealing something about ourselves, our politics, and our position in the world. We have personal connections to the stories we choose to share on our social media properties, and we communicate a truth about ourselves without saying so each time we post a link. So my friend, depressed by the election news but mesmerized by Leiomy, shared this video as if to say that he too is storming into Trump's America like a confident, fierce Leiomy, a brown trans body on a catwalk who will use creativity and fierceness, a kind of aesthetic violence, to not be silenced under the Trump regime. She will use the dance floor and the catwalk to make her voice known despite all the odds.

A few years ago when I was living in Williamsburg, Brooklyn, before Williamsburg reached its Whole Foods–having, luxury-condo apex, there was a tiny gay club I used to go to called Sugarland. Pizza joint by day, gay club at night. My friend Jeremy and I went there one weekend, not quite the opening weekend, but the venue had not been open all that long, and we watched a queer underground New York electronic music group called The Ones perform their hit song "Flawless." They were fabulous and, I should point out, the three met while working as stylists at Patricia Field, another example of how the boutique served as ground zero for underground, fabulous queer performance in New York City. There the trio stood on a tiny stage in futuristic costumes, like black queer superheroes, sing-chanting the words "Just like perfection. Absolutely flawless" over and over again to a house-flavored beat. I've seen a lot of queer musical performances in nightclubs over the years, but this is still one of the most memorable acts I've seen, not for anything like virtuosic stage pyrotechnics or amazing vocals but because the message was so clear: You're flawless. Own it. When Jeremy and I left the venue we had "Flawless" stuck in our heads, singing it at 3:00 a.m. all the way down Bedford Avenue, marveling how you could make a whole dance track focused only on feeling good, looking flawless.

Much of dance music focuses on looking good, wearing the right clothes, and being in all the right places at the right time. In "Flawless," The Ones are there to tell you that "naturally your entrance is grand. Red carpet rolls out, on the side they stand, worshipping you like a goddess." In a famous 1979 essay on disco, Richard Dyer highlights that one of the major characteristics of the genre, and one of the reasons people didn't like it initially, is its blatant commercialism. "Much of the hostility to disco," he wrote in Gay Left, "stems from the equation of it with capitalism. Both in how it is produced and in what it expresses, disco is held to be irredeemably capitalistic."[1] This commercialism is at the level of specific disco fashion and disco balls, of course, but it is also mirrored in nightclubs, materialism, and slick production values. But for Dyer, the commercialism in gay-oriented music is turned on its head because it is produced by oppressed groups, and here I'm talking about both queer and brown communities, disempowered groups that make their own culture via commodities that were not initially intended for them.

This was, I think, the point of American celebrity drag queen RuPaul's 1993 single "Supermodel (You Better Work!)," an upbeat dance track people knew from New York to Kentucky and which peaked at 45 on the Billboard Hot 100.[2] "*Work!* Turn to the left. *Work!* Now turn to the right. *Work!* Sashay, shantay!" RuPaul sings on the track, imploring us to "shantay" down the runway. *Shantay* means nothing more than feeling fabulous. But when RuPaul asks us to "work!"—can you hear her now?— what is she asking us to do? When used in a queer performance context, "work!" frames labor we reclaim because it is creatively fulfilling. You can spell it a number of ways: werk, worq, werq, worrrrrk, and on and on— purposeful, playful misspellings that actually do the job of tying queer aesthetic labor off as work you do because it's exciting, creative, and embodied, and finally because it reflects a core aspect of yourself. RuPaul's fabulous, catwalk-heavy anthem, like "Flawless," highlights "work" not as commercialism or owning labels but as queer imagination. "And it don't matter what you wear," RuPaul sings on the track. "They're checking out your savoir faire. And it don't matter what you do, 'cause everything looks good on you!" Instead of insisting we own labels as a key to fabulousness, RuPaul as cultural theorist points to the value of everyday small gestures of fabulousness. But why does so much popular queer performance, and black queer performance and music in particular, focus on the allure of fabulousness and working the catwalk? What's queer about the catwalk?

I've always been drawn to the fashion catwalk as a space where you're meant to see and be looked at, a moving display case of identity in which the job is to tell a story, and sell garments, simply by walking straight ahead. As a closeted queer teenager growing up in Ferguson, Missouri, I fed my fashion fetish by secretly watching hours and hours of runway shows on Fashion TV because I was fascinated by runway modeling as affect. I loved watching the models come out from backstage, walking toward me in my midwestern living room, going back and forth, back and forth. Even though what they were selling to the room were the garments themselves, what captivated me was the allure. The production. The sensuality, the opulence, and of course the attitude. I liked the fantasy, what they did onstage, how they walked. They were moving forward, or being propelled to someplace fabulous, really, and I wanted to be wherever they were going.

If I wasn't watching footage of fashion runways then I was focused on reality television shows about fashion models, from *Project Runway* to the Tyra Banks–led *America's Next Top Model* and the more recent *The Face* starring Naomi Campbell. *Project Runway* was always about the designs, never the models. And though *ANTM* did include catwalks at certain points throughout the show, they were usually way over the top, *Fear Factor* meets high fashion, and were never grounded as the main feature of the series. *ANTM* focused primarily on how to take pictures, how to pose as though you were already a picture. Bravo's *Make Me a Supermodel* premiered in 2008 and the catwalk was a major part of the weekly competition and elimination process. On *Make Me a Supermodel* contestants were judged both on their ability to take editorial pictures and on how they worked the runway.

I love the performance space of the catwalk so much that even when I go dancing one of my signature moves is walking around the room to the mood of the music like I'm on a catwalk, not at all an uncommon sight if you're at the club and there are brown queens in the room. No matter how packed the dance floor gets, I will still find some sliver of real estate, a corridor just long enough, and my friends and I will take turns walking to the music, working the room, going back and forth, back and forth, looking at each other, commenting on each other's moves. What makes fashion modeling interesting visually is not just the clothes but the fact that the clothes are on the run. The clothes are dancing. Clothes have to be worn to have cultural meaning, as Anne Hollander has shown, but these looks must also move around and be seen in the urban environment. One of the earliest examples of the marriage of the city and the catwalk as a space for the spectacular display of self was the mirrored Peacock Alley of the 1897 Waldorf Astoria Hotel in New York City. Guests arrived at the Waldorf Astoria by horse-drawn carriage and strolled (or shantayed) down an elegant, three-hundred-foot-long mirrored corridor lined with sumptuous sofas and chairs that led from the carriage entrance outside to the hotel's exclusive restaurant, also called Peacock Alley.

I want to think about what the catwalk allows as a performance space, especially as a space for performances done by people forced to the margins. What is possible on the catwalk and in catwalk performance that is not in everyday life? When Beverly Johnson, the first African American model to appear on the cover of American *Vogue*, worked the catwalks in the 1970s she transformed the room with her elegance. She was giving a fantasy. Supermodel Naomi Campbell, in her turn, has long been celebrated for her iconic power walk. "Do the Naomi Campbell walk, Naomi Campbell walk, walk across the room like Naomi Campbell," Beyoncé sings in her 2006 song "Get Me Bodied."[3] Through movement, makeup, and accessories, models draw you into their world, and it's this sense of imagination and otherworldliness that has always interested me about the performative possibilities of the runway.

But when brought out of a commercial context and used solely for performance purposes, the catwalk is nearly always about self-assertion, creativity, ownership, and fierceness. A go-to example of what the catwalk does when it is brought out of its shell is the music video for "Free Your Mind," the 1992 single by the black female R&B/funk rock group En Vogue. Dressed in edgy black high-fashion looks and leather knee-high stiletto boots, with opulent hair and headpieces on top, these divas are dressed to impress. They stomp around a long catwalk lit from below while paparazzi are positioned below them on either side of the platform. As they take control of the runway—seizing it, really—they are making a commentary about the lack of visibility of black women's bodies in commercial fashion media. And as they take control of the catwalk as well as the picture frame, they also insist on their visibility and its immediacy. They're not asking for permission or waiting to be seen and noticed. They're making us notice them right now. Instead of coming onto the catwalk to show a garment they use fashion, personal style, and dance to perform their worth as black female bodies.

Soul Train, which stretched from 1971 to 2006, is the longest-running black television series in history. The show is unique not only because of the way it highlighted black visibility through black music but because it also used dance, personal style, music, and the catwalk to show the power of black joy and personhood. As Mark Anthony Neal has shown, *Soul Train* provided television audiences the opportunity to see a creative "black communal ethic," transforming the dance floor and the catwalk into a space where the black community "reintegrated with itself." For Neal, *Soul Train* reflected the cultural importance of the dance hall of the 1970s as one of the most important spaces for black community and expression.[4] The visual signature of *Soul Train*, the show's "zip," was the *Soul Train* "line," a catwalk where joyous, well-dressed black Americans stood across from one another creating a catwalk-like space between them, allowing dancers to go down the runway to the groove of the music.

Many user-generated compilations of the *Soul Train* line live on YouTube, including more than one tribute to Rosie Perez. But one fan video that stands out for its originality and unbridled black queer sensibility is "Soul Train Babies" uploaded in January 2014 by Darrell J. Hunt. The clip shows a typical *Soul Train* line, but what's unique about Hunt's interpretation is that he dubs a sassy commentary about each dancer's performance as they go down the line. "How you do all this in shoulder pads? C'mon on, pumps!" he says to one dancer. "C'mon, mama! Ain't been to a single dance class but got on leg warmers—I live!" he says to another.[5] The whole clip is centered around his positive reactions to the dancers as they hit the line, and it specifically connects to the practice of chanting in voguing culture. The *Soul Train* line was already a space where fabulous dancers of color worked a look and their dance moves on the catwalk, an early example of the catwalk as a parade ground for identity, creativity, and personhood. The added black queer vocal overlay highlights the connection between catwalk performance and queer performance. Here, the catwalk is a queer performance space where individualized fabulousness is turned on, animated, and where fabulousness shows itself as being about creativity and self-assertion through the optics of style. In the process of such queer displays of fashion, fabulousness turns out to be very much about storytelling, a poetics of the self, and narrating that self through movement and pose.

One of the phrases you'll hear again and again during a vogue battle is "Hold that pose for me," an indication to performers that the moment is over. They should hold their pose while the judging panel makes a final decision about who wins the round, who snatches the trophy. In a series of Facebook status updates called Ballroom Tings, veteran DJ and ballroom pioneer Vjuan Allure articulates the meaning behind holding that pose: "Hold That Pose—the importance of holding that last pose— almost everything in Ballroom is a snapshot—that final pose to your performance, walk, selling it, whatever—it's your exclamation point—end of scene. It's catching a moment in time to see if you can put the whipped cream on top of your performance! Hold it, Seal it! It's called a final pose for a reason—stop moving."[6] The pose is essential for recording the final moment of the performance as well as for putting an exclamation point at the end. And this is right in line with Craig Owens's idea of a pose as already being a picture. At the end of the day, a pose tells a story. It is the ultimate poetics of the self.

Nowhere is this clearer than in the dance track "Walk for Me," an ode to the ballroom scene produced by New York performer Paul Alexander. In a 2006 performance of "Walk for Me" at Bank, a club that was situated on the corner of Houston and Essex on the Lower East Side, Alexander chants, "I want you to take to the catwalk, *darling*. You sure look gorgeous! Walk for body, walk for face. Walk it and snatch first place. *Walk for me*." Here, the references to voguing and house ball culture, such as "snatching first place" or winning the top prize, and "walk for body, walk for face" are unmistakable. But what makes this performance stand out even more than the lyrics themselves is that while he chants, New York nightlife queen Kim Aviance, of the House of Aviance, stands beside him, dressed in a full look. As he says "Walk for me" she turns her body and starts walking sensuously in place on a treadmill. There she is, walking, working, dressed to impress, working the treadmill like a catwalk. In this performance a walk has been turned into performance, but even more than that, a treadmill, a machine meant to whip bodies into the correct physical shape, is repurposed into a tool of fabulosity and "sickeningness."

As Aviance works the imaginary catwalk with fierceness she highlights that for minoritized groups, the simple act of walking is a parade ground of pride in the face of extreme duress. Walking fabulously on a real or imaginary runway may be dance, but when transposed out of the framed, idealized nature of queer performance space, walking-while-fabulous is actually about survival when you're already a spectacle. In his earliest discussions of power in *The History of Sexuality*, Michel Foucault shows how one effect of power is what he calls "negative uniformity," or how power restricts what can be done, said, shown, and even experienced. "Renounce yourself," he wrote, "or suffer the penalty of being suppressed; do not appear if you do not want to disappear." You can exist freely as long as you completely blend in, suppressing any traces of spectacle. The fear of difference creates a relentless uniformity by "submission in the one who is constrained by" the norm, and that transforms us into obedient, conforming subjects.[7] When you're out doing fabulousness, in whatever way, you could be a target, and that means even walking to get a sandwich could be dangerous. In this context, when walking is elevated to the level of performance, what it underscores is survival and assertion—taking space, not waiting to perhaps one day be given it.

In ballroom, the runway is both a performance space and a place for the articulation of a fabulous queer self. "The whole idea," Grandfather of the House of Ninja Archie Burnett said, "is I'm fierce and I know it."[8] Bringing this trope of fabulous walking into a queer lifeworld shows the extent to which performing fabulousness at the vogue ball is ultimately about a poetics of the self. At the Janet Jackson Tribute Ball I attended in June 2014 at the Paris Social Club, the "Runway Diva" category especially highlighted fabulousness as about selling yourself. Rather than sitting at the front of the "stage" area, where people ended up as they walked down the runway, I stood at the back, the "backstage" area, so I could be there when people entered and left the runway. I saw them looking prim and fabulous as they emerged (or, often, *ran*) from the bathroom cum dressing room when their categories were called, and I saw them out of breath and sweaty when they left the floor at the end of their number. "I wanna see a bitch walking for me. I wanna see a bitch turning for me. I wanna see a bitch walking for me for *run, run, run, run, runway*," New York vogue legend Dashaun Wesley chanted to the Paris crowd. Dressed mostly in black, the contestants came out onto the catwalk, often with hand-embellished or handmade looks, and sold their garments, their ideas, and their sense of self to the room. "Which bitch is walking the runway? Which bitch is turning the runway? Which bitch is serving the runway eating the runway, ow!" There they walk, back and forth, back and forth, each giving attitude, fantasy, and unbridled queerness. The whole thing was about what you can do to stand out creatively.

Curious about the dynamics of the runway and how it has been brought to a queer performance context, I took a one-day runway workshop intended for voguers. We began by walking like our normal selves from one end of the room toward the mirror of the dance studio. This was the most important task, the instructor told us, because even though a model walk doesn't seem natural, it should *feel* natural. He didn't want any of us to walk the way we thought models were supposed to walk. From there the instructor prompted us to walk like we were in a hurry to meet our friend for a drink, and we did this back and forth for a few minutes. Then we were told to walk like we were on our way to a hot date, an altogether different kind of walk. Try this sometime. Each of these walks has a different attitude, all inspired by a specific theatrical impulse or setup, and he was mainly encouraging us to think about the way we move in our own bodies. At all times he told us not to walk the way we think models are supposed to walk, and this was his way of allowing everyone to tap into their own inner confidence.

As we went through the exercises in the dance studio I realized there was already an empowering aspect of the runway workshop, even if you weren't competing in the ball. It was all about having and selling confidence. "Don't walk to the music," the instructor would say. "Walk to the attitude." "You're worth it!" he screamed over and over as we walked toward the mirror, and just the fact that he said "You're worth it!" actually made you feel worth it, like you had a sense of value. This is ultimately, I think, what the runway is about, especially within a queer performance context. It's not about asking for value or asking for permission. It's a declaration of value, self-worth, and possibility.

After the group exercise of catwalking toward the dance studio mirror with various scenarios, at the end of the class we did a mini runway show in which each of us walked on our own to music as a way of showing off what we'd learned. This time our only prompt was to find something about ourselves and sell it to the room. It could have been a piece of clothing we already had on or one of our defining features. I'd never been more nervous than I was then. One girl piled her long hair into a ponytail and held it at the top of her head. The experience was cathartic in a lot of ways because walking down the runway ushered in the confidence that comes with working with what you have. Coming away from the runway seminar taught me how much voguing and runway work (*werk*) is about confidence. That much may seem obvious, but in fact loving and selling yourself as a marginalized body has a much more pronounced impact when you live in a world that constantly devalues your sense of worth, where walking down the block just to get a sandwich could be a dangerous scenario.

The most memorable participant in the runway category at the Berlin Voguing Out Festival in 2014 was Ruda Puda, a Berlin-based fashion designer who stunned the room even before he began his walk down the runway. He was flawless in a tight gray lamé jumpsuit and bejeweled eyelashes, lips, and a sequined Mardi Gras–style headpiece with a thick, long, black ponytail attached to it, evocative of a horse's mane. The audience roared enthusiastically even before he fully emerged from backstage, an acknowledgment that his look was *working*. No holds barred, he pumped down the runway with sass, an unstoppable vision of fabulousness. "It's a pass, honey, it's a pass!" Georgina Leo Melody excitedly shouted into the mic, meaning he would advance to the next round of competition. Before he reached the end of the catwalk, before he even finished his performance, the judges had already leapt out of their seats, showering him with 10s across the board—the highest possible score— each of them actually fanning him off with their score cards, a show of affection in the ballroom scene. He was that hot. What I love about this particular catwalk performance is that even though Ruda Puda knew he had secured the highest score, even though Georgina had told him he'd already advanced to the next round, he simply stood there, much longer than necessary. He lingered, did an extra spin so the audience could get another good look at him, tossed his mane, causing the crowd to go even more wild. He accentuated his face with his hands, paused.

The crowd screamed. They were joining Ruda Puda in celebrating his self-worth, his fabulousness, as well as all the creative labor it took to bring this particular look to life. That creative labor includes all the drawings and sketches, the putting on of makeup, editing the look down, sewing the catsuit, getting *into* the catsuit, figuring out a solution when something suddenly doesn't fit right or goes wrong at the very last second. Here the audience believes it is looking at Ruda Puda when in reality it is actually Ruda Puda, in all of his fierceness, who is staring back at the audience. He already knows he looks good. The point is to make sure *you* know he looks good.

I'm theorizing the catwalk as a space to demand self-worth, a line of critique that joins Joseph Roach's reading of the parading Mardi Gras "krewes" like Rex and Zulu, who traditionally throw objects at the crowd. Though throwing things is technically illegal, Mardi Gras krewes "appropriated the insulting act of throwing offensive materials on passersby, a time-honored carnival prank, and transformed it into the condescending but apparently good-hearted act of throwing cheap baubles to the acquiescent crowd, whose members continually plead, 'Throw me something, Mister.'" Krewes are street gangs whose members have labored extensively to create Mardi Gras looks as a way to one-up or out-fierce other rival street gangs, and here Roach shows that the confrontation is not about urban violence but beads and sequins.[9] The simple act of throwing objects at an audience is about demanding presence, and as Ruda Puda stands there in front of the crowd, throwing not beads but a fierce look, he's also demanding recognition of his queer aesthetic labor. Mardi Gras krewes, like voguers and runway queens, compete with one another through fierceness as they *seize* their individuality during the length of the runway or parade route.

On May 4, 2015, FKA Twigs, loved by cool kids and the edgy fashion press alike for her artistic brand of electronic R&B, went to the annual Costume Institute Gala at the Metropolitan Museum of Art in New York with her fiancé, Robert Pattinson, star of the *Twilight* franchise. The gala, produced by *Vogue* editor in chief Anna Wintour, is by all measures one of the most fabulous red carpet moments of the year, with televised fashion coverage featured on all the major networks. The gala always serves as a preview of the newest summer fashion exhibition at the Costume Institute, that year's being *China: Through the Looking Glass,* which centered on the impact of Chinese print in Western fashion. Just a few hours after the ball, Twigs and Pattinson went downtown to a very different kind of function, this one on the corner of 39th Street and 8th Avenue at Escuelita, a gay Latino dance club known for its weekly Monday party Vogue Knights.[10] In video footage of the couple uploaded to the YouTube channel Ballroom Throwbacks, Twigs and Pattinson drink champagne, kiss, and have a front-row seat to the performances. One person commented on the video wanting someone to "please explain to my country ass . . . what is Robert Pattinson and his hundred-million-dollar self doing here? I mean, really?"[11]

This was not the couple's first time at Vogue Knights. In November 2014, Twigs was seen at Escuelita, only this time she didn't just sit and enjoy. She showed her chops. Like many pop stars before her—from Madonna to Jennifer Lopez—Twigs regularly brings voguing into her stage and video performances. The majority of her music video "Glass and Patron," for instance, takes place at an imaginary, highly stylized vogue ball. Dancers pump down the catwalk like they're competing for a trophy, most of them performers of color, and each gets their moment to shine on the runway. "Come on up here, come on up here," the commentator says as he brings Twigs to the floor at Vogue Knights. "We know you're up in the place with your man but we're not going to say his name, honey." He congratulates Twigs on the release of "Glass and Patron" before he slips into a chant, a uniquely ballroom sound that Marlon Bailey sees as scat-like, improvised rhythmic speech.[12]

"You wanna let it out, don't you? You wanna let it out, don't you?" he chants as Twigs hits the floor and vogues. She's so fabulous she gets snaps from the audience, and she ends her quick foray on the voguing runway with a quick spin and a dip or "death drop," a dramatic dance move that looks like a sudden drop to the floor with one leg pointing in the air. Her performance is so strong that one audience member screams, "*Ow!*" the ultimate sign of approval in the ballroom scene.[13]

Ballroom is a black and Latino queer underground world of fantasy that captivates the popular imagination.[14] At its heart voguing, which is only one aspect of the ballroom community, is a movement language that transforms poses into dance, but today vogue femme in particular is the most recognizable style of vogue, a form built by trans women of color. "There's an iconic chant—'butch queen voguing like a femme queen,'" Leiomy told me in an interview for *Out* on the problem with *realness*—"which is basically gay men emulating trans women while dancing." But now, Leiomy says, a lot of gay guys don't respect trans women. "They put trans women in the back now instead of having us in the forefront."[15]

Broadly speaking, there are five elements of vogue femme, the most popular strand of vogue: hand performance, which is about dramatic storytelling with the hands; the duckwalk, a type of low, crouched movement in which the dancer walks "like a duck," often framing the face and kicking the legs out in a gesture of femininity; the catwalk, or how you parade yourself down the catwalk with an air of fierceness; floor performance—my favorite—which is about how the dancer works her or his relationship to the flatness of floor; and finally spins and dips, a pirouette-like gesture in which the voguer spins graciously before dramatically dropping to the floor, slamming it down with a leg opulently pointed in the air.

FKA Twigs fits into a broader range of female pop performers drawing inspiration from the visual language of vogue, from Madonna and Cherie Lily to the French cult electro group Yelle. References to voguing, a historically underground black and Latino LGBTQ cultural form, can be found in many corners of mainstream popular culture today. Leiomy Maldonado, for instance, first became a household name as a member of the dance group Vogue Evolution on MTV's *America's Best Dance Crew*, and since then her signature hair flip, the "Leiomy Lolly," has inspired the hair choreography of a range of pop divas, from Willow Smith and Bey-oncé to Lady Gaga and Britney Spears. Other celebrities like Olivier Rous-teing, the Instagram-savvy creative director of the French fashion house Balmain, Tamar Braxton, and Rihanna have embraced voguing, leading one journalist to write an article entitled "Nah, Rihanna: A History of 'Vogue' Exploiting Queer People of Color." Transgender DJ Terre Thame-litz, who performs as DJ Sprinkles, commented on the mainstreaming of Madonna's version of vogue this way: "Madonna was taking in tons of money, while the Queen who actually taught her how to vogue sat before me in the club, strung out, depressed and broke. So if anybody requested 'Vogue' or any other Madonna track, I told them, 'No, this is a Madonna-free zone! And as long as I'm DJ-ing, you will not be allowed to vogue to the decontextualized, reified, corporatized, liberalized, neutralized, asexualized, re-genderized pop reflection of this dance floor's reality!'"[16]

Voguing is a popular cultural form because it represents what dance scholar Barbara Browning has called "infectious rhythm," or how the seductive poly rhythms of the black diaspora make their way through culture like a virus.[17] These cultures spread because they're contagious. Here, Browning echoes Paul Gilroy, who has powerfully argued that part of the reason black performance cultures spread the way they do is that they are inherently promiscuous, and promiscuity is part of its livelihood. "Promiscuity is the key principle of its continuance," Gilroy wrote, high-lighting the way black performance practices are regularly spread, used, commercialized, exploited, and appropriated. As long as there is black culture and black creativity, they will always be promiscuous.[18]

The problem with the appropriation of black and brown cul-tural forms is twofold. On the one hand, white artists—and I'm thinking of Miley Cyrus and Katy Perry in recent pop music history—in desperate need of an "edgy" career refresh hastily put on black and brown cultures in an act of body snatching. They do it uncritically, as if they've some-how invented a new paradigm, as if culture has never seen a white art-ist take on black culture. But the paradigm is just as easily thrown away when blackness no longer serves them—when it no longer brings cash and dividends, as in the case of Miley Cyrus who, after years of appropriating and objectifying black women, announced a return to country music, leading Black Twitter to joke about her "return" to whiteness. Cultural appropriation looks like Madonna, who told *Rolling Stone* in 1989 that she felt black. "All of my friends were black, and all the music I listened to was black," she said. "I was incredibly jealous of all my black girlfriends because they could have braids in their hair that stuck up everywhere. So I would go through this incredible ordeal of putting wire in my hair and braiding it so that I could make *my* hair stick up. I used to make cornrows and everything."[19] In short, cultural appropriation is about how white people get to put on blackness and other cultural forms while still claiming the financial, personal, and political benefits of white privilege.

Used widely across all of the cultural industries, from fashion and film to music and advertising, cultural appropriation is upsetting because instead of simply casting black models in a fashion campaign or editorial, for instance, casting agents would still rather cast white models and paint them black. Why? The bottom line is that cultural appropriation has less to do with what gets appropriated and more to do with who gets paid—how the appropriated thing is straightened out and then whitewashed so much that the new version is white, neutral, and "appropriate." The problem with cultural appropriation, then, nearly always has to do with who makes money off a sterilized aspect of culture that originated in black and brown communities. Why do brown folks so rarely make money from their own cultural innovations?

As creatively exciting as vogue is, the problem with its explosion in contemporary popular culture is the way media outlets, always on the hunt for the latest trend, regularly suggest that voguing is "back." But where does it actually go when the media isn't writing about it? This was the implication of a fashion story published in the *Guardian* on November 18, 2014, titled "How Voguing Came Back into Vogue," the irony being, in fact, that voguing has not gone anywhere or been out of vogue since it was originally created in the 1980s in New York by a group of disenfranchised black and Latino queer youths. The only thing that changes, actually, is the singer, artist, journalist, or media outlet choosing to pay attention to it at the time.

Ballroom, a rich underground culture and dance form that emerged in New York City drag balls as early as the 1960s and was exposed to the mainstream for the first time in Jennie Livingston's 1990 documentary *Paris Is Burning*, is a rich site to understand beautiful eccentricity as a practice of everyday life. As with any good story, the origins of voguing are subject to rumor, but one thing is certain: it participates in a wide range of black diasporic sonic and movement practices. One story suggests that Pepper LaBeija, who had an interest in couture and high fashion, naturally incorporated fashion poses into his performance. LaBeija studied runway walks and re-created these gestures on the dance floor, and his moves eventually caught on.[20] Another, more gossipy story suggests that Paris Dupree was seen dancing in a nightclub with a *Vogue* magazine in her bag. As she danced, she took the magazine out, opened it, and posed right on the beat like the model on the page, then turned to another page and stopped in a new pose, again on the beat. Then a queen approached Paris and did her own pose, and Paris responded with yet another pose—each trying to be more fabulous than the other through the optics of posing and fashion.[21]

"*Pop! Dip! Spin! Vogue! Dip! Crawl! Turn! It! Out!*" the commentator shouts over a loudspeaker in *Paris Is Burning*, while fierce queens slide into and out of poses on the beat of the music. "No touching—and if you touch, I'm chopping you": these are the rules. There are maybe a hundred people in the room, all of them LGBTQ blacks and Latinos, and they all look fabulous. They cheer the dancers on. With the fluidity of Brazilian capoeira and the language of a dance battle circle, two queens move around the runway to the beat of the music with their arms constantly in motion, each trying to out-fierce the other through improvised poses taken from the visuality of fashion modeling.

But if the point of the routine is to outshine the competitor, one participant has a better idea: instead of doing the moves on her feet, she'll show everyone up by pressing her back against the hardwood floor, slithering, crawling up the floor, constantly moving, posing, making sure to hold each pose a few seconds before inventing the next. The category is floor performance. "Work!" the commentator shouts as the voguers battle to display their fierceness. When Willi Ninja comes to the runway, he bounces his shoulders and does some hard, angular poses that look like a combination of Egyptian hieroglyphics, jazz dance, and gymnastics. As the ball continues, it becomes clear that in this unique social world, the runway is the battleground for displays of fierceness, a confrontational arm of eccentricity that is about self-assertion and creative labor.

Voguing, then, is ultimately a battle for fierceness. It is a defiant and spectacular way for marginalized bodies to inhabit the world by using the performance of style to assert our agency and to call out normativity with a single headpiece. Even if fierceness cannot change the social order and make things right once and for all, it still challenges the social order in the first place, revealing its seams and crevices. In this way fierceness actually cracks open normativity: when fierceness pumps through a room, part of the confrontation it stages has to do with how it underscores how normal everything else there seems to be. Fierceness is a creative, transgressive working or "werking" of the self through the creative labor of fashion, performance, and self-styling. Because fierceness never asks for permission to exist on its own terms, as a queer aesthetic this further highlights how fabulousness is nearly always about urgency, agency, and the temporal — about asserting yourself aesthetically, right now.

What would it mean to think about fierceness—style—as a form of violence? The *Oxford English Dictionary* cites 1382 as the earliest usage of *fierceness*. There, the term is described as "formidable violence; intractable savageness of temper; lively; vehement and merciless fury."[22] I'm drawn to this definition because it actually posits fierceness as a powerful force—as sheer energy. But what if this violence, this savageness of temper, isn't physical violence? What if it is a kind of *creative* or *aesthetic* violence? As aesthetic violence, fierceness creates a breach in the omnipresent yet imperceptible seams of normativity through the urgency and immediacy of style. This breach changes the dynamics of lived space and does important work in crystallizing, highlighting, and pushing back against limiting identity categories. If there is resistance where there is power, fierceness is an aesthetic tool that breaks from an established (boring) uniformity to create new potential.[23]

There's a line of thought within certain theory circles that if you're not pointing at negativity, then you're not doing criticism right. If you find positivity or celebration in anything, you're uncritical. But when you are brown, queer, and marginalized, you're political the second you wake up, the moment you walk into a room. You wade through the waters of negativity, depression, self-doubt, self-loathing, critique, and ridicule every single day. The next micro-aggression is waiting right around the corner. Instead of pointing out more and more social ills, we need ways for thinking about the immediacy of art, beauty, creativity, and ideas because when you're brown, queer, and marginalized, sometimes your creativity is all you've got.

These ideas draw on what José Muñoz calls "critical idealism," a way of living that privileges hope and possibility instead of the suffocating anti-utopian negativism that is often de rigueur. For Muñoz, queerness offers a rejection of a "here" and "now" while daring to imagine the potential or possibility of another world.[24] Queerness—much like fierceness and fabulousness—is an essence that escapes the present and lunges forward toward a future place that is not here, now, but *there*. It is a horizon we may never reach but a dreamy place we can continue to reach for, a future island just as important as the work we do to get there. The story of fabulousness draws on utopian world-making practices and takes up Muñoz's call to teleport to that future place. Dangerous style seizes that future utopian space and brings it into the here and now, and in real time. Beautiful eccentrics, a genderless/gender-avoidant army of expressive creative renegades, walking through the streets of Berlin, Mumbai, London, or rural Pennsylvania, are not theory or potential: they are very real, and their existence is risky business.

With Muñoz in mind, fierce, dissenting style uncovers possibilities for a queer future, a future where renegade glamorous eccentrics are not the exception to the rule but the rule itself. A future where, in the words of performance artist Alok Vaid-Menon, gender doesn't exist, and a future where gender-nonconforming, nonbinary bodies are not penalized or harassed on the street or denied love and romance. Fabulous eccentrics are not concerned with the (boring) normative rhythms of everyday life but with the excitement of what is possible through style. Fierceness provides the blueprint for queer futures because it allows us to turn ourselves into our own version of utopia. Fierceness says: here's what life would be like in the world I dream of inhabiting. As a "remaking and rewriting of the dominant script," fierceness creates the possibility for transcendence, for exploding ready-made conventions and reassembling them to explore alternative possibilities not as a theory, but as immediacy.[25]

Immediacy is what makes voguing the viral cultural form it is today. By the late 1980s voguing had already fascinated the mainstream. The lead article in the February 1989 issue of *Artforum*, for instance, was an exposé of the underground culture of voguing in New York City. Written by John Howell, "Voguing" described the phenomenon as performance, a solo dance form that borrows from break dancing, gymnastics, and the poses of high-fashion modeling. The vogue balls themselves, which Howell vibrantly illustrates as a cross between a pep rally and a prayer meeting, are spaces where what he calls "triple minorities"—poor gays of color—raise important questions about existing on the fringe of the social norm, where the traits that marginalize one in everyday life are made fabulous in the ballroom, giving one a sense of value.[26] The fact that Howell's piece was the lead article in one of the most important magazines of art criticism suggests the level of interest the voguing phenomenon had at the time for the mainstream art public.

Willi Ninja leans against a tree, opens an invisible powder compact, and pantomimes the act of patting his face. Next he "puts on" blush, eye shadow, and lipstick. The process is expressed through the rigidity of the fashion pose, and the scene is most memorable for the way it illustrates the angularity, rhythm, and motion of the pose; Ninja never stops moving until the routine is complete. As Ninja describes, this dance form had to be called "voguing" because the word *vogue* itself is already evocative of a powerful stance, and his point is crucial for thinking about fierceness as a demand for presence. A dance called the "Mademoiselle," Ninja said, would not have the same urgency.[27]

Jonathan David Jackson, one of the earliest scholars to write about voguing, described it as a working-class, primarily LGBTQ black and Latino aesthetic community that emerged in the 1970s.[28] In New York City, the history of the drag ball stretches back to late nineteenth-century Harlem and Greenwich Village, where female and male impersonators staged lavish drag contests. In his analysis of the Hamilton Lodge Ball, which threw its first function in 1869 and held one every spring into the 1930s, George Chauncey described Harlem as a space that may have facilitated new patterns of black visibility, but it was also the place where black gay men could gather socially. These men, who were frequently unwelcome in majority-white nightspots, transformed parts of Harlem into a self-sufficient gay social world. The event that framed that world was the Hamilton Lodge Ball, which attracted hundreds of drag queens, male impersonators, and thousands of spectators, most of them black. By 1925 there were an estimated eight hundred people in attendance, and five years later, in 1930, there were fifteen hundred.[29] In his autobiography *The Big Sea*, Langston Hughes refers to the Hamilton Lodge Ball as "spectacles in color": "For the men, there is a fashion parade. Prizes are given to the most gorgeously gowned of the whites and Negroes who, powdered, wigged, and rouged, mingle and compete for the awards. From the boxes these men look for all the world like the very pretty chorus girls parading across the raised platform in the center of the floor."[30]

The central feature of these balls were the inventive, creative costumes that turned the parties into a unique space in which gender and race were launched into suspension and critique.[31] In one image from the early twentieth century, a man named Phil Black appears in a glamour triptych. The first image shows him as Phil Black, in his male drag. The second two images introduce Cora Black, Phil Black's female alter ego. These images show that the drag ball, which the tradition of voguing emerges out of, has for more than 140 years been the space where queer people of color have removed themselves from the gendered and racist politics of everyday life and created their own unique social worlds, allowing them to live out alternative versions of sexuality and gender performance.[32]

There are many films that chronicle the history and culture of the voguing and ballroom scene, like *How Do I Look?* directed by Wolfgang Busch, *Kiki*, directed by Sara Jordenö and cowritten by Twiggy Pucci Garçon, and Elegance Bratton's crowd-funded documentary *Pier Kids: The Life*, but the urtext of the ballroom scene is currently still Livingston's *Paris Is Burning*, a film the *Washington Post* described on its debut as an "unexploitative examination of a subculture that until now has been invisible to most Americans."[33] *Paris Is Burning* portrays the underground world of voguing as an alternate social universe made up of black and Latino gay subjectivity and social experience. It is a story about how these disenfranchised bodies, many of whom have been kicked out of their homes, are sex workers, or are in the process of gender reassignment, make a place for themselves by mirroring the world of fashion and financial success. In an image I found taken at one ball, Pepper LaBeija, Mother of the House of LaBeija, holds a newspaper with the explosive headline: "EXTRA: PEPPER LABEIJA NAMED CHAIRWOMAN OF MERRILL LYNCH," an unsubtle story line that grasps for visions of white upper-middle-class visions of success.[34]

Paris Is Burning was produced with a budget of $500,000.[35] Jennie Livingston originally had the idea for a documentary about the balls after going to Washington Square Park in New York City and seeing a group of young men do a stylized dance that made them look like fashion models. Since *Paris Is Burning* debuted—eventually the film won Best Documentary at the Sundance Film Festival—scholars have taken an interest in voguing by criticizing the roles that whiteness, subversion, and exploitation play in framing the film's narrative.[36]

Philip Brian Harper, in his widely cited review of the film, takes issue with what he calls the film's "reputed subversiveness"—the idea that somehow a film about queer of color drag queens is subversive or revolutionary. For Harper, what's at stake is how Livingston exploited the ballroom community for cultural and financial gain and in the process positioned herself as the voice and interpreter of the ballroom community, a throwback to the problems with cultural appropriation. Harper describes how Livingston was sued by nearly all of the film's participants, with Paris Dupree claiming as much as $40 million in damages. Dupree appears in the film for fewer than three minutes, but her 1986 ball Paris Is Burning gave the documentary its title. Yet the queens had already signed "releases," so legal action against Jennie Livingston, as well as Miramax, the film's distributor, was dropped. What was "released" once those papers were signed? Harper asks. While it might seem that the personalities in *Paris Is Burning* enjoy a sense of agency within the film itself, for Harper as well as for other critics of utopian spaces, they lose that agency as soon as they leave the dimension of the ball world and hit the streets.[37] That's fair and very real. But the issue isn't the drive for or the creation of a separate dimension. The issue is the institutionalized way in which society marginalizes black and brown folks, queer and trans folks every single day so that we need separate dimensions in the first place. The heteronormative, homonormative capitalist system is what needs to change, not ideas, joy, creativity, or expressions of dissident fashion—although bad fashion should be stopped too. My point is that it's even more demeaning to ask folks whom society marginalizes to wait, hold on, and be still until things are amazing, perfect, and utopian once and for all before they can express themselves. What if that day never comes? Should we sit in a cold room, desperately waiting for our number to be called, or should we live vibrantly, immediately, and in the present?

Voguing may not be a world that exists beyond the confines of the ballroom floor or the catwalk, and it may not even be utopian but, like all fabulousness, it suggests an exhaustion with the here and now and is at the very least a portal to another dimension. Fabulousness, creative strangeness, eccentricity—these are all portals to a separate world that indicate boredom with and exhaustion of the structures of the present. Jonathan David Jackson observed that negative critics of voguing overlook the capacity for members of the ballroom scene to create and invent their own rules of existence.[38] This, to me, is what is so timeless about voguing as a form of creative expression and so viral about fabulousness by extension. Rather than focusing only or primarily on disenfranchisement, we should also think about how that duress is transformed into creativity and beauty. The sentiment calls to mind queer theorist Eve Kosofsky Sedgwick, who in 2003 criticized the obsession in queer studies with focusing on the surface only as a way to uncover an unknown oppression, as if revealing all oppressions will set us free once and for all. "In a world where no one need be delusional to find evidence of systemic oppression," she writes, "to theorize out of anything *but* a paranoid critical stance has come to seem naïve, pious, or complaisant." Calling this critical stance a "paranoid" reading, Sedgwick believes we do a disservice when being "paranoid" becomes synonymous with deft or innovative critical reasoning.[39]

A typical—and valid—critique leveraged against *Paris Is Burning* is the value it places on whiteness. In a queer of color utopian social world that is supposed to be about brownness, queerness, and creativity, it's suspicious that the only beauty ideal ever savored by the queens is whiteness. But whiteness is difficult to unlearn, to unhinge ourselves from, particularly for people of color, because images of whiteness and white beauty standards have permeated popular and beauty culture for hundreds of years. Angie Xtravaganza, who went through gender-reassignment surgery during the making of the film, said she wanted to live "like a white woman" because anything they want, they can have. For bell hooks, this focus on whiteness is the principal failure of *Paris Is Burning* and, by extension, of ballroom culture. She's interested in how black bodies continue to worship at the altar of whiteness. Rather than showing brown folks mirroring strong brown folks, *Paris Is Burning* shows how the queens glamorize white femininity exactly as it is in Hollywood and on the covers of mainstream fashion magazines. For hooks, the form of femininity the queens perform is so deeply wrapped up in the fetishization of whiteness that "womanness and femininity is totally personified by whiteness," a line of critique that certainly gets at the inner workings of white supremacy and beauty culture.[40] It is worth noting, though, that Marlon Bailey, in his ethnography of voguing in Detroit, has shown that in that city there has been a long tradition of black drag queens emphasizing black women performers.[41]

Even in the contemporary queer of color drag scene many performers use phrases like "rich white lady," "I'm serving rich white lady," and "Caucasian" to press play on certain imagined, *Dynasty*-like fantasies of whiteness, class, and unbridled opulence. Describing things as "Caucasian" is a popular trope in queer of color circles. The best example of this is Joanne the Scammer, a social media drag star in a full beard, fur coat, and bad wig who makes hilarious videos about her many scams. Beneath the surface of her "scams" lies an appraisal of whiteness. In the videos Joanne almost always talks about how she is a white woman, even though she is very clearly black, and that's part of the joke. "Getting Scammed by My Boyfriend's Ex (ft. Joanne the Scammer)," a skit in which Joanne drops in on a Christmas party at her ex-boyfriend's apartment, goes like this:

> **JOANNE:** Well, well, well! If it isn't my ex–love interest Phillip, and his ethnic housekeeper.
>
> **LILY:** Uh, hi! My name is Lily, I'm Phillip's girlfriend. Nice to meet you.
>
> **JOANNE:** Oh, I see. You've downgraded from a Caucasian to *this peasant!*
>
> **PHILLIP:** Joanne, please. Just leave us alone!
>
> **LILY:** Wait, what? *Caucasian?* I mean, you're not even close to white.
>
> **JOANNE:** You know, honestly, I cannot stand you people telling me who the *hell* I am! I . . . am a *white woman.*[42]

Joanne the Scammer's videos are less about aspiring to whiteness and more about poking fun at whiteness and the stereotypical things white people say and do, subtle racism and micro-aggressions included.

By now *Paris Is Burning* is a canonical text about the culture of voguing, taught in any queer studies, black queer studies, or film studies course worth its salt. It's still a fascinating piece, but the zeroed-in intellectual focus purely on *Paris Is Burning* as the dominant text of the ballroom scene actually eulogizes an otherwise vibrant culture, locking it in a 1990s time capsule rather than seeing it as a vital global culture of creativity and performance that is still contemporary, still innovating, and still "sickening." In May 2015 a special screening of *Paris Is Burning* at the Brooklyn Museum sponsored by BRIC Arts, a Brooklyn-based arts organization, created a social media firestorm when it was discovered that only Jennie Livingston and queer musician JD Samson, of the feminist punk band Le Tigre, had been invited to help present the film. Not a single person of color, not a single member of the ballroom scene was on the bill. Why not? How on earth did it not occur to the organizers that producing this event about the lives and livelihood of queer people of color without engaging the ballroom community in any way was an act of cultural gentrification? In response, a petition to boycott the screening was launched on Change.org, calling BRIC out for thinking it was appropriate "not only to show this documentary, but with an ALL-WHITE entertainment line-up. This is the appropriation of our narratives for the sake of entertaining a gentrifying, majority white audience that seeks to consume us and call it paying homage."[43] Recognizing its error, BRIC issued a public apology on the event's Facebook page and announced an updated program that included ballroom mainstays Vjuan Allure, Junior LaBeija, Hector Xtravaganza, and Dr. Sol Williams Pendavis. This should have been the program from the very beginning.

In the years since *Paris Is Burning* was released, voguing has become much more international. Willi Ninja did say he wanted to take voguing to the real Paris, and now it's there, but it's also in Russia, Germany, the UK, the Netherlands, Slovakia, and Sweden too, in scenes that are often spearheaded by white straight female professional dancers who are trained in other forms of dance. Voguing is now taught in dance studios around the world to voguers and nonvoguers alike. It has become choreography that can be perfected and learned in a dance studio. In general, European voguers come from a dance background. "They've been doing hip-hop, they've been doing waacking," Paris-based DJ, vocalist, and producer Kiddy Smile told me. "They've been doing other things. And then they realize there's a new thing they think they can be good at."[44] The origin of vogue was about creating black queer space, a safe space, for the brown gay community to express themselves. It was never about dance studios. "One cannot really go to a school and learn how to vogue," the artist Rashaad Newsome has said.[45] "You go to where it's happening, learn the language, and make it your own," producer, DJ, and RuPaul collaborator Vjuan Allure agreed. "You have to go to the club. We used to go to the clubs. We went and we was *gettin'* it. You weren't there for a ball. You just vogued. And it wasn't choreography."[46]

YouTube and Facebook Live have also changed the way voguing and ballroom culture are shared and experienced. What used to be invitation-only, super-underground functions can now be streamed online to all your Facebook friends or uploaded to YouTube, and performances can be watched repeatedly. Voguing, which goes viral because it is a performance of optimism, is accessible from nearly any corner of the world. It's possible to see dancers of all stripes, not all of them a part of the ballroom community, offer step-by-step videos on voguing, treating it like choreography. "How to Vogue," a video uploaded by ThePhilOfIt in 2013 that veteran vogue DJ MikeQ shared on Facebook as a prime example of "how to get chopped at a ball," is just one example of how voguing has spread online.[47] YouTube is both a blessing and a curse in that it provides access to the culture with the unfortunate trade-off that many people assume you can watch a YouTube video, perfect the moves, and then go straight to a vogue ball. But a word to the wise. It's not gonna work like that. Voguing is not choreography. It's a feeling, a mood, a conveyance of attitude, personality, creativity, and optimism.

"What a lot of the kids are saying," Vjuan Allure told me, "is that you're just imitating what you're seeing on YouTube. You're not really *voguing.* You're not thinking in your head what *my* moves are. You can tell when it's not your performance, when it's somebody else's performance that you *saw.*" You need to be part of the culture to really learn vogue. "You have to go to the club," he said. "We used to go to the clubs and I didn't care about the promoter. We went and we was *gettin'* it. You battled. You weren't there for a ball, you just vogued. And it wasn't choreography." Now, though, with the prevalence of YouTube and the internationalization of voguing, what we're seeing are people who watch a few videos at home and think they're ready. "If you're learning in another country," Allure said, "they will probably let you walk in a ball because it's catching on. In the States, *no*. If you come down there looking like a mess . . . *chop*."[48] Lasseindra Ninja agreed. "You can't watch a video and come to a ball. No, baby. If you want to make a cake, you need to have some eggs to make a cake. If nobody taught you that before and you come to a ball—no, baby. It's not gonna work like this."[49]

Finally, voguing has found a place in the art world. "I feel that the practice of vogue," black queer performance artist Rashaad Newsome has said, "is very much a part of performance-art history, and as museums care for, conserve and collect artefacts and objects of artistic, cultural, or historical importance, I can think of no place better for the pieces to live."[50] He's right. But voguing is not simply being collected and supported by arts institutions. It's also now creative material for performance art, dance works, and installations, including Newsome's own, and as a form of contemporary dance, it is now taught, learned, and practiced in studios around the world like other canonized styles of dance.

Ballroom consists of two elements: "houses" and the actual balls themselves, social events where fabulousness, fierceness, and queer aesthetic labor become a creative competitive sport. Houses are unique, self-contained kinship networks that allow members to challenge the narrative of family as a stable, unchanging unit. In ballroom, "family" can in fact be created and made up, as the anthropologist Kath Weston has explored.[51] When you are gay or queer, choosing your own family is powerful, especially if you have been severed from a biological family because of sexual orientation or gender. In ballroom, these family units, or houses, are often named for positive ideals or high-end fashion labels.[52] Father of the House of Saint Laurent remembers how he came up with his house name:

I remember being at a club called the [Paradise] Garage, and we decided we were going to form our own house. So it was myself, Chris, Octavia

**and another friend of ours, Terence, and we all
sat around thinking, "What name are we going
to call our house?" And we were going to be
doing this, and we were going to be different
from everybody else. We were going to be, you
know, fabulous. We were thinking about names
and someone said, "How about the House of Yves
Saint Laurent?" but for some reason it didn't feel
like we were the House of Yves Saint Laurent. So
we just dropped the Yves and we became Saint
Laurent.**[53]

The house system emerged in response to the often racist drag pageants
of the 1960s, which were frequently exclusive and hostile environments
for black queens. During the 1960s, mainstream beauty pageants in general were not spaces for celebrating black beauty. Black women could not
compete in the Miss America Pageant, for instance, which in 1968 led to
the development of the Miss Black America pageant as a form of protest,
supported by the NAACP.[54] The rejection of black beauty stretched even
into the world of drag, as seen in Frank Simon's 1968 film *The Queen*, a
documentary about the 1967 Miss All-American Camp Beauty Pageant—
RuPaul's Drag Race before *RuPaul's Drag Race* was a thing. A frustrated
contestant named Crystal LaBeija rolls her eyes in distaste as her name
is announced as the third runner-up. As a black drag queen fighting her
way through a white supremacist gay culture, LaBeija knows that race
has everything to do with why she didn't win. She stands with the other
contestants while Rachel Harlow, one of the three white semi-finalists, is
crowned. Then, in an iconic, jaw-dropping seizing of the moment, LaBeija
storms offstage, foaming at the mouth about how the entire competition was rigged from the beginning. The other queen didn't deserve to
win. "Get a picture with me and Harlow and see which is more beautiful, *darling*," LaBeija says to the camera, completely shading the winner.
"Do you think she deserved it?" a white contestant asks backstage. "You
know she didn't deserve it," LaBeija says. "*All* of them—the judges knew

it too. 'Cause she was *terrible!*"[55] Many in the black gay community have a deep affection for this scene, pointing to this moment as the pinnacle of the black queer practice of "reading." As E. Patrick Johnson described in an early essay on the subject, "To read someone is to set them 'straight,' to put them in their place . . . usually in a way that embarrasses a third party."[56] Determined to create a place for herself, Crystal moved beyond the shade and produced her own functions in which black queens could find a unique space to compete against one another without having to deal with the exclusivity of the white drag pageant world. These balls birthed the first "houses," and LaBeija was the first house.[57]

LaBeija's tirade links up with what Lauren Berlant has called "Diva Citizenship," or the process of emergence that allows for people at the margins to rise up and speak out against the ways in which they are violated by normativity. For Berlant, Diva Citizenship means "when a person stages a dramatic coup in a public sphere in which she does not have privilege." This certainly describes Crystal LaBeija's dramatic scene at the Miss All-American Camp Beauty Pageant. "Flashing up and startling the public," Berlant writes, the diva "puts the dominant story into suspended animation."[58] The creative work of the diva is to publicly challenge traditional narratives. LaBeija was less upset about losing a pageant and more annoyed that, in standard operating procedure, whiteness settled in to limit her potential.

Walk into a vogue ball and the first thing you notice is the sense of community and togetherness—the sense of being in an optimistic "black queer space."[59] Guests sit at tables labeled with their individual house names, as if at an awards ceremony, and a crowd gathers at the foot of the runway, cheering, chanting. It's noisy. The DJ keeps the music flowing, and the commentator, who raps when he speaks, introduces a new category once the last one has ended, inviting anyone from the floor to come onstage. The commentator plays a pivotal role at a ball because he is simultaneously the voice of the function, the master of ceremonies, a keeper of the cultural traditions of voguing, and an additional rhythmic element that makes voguers want to walk.[60] Commentators like Dashaun Wesley and Kevin JZ Prodigy are remarkable in their improvisational prowess, quick-wittedness, and the fiery way they narrate what happens on the stage. They react to what the performer does at the same time as they give her or him the attitude they need to pull out a sensational performance. Lasseindra Ninja, Mother of the Paris chapter of the House of Ninja, underscored the importance of sound, the DJ, and the commentator at a ball. To give a compelling performance she needs a "good motherfucking beat. I need the 'ha.' I need a hard beat and then I need the commentator and *then* the commentator gives me the juice to give what I want to give. And then the crowd. If the crowd is reacting to what I'm doing, then I'm going to do more."[61]

One of the most awe-inspiring and beautiful aspects of voguing is the "suicide dip," a form that ties voguing to other forms of black dance including hip-hop, break dancing, and capoeira. Because they can happen anywhere, at any time, and due to the spiraled nature of the moves, dips are about physically seizing space. Vjuan Allure, one of the most important DJs on the ballroom circuit and member of the House of Allure, told me that the suicide dip has been going on since the late 1990s and that at one point it was called "the dying swan," which presented a more graceful fall than the sudden drops of today. "The Timber" was another name for the dramatic move, "where you just stand up and timber into a dip."[62] The suicide dip is the most recognizable and impressive aspect of voguing to everyone, from members of the voguing community to passive onlookers. In one viral YouTube video filmed in 2013 at the yearly STREET-STAR dance festival in Stockholm, Leiomy takes to the stage to demonstrate her voguing prowess and iconicity as the queen of vogue femme. As Dashaun Wesley announces her and as Vjuan Allure pops the beats, Leiomy starts with some wild hand performance before she spins and falls into a dip—in heels—much to the excitement of the audience, leading Wesley to chant, "She *de-de-de*-fies gravity!"

Countless other YouTube videos, now the dominant medium for experiencing voguing, what Tommy LaBeija has called "virtual balls," show how deeply the suicide dip has penetrated the ballroom scene.[63] These videos range in scope from voguing in the privacy of a bedroom to voguing "how-to" videos, not to mention the video documentation of actual ball events. Nearly all the videos I have seen of vogue femme showcase the dip, but one clip in particular, a favorite among lovers of vogue, fully captures this move as a kind of embodied fierceness. The performance begins with one, then two, then three people on the runway, but by the end, there are a dozen people dancing. On the crash of the beat—the "ha"—all the queens slam their bodies against the floor, back first, while still managing to pose. As the song progresses more people enter the runway, one by one, slamming their bodies against the ground on the beat too until, at a certain point near the end of the clip, there are a dozen people on the stage with little space left to dance, and we see a creative battle for who can do the fiercest dip.

With the dip as such a trope in contemporary ballroom culture, I asked Allure how one learns to do the gravity-defying move. Is it as difficult as it looks? "What I did was, we would be at someone's house and we would just practice. They would be like, 'We want you to get into a dip in five moves. Okay, now do it in four. Now do it in three. Now do it in two. Now do it in one.' And when you fall, you're going to be in the dip. You learn to do it—you get used to the floor."[64]

A vogue ball is as intensely sonic as it is visual, and there are at least three levels of sound at a ball: the music coming from the DJ booth, often self-produced vogue beats or vogue remixes of popular music, usually played alongside ballroom or house classics; the chants, applause, and cheers from the audience, which is about encouraging each voguer while also creating a second layer of sound and excitement; and the commentator who, "like a scat singer in jazz," uses the voice to imitate rhythm.[65] The name for this unique style of sound is chanting, and Allure tells me that it is used in the ballroom scene because it creates rhythm in addition to the rhythm already emerging out of the DJ booth: "When you're coming out on the runway, it's like the beat is there, and you're *working* to the beat, but the commentator is giving you *extra*. Most of the time they're around the person, which makes you go for it even more. It adds to the crowd, it adds more."[66]

The commentator adds intensity to the space and encourages the voguer while he or she is on the runway, all in service of pushing each performer to be hot like fire. This sonic intensity is captured especially well in a 2011 track by MikeQ called "Feels Like" featuring Kevin JZ Prodigy. The track, framed by the dip-inducing nature of the "ha," starts with Prodigy chanting, "Cunt, cunt, cunt, cunt. Cunt to the feminine or what," the word *cunt* not unproblematically reappropriated here from an insult to facilitating a specific performed "real" femininity on the dance floor, what Marlon Bailey sees as femininity performed in a way that totally eliminates "any sign of deviation from gender and sexual norms that are dominant in heteronormative society." The best known use of "cunt" is "Cunty," a 1999 track by drag performer Kevin Aviance that also opens with the word repeated again and again in a rhythmical fashion. While the use of such a derogatory and not totally unproblematic term may reveal misogyny within black gay culture, members of the ballroom community use this special form of language as a term of endearment to actually celebrate queer aesthetic labor and the occasion of performance.[67] "Feminine soft cunt to the what, cunt," Kevin JZ Prodigy chants. "Feminine soft cunt to the cunt, cunt," the emphasis on the word *cunt* holding such force that it evaporates into a sound, a rhythm with no meaning attached. To my mind, "Feels Like" highlights the illusory nature of gender because the first time he says "feminine" his voice is sent through an audio effects processor in a way that swallows the word, chops it up, stutters it, creating a sonic mirage of gender.

It's difficult to talk about voguing without also pointing to the problematics in voguing around misogynist language, gender, and "realness" in particular. Inasmuch as voguing offers a portal to another dimension, perhaps not necessarily a safe space but *another* place, it is not a perfect utopian field. For one, words like *cunt, bitch,* and *pussy* will always be derogatory for some, just as they will be benign and fun for others. TS Madison, a popular black trans activist, adult entertainer, and YouTube personality, popularized the colloquial phrase "Step your pussy up," for instance, which is meant to be an uplifting way of saying you need to do a better job. Believe in yourself! On RuPaul's "Step It Up," a track on her 2015 album *Realness,* she sings, "Girl, you gon' have to step your pussy up / If you're trying to be somebody, girl, you better step it up."[68] Realness, for that matter, offers another complication in the world of voguing, where realness categories often uphold essentialist gender norms as competitors are judged against heteronormative gender ideals. "If you lose a category called 'realness,'" Jamel Prodigy wonders, "does that mean you're fake? What does it mean to not be *real*? People think it's just a ball, or it's just extracurricular, or it's just nightlife. But realistically, you take that in and the natural competitive instinct is going to make you want to do something to make you more real."[69]

But the story gets even more complicated as "realness" can be a space of misogyny and enforced gender norms, where certain performance categories are often segregated according to gender and where there are often "women's" categories intended for cisgendered women that are not always inclusive for trans women, nonbinary, or transfeminine people. The idea is that ballroom is open to everyone, so cisgendered women should compete with other cisgendered women, and trans women with trans women to keep things equal. Things blew up during the Women's Performance category at the twenty-third annual GMHC Latex Ball in August 2013 when Mariah Lopez Ebony was ridiculed onstage and told that she wasn't eligible to be in that category because she was a trans woman. "If she wanted to walk the category and she feels like she's had her full surgery and she feels like a complete woman," Leiomy said, "why wouldn't she be able to walk?"[70]

To make things even more complex, realness can often be a lifesaver at the same time that it enforces hetero-patriarchal gender norms. As Marlon Bailey describes, realness is essentially a theory beyond ballroom that shows the ways all heteronormative genders and sexualities are performed. Realness "is at once about authenticity and illusion," and it can be a survival strategy that can get you home safely at night.[71] To be "real"—to plug into heteronormative gender standards—is to go undetected, to pass, and that means at the very least that you may be able to move through society with relative safety. In ballroom, nothing is cut and dried.

Voguing is a uniquely black and brown LGBTQ culture that has expanded globally. But what happens when black queer space exists in translation, when it is figuratively translated into Swedish, Dutch, German, or Slovakian? Produced by Mother Georgina Leo Melody, the House of Melody, and publicist Mic Oala/Ranma 007, the Berlin Voguing Out Festival launched in 2012 and is to date the center for voguing activity in Germany. In 2014 the festival included a screening of the film *How Do I Look*, a 2006 portrait of the ball scene directed by Wolfgang Busch, and a talk-back with ballroom legend Vjuan Allure, runway coach Archie Burnett, and Berlin-based arts writer Jan Kedves. During the talk-back Burnett reminisced about how he learned to vogue in New York's Washington Square Park, which is also where I remember seeing it for the first time—there or along the Hudson River Pier or on Christopher Street in the West Village, where underage black queer youth emerged from New Jersey on the PATH train and hung out because they were too young to go to the club. Today, cupcake shops and candy stores have replaced the saucy gay sex shops and booming gay bars that used to be in the neighborhood. Now that New York is so gentrified, I asked during the Q and A, what does voguing look like? Vjuan Allure jumped in immediately. "It looks like this," he said, pointing out to the audience, subtly reminding everyone how white the room was. And it was true. The room was full of young, white hipsters. He didn't say it was a bad thing, just that this is the way culture always proliferates, recalling Gilroy's notion that black culture is always already promiscuous business. Allure didn't seem at all concerned about the appropriation of voguing by a white audience, though, because "by the time you all catch on to voguing, which we have been doing for years," he said with just a hint of shade, "we will have already moved on to the next thing."[72] For Allure, blackness and queerness are constantly innovating new aesthetic paradigms.

That year, the BVO Festival was held at Prince Charles, an arts venue in Kreuzberg at Moritzplatz right around the corner from Motion*s, the dance studio where voguing workshops took place all week. If a vogue ball is notable for how it looks and how it sounds, it's also remarkable for the way it seizes social space and makes it queer. I mingled with people as they arrived at the venue, taking in their looks, which ranged in severity from the most masculine to the most outrageous; sometimes people arrived with only half their look on. After the function, as the ball disintegrated into a party, people worked their way around the room, and their creative effort was immediately celebrated with affirmations like "Yes!" "Work!" and "You look *fierce*, Miss Honey!" A claim to creativity and fierceness was at stake, an aesthetic fight in the attention economy for the most "sickening" look. The vogue ball became a parade of difference, a symphony of creativity.

I remember being impressed by the scale of the function; I'd never been to a ball that felt so high end. Most of the balls I've been to in America were staged in halls or else a place like Terminal 5, formerly Club Exit in New York City, hardly a beautiful space, where the focus was less on your experience of the room and more on your performance. As music journalist Julianne Escobedo Shepherd has written, New York vogue balls had been held mostly in community centers, but Susanne Bartsch's Love Ball, a fund-raiser for AIDS research that took place in 1989, was one of the first to go high end and be judged by fashion royalty like Iman and André Leon Talley.[73] That August night in Berlin, to be in Prince Charles felt like the privilege of attending a major fashion show by a major international designer, the room anchored by a long, pristine white catwalk, matching foldable chairs on either side, and big theatrical lighting. The only thing missing was Anna Wintour.

I found a place in the front row, eagerly waiting for the performances to begin, not quite sure what to expect. The sleekness of the production framed voguing as, and elevated it to, an art form, the room doubling as a contemporary art gallery. As the art critic Brian O'Doherty shows in his theorization of the white cube, the whiteness of the gallery acts as a source of power and permanence at the same time as it removes the artwork from a social context, thereby highlighting its formal existence and financial-cultural power as "art."[74] But far from removing voguing from its brown queer social context, the white cube-like space of Prince Charles had the effect of elevating brown queer creative innovations, already in translation, to the highest aesthetic platform.

That said, it's hard to underscore how white the ball was, not only in terms of the audience but the voguers as well. This was a new aspect of the ballroom scene I'd never experienced in the United States. I've been to balls in New York, in Washington, DC, and along the East Coast, and though there is often a white person or two in the room, balls, even the ones captured on YouTube, are mostly full of brown, queer, and trans bodies. Though I knew the Berlin Voguing Out Festival would be somewhat white, I was shocked to discover it was *so* white, and not always queer. "That's why we always try to have Archie or other legends from New York," Mic Oala told me, "because they created this whole thing. It's important to work with the people who are still alive from this scene and who are black from this scene." This preservation of the brownness and queerness of voguing, which I have noticed at every ball and voguing workshop I have attended in Berlin, is why, for instance, the white cube feel of Prince Charles is less about erasing the blackness and social context in translation and more about *amplifying* the blackness and the social context. "We try even at our mini-balls," Oala said, "to make sure it's not a panel of white people who feel entitled to say, 'Okay, I *know* how to judge voguing.'"[75] There's an element of anti–cultural gentrification in the Berlin ballroom scene in the sense that when legends from New York or the more "authentic" scenes are on the judging panel, they pointedly focus on educating the audience about the history of voguing. They remind the onlookers that this is an expressive form that does not belong to white people, even though they are welcome to play too. Voguing is deeply rooted in the struggle for brown, queer, and trans livelihood, and it is important to understand and respect the rules as well as its queer of color history if you want to participate.

This anti–cultural gentrification is especially clear whenever Lasseindra Ninja, Mother of the Paris chapter of the House of Ninja, sits on the judging panel, as she did at the 2015 BVO Festival. Despite the spread of ballroom throughout Europe, she told me, the Paris scene is "the *real* scene of Europe. Why? Because [we're] black. And that's why we're the truth. The girls from the rest of the countries—they're white. When you watch the YouTube video clips you see that. You see the difference.

They don't feel what we feel. They don't live what we live. Being black is not just being black. You have all the consequences of being black in this world."[76] Kiddy Smile, a French producer and member of the House of Mizrahi, feels the same way. The ballroom scene in Paris is the "real scene of Europe because it's the first time outside the U.S.," he told me, "that a real ballroom scene is born, meaning it's actually by and for black people, people of color, and gay people."[77]

Lasseindra built the ballroom scene in Paris along with Mother Stephane Mizrahi, throwing the first ball in 2012 at the Velvet Club. Since then she has solidified her position as the most famous voguer in the European scene, building the reputation of Paris as a hot spot for vogue performance. In *Proletarian French Voguers*, a brief documentary on the Paris ballroom scene produced by *Vice* in 2014, Mother Steffie shows the critical importance of voguing for brown people in Paris: "It allows the girls, because they're gay, to find their true identity, to accept who they are. And that way they gain more self-confidence so they can really be like, 'I'm that bitch,' you know? But if you want to be like, 'I'm that bitch,' you gotta go somewhere to confront people. That's what the balls are for."[78] Being "that bitch" is about being creative, asserting yourself through performance and style. It's about not asking for permission to exist but about existing anyway, right now, and on your own terms. For queer people of color, being "that bitch" is about queer livelihood and ethical self-making, particularly when you are forced to exist in a world with norms that were not created with you in mind. "Ballroom life is not about what you *could be in real life*," Kiddy Smile believes, "but how you transcend what you *couldn't* be in real life."[79] To curb the trivialization and cultural gentrification of voguing in translation, Lasseindra is quick to chop anyone who is not fully bringing the category. "When I'm on the panel I chop them, but also I'm telling them why I chop them, and I say it in front of everyone so that the next girl has a chance for the next ball." Unfortunately, not everyone takes kindly to being called out in the middle of their performance. "Sometimes they think I'm being rude or shady or whatever," she said. "But that's the only way they can learn."[80]

The point is certainly not that straight white people can't vogue or participate in the culture, but that they are often met with skepticism or a sense of their inauthenticity on the scene. It's thought that they don't really understand the culture. Mic Oala/Ranma 007, a cultural producer and activist based in Berlin, described her first Paris ball experience this way: "I went to my first vogue ball in Paris a few months ago, and as soon as I walked in everybody had their arms crossed, like, 'Who is this white girl?' but then when I danced they were more at ease and saw that I was one of them." Her anecdote gets at the crux of the internationalization of the voguing scene, and when I asked her why the room at the festival was so white and straight, she told me that a lot of the male attendees come because they are there supporting their girlfriends who are dancing.[81] And that means they might not have any direct connection to queerness or queer culture besides this. That's why the panel of judges, almost all legends from the New York ball scene, do a lot of work to educate the audience about ball culture. They remind the room that this is a brown queer culture. They do much to preserve the culture in terms of specific dance moves and performance categories to ensure that the integrity of voguing and ball culture doesn't evaporate.

But even in translation, vogue still maintains its values of imagining livelihood for queer people and people of color, using creativity to assert your agency right now. For Zero Melody, a professional dancer based in Berlin, performing fabulousness through voguing allows him to feel free. "Back in the days when I was in the tenth grade," he remembered, "because I was gay people were really mobbing me and it was kind of hard to be 'me,' to be free. Nowadays, because of voguing, it's like I really don't care. I like to walk with heels or dance with heels. This is me. This belongs to me."[82] Georgina Leo Melody, who is Afro-German, also struggled with her blackness growing up in Düsseldorf. She didn't think she was pretty:

Obviously, growing up in Germany there's a lot of white people. As a teenager I never saw myself as an attractive person or as a person that

guys might be interested in. My best friends were three blond girls, probably not the best choice! It wasn't until I was in my twenties—and I think it really changed with voguing, how I carried myself. Onstage people would be like, "Wow, she's a power woman!" I think there's something that came through voguing where I was like, "Okay, I'm *pretty* attractive. Maybe they don't talk to me because they're scared!"[83]

All vogue categories are about asserting yourself creatively, about bringing something unique to the stage, to the moment of performance, and then leaving a memorable trace. But two categories that, to my eyes, are expressly about creative power and agency are runway and sex siren: the runway itself, as a space, lifts up and frames queer aesthetic labor, and sex siren is about body positivity, confidence, and selling sex appeal.[84] When done by marginalized bodies, the performance of sex appeal in the safe space of the ballroom scene is critical because these are people who don't always get to be on the covers of magazines, who aren't necessarily first choice in being cast for photo shoots, and who by and large sit at the bottom of the totem pole in media representations of beauty.

With the increased commercialization of voguing by large-scale multinational corporations, we see the ways that brown and queer bodies are starting to be written out of the stories they've created for themselves. Mic Oala, who works closely with European creative industries, is regularly approached by members of the entertainment industry when they are looking to cast voguers for a corporate function, like the 2015 Smirnoff Presents Voguing: We're Open video campaign, which featured Vjuan Allure, Georgina Leo Melody, Leiomy, and Aviance Milan. Often, though not always, it's difficult for Oala to cast queer dancers and dancers of color. "They call and say, 'Okay, we want to have Georgina Leo Melody, and can we have this blond girl and can we have a male dancer who

doesn't look gay?' Sometimes they come up with bullshit, and then sometimes they even say, 'Yeah, we don't want to go *that* exotic.' And I'm like,
what? I don't want to be rude but these dancers are from Düsseldorf, a
German province! What's so exotic about that? It's really, really racist in
this business. They often say, 'Yeah, they look pretty but we don't want to
have it too brown.'"[85]

    There is a power of voguing in translation that I would argue
does not exist in an American cultural context. Voguing in the United
States is still by and large the brown queer space that it always was, but
when this space is translated it becomes a site where black and brown
bodies in countries with relatively low ethnic populations learn to love
their ethnic traits, discovering not only their queerness but their sex appeal too. I think about Zoe 007 from the House of Melody, a biracial
Afro-German with huge kinky hair who first came to voguing as a way
of expressing herself creatively. Through voguing she learned to love the
texture of her mixed-raced hair:

> **I used to wear my hair braided because I hated
> it. Here in Germany you don't have that many
> mixed-race girls with curly hair, and you don't
> get taught how to use your hair, and I started to
> straighten it. And then when I started voguing
> I saw clips of girls using their hair while they
> dance. When I met Leiomy she told me, "Yeah,
> girl! Wear your hair natural! Use your hair! You
> got a lot of hair—use it!" At first I was like, okay,
> I kind of like it, but now it's *really* my signature.
> For me as a mixed-race girl who was really sur-
> rounded by white girls when I went to school,
> every time I wore my hair natural they said, "Oh
> my god, I need to touch it!" so I hated it. Now I
> love it, and it's because of voguing, the dance,
> the culture of being fabulous that I learned to em-
> brace myself and embrace my curly hair.[86]**

In translation, voguing gets an additional layer of meaning as it creates space for black and brown Europeans in countries with low ethnic populations to learn to love their skin color and hair texture, in places where it's even difficult to find the right products to manage ethnic hair at all. Performances of fabulousness help them realize that they are desirable bodies despite growing up in majority-white environments.

In the fashion industry as on the vogue ball floor, the catwalk is always about selling it, whatever you're selling, and making audiences fall into the fantasy. Selling something on the catwalk is a metaphor for performance itself, but it's not just about bringing something to the table, as Lasseindra Ninja told me. It's about "how you yourself can put things *on* the table," meaning, in other words, what of yourself can you bring creatively that hasn't been seen before?[87] Fabulousness, then, is about the confidence of approaching the table but then putting something *on* it. Through spectacular performance and make-believe it is possible to gain confidence, express yourself creatively, and imagine your own utopian version of the world in real time.

Performance is the space where queer utopias are enacted, and the stage is the actual platform where utopian visions can be realized. To my mind, the catwalk is precisely the utopian space where queer personhood, personality, creativity, and innovation can be claimed. Instead of selling clothes and garments to magazine editors and tastemakers, what you're actually putting up for show are your ideas, imagination, and creativity. This sense of peacocking, of parading yourself around, is important for all kinds of brown and queer performance practices, because brown and queer people are constantly told to wait, that we are not good enough, that we don't get to sit at the table, that we don't have rights, that our votes don't matter, that our lifestyles or bodies are invalid. On the catwalk—a space that could be at the vogue ball or anywhere we go, even just a casual pump down the sidewalk—we get to shout, for all to hear, that we may be brown, and we may be queer. But we are here, we are creative, and we are fabulous.

Paris Is Burning
A Conversation with Lasseindra Ninja

IN AN ICONIC LINE FROM *Paris Is Burning,* Willi Ninja says he wants to take voguing to the "real" Paris. Voguing has spread across Europe, and new scenes are emerging in South America, for instance, but by far the richest, most interesting scene outside of the United States is Paris. In 2013 the Paris Xclusive House of LaDurée became the first French vogue house. Lasseindra Ninja and Stephane Mizrahi are two important co-conspirators behind the Paris ballroom scene who helped shape it into the robust community it is today. Heavily documented on Paris Ballroom TV, an online video platform that documents and archives every important Parisian function, the Paris ballroom scene includes stars like Matyouz LaDurée, Keehdi Mizrahi (Kiddy Smile), and Keiona Revlon. Here, Lasseindra talks about what makes the Paris ballroom scene such a lively space, one exploding with creativity and ideas.

Voguing is so much about communicating your fabulousness—expressing yourself on the dance floor but also in your creativity.

Fabulousness is about creativity. But it's also about yourself and how you're going to bring yourself to the world. It's not that one thing can be fabulous. It's that a lot of people can

211

be fabulous. Creativity is not something you can touch. Creativity is something you see, so it's not only physical. It's not only an outfit or shoes. It's more about creating something in the air. It can be an idea, something in your head. You just have to bring it out. It's how you can bring yourself to the table, and how you yourself can put things *on* the table.

You told me that you discovered voguing in 1998. What was that like?

The dance I discovered when I was walking in Harlem. I saw people dancing but I didn't know what they were doing. In 1998 I took my first step into the scene. I went to the club and the first thing I said to my friend was, "I want to learn how to do *that*." I started with a friend—she's not even a voguer— but she's always at the balls, watching people dancing. So that's how I got into voguing.

Willi Ninja said he wanted to bring voguing to the real Paris, and now it's there.

We are the *real* scene of Europe. No, for real. It's still a baby scene because lots of people still don't know about the real culture, the real meaning. But they know about voguing. They know the feeling it comes from. Why? Because they're black. And that's why we're the truth. The girls from the rest of the countries—they're white. When you watch the You-Tube video clips, you see that. You see the difference. Paris is the real scene of Europe because the rest of the scenes don't know the purpose of what they're doing. They don't *feel* what we feel. They don't *live* what we live. Being black is not just being black. You have all the consequences of being black in this world.

Culture—especially black culture—is bound to spread and it's hard to control where it goes and when. You're saying that Paris is the real scene of Europe because black and brown folks there are being creative under duress.

You're being excluded from your own community because you're gay, and by your own community I mean black people who don't "see" you because you're gay; to them "gay" doesn't exist. You cannot be that, because that's more of a "white thing" in the black community. You will have no family; you will be by yourself. And that means you will have to figure everything out for yourself from a young age—fifteen. Having your parents say, "You're not my child anymore"—it can happen to a white girl, yes. But when you're black you have *everybody* in the community saying, "You're not a part of this community anymore." That's really different.

Do you think this duress makes you want to dance harder or be better on the catwalk? What does the reality of racism and living while black do for the performance itself?

My performance is an expression of myself. I don't need nobody to say what the fuck I have to do. I'm doing what I want to do. This is my world. It's also a way to release my frustration, something to express yourself. My body is expressing what I feel. My performance is all about me. Me.

One thing Vjuan Allure told me is that people will watch YouTube videos, learn those moves, and then go to a ball and try to compete.

They're not expressing themselves. We had this in Paris the first time and I had to cut it. I had to cut people. I had to put them in their place. I mean, you can learn moves from a video. But you cannot learn and know yourself through someone else's video. You need your own experience to know yourself and to give something in your performance. You know what I mean? The only thing you're gonna give is their moves, not yours. That's really the new world. I didn't learn on YouTube because I had the chance to see people do it in front of my eyes. That's how I learned. But for the new girls sometimes it's the only way to learn something.

When you're judging a ball how do you decide when a person should be chopped?

If she's not bringing the category—she needs to know what she's walking for before coming to the ball. You can't watch a video and come to a ball. No, baby. If you want to make a cake, you need to have some eggs to make a cake. If nobody taught you that before and you come to a ball—no, baby. It's not gonna work like this. Sometimes they think I'm being rude or shady or whatever. But that's the only way they can learn something. When I'm on the panel I chop them, but also I'm telling them why I chop them, and I say it in front of everyone so that the next girl has a chance for the next ball.

Can you tell me a little bit about the House of Ninja?

Legendary Iconic House of Ninja, founded by Willi Ninja. This house is more runway, new way, and old way. The girls that are in vogue femme are all very, very good. We're more classic. We're not like the other houses. We're iconic. We're not walking every ball, we're just choosing balls to walk. Sometimes it's good to just lay back, watch, and come back.

What do you need to do to give a great performance?

It's the music, the DJ, and the commentator. And it's also the feeling. How do you feel today? It's also about how are they going to drop the beat too. Because you never know what he's going to drop. A good motherfucking beat. I need a hard beat and then I need the commentator and *then* the commentator gives me the juice to give what I want to give. And then the crowd. If the crowd is reacting to what I'm doing, then I'm going to do more.

Voguing is a cultural form that has long been snatched up and gentri-fied by corporate interests—most recently by Nike, which launched a Pride-centric ad starring "Wonder Woman of Vogue" Leiomy Maldonado. Media outlets—always the taste makers—regularly declare voguing is "back in vogue," but the question that remains is where do media outlets think voguing goes when they aren't writing cover stories about it? Where does voguing go when singers aren't co-opting it, appropriating it, and using it in their performances? The reality is that voguing doesn't go any-where because it's not just a trend, a style of movement, or a choreog-raphy. As a marriage of music, beats, style, dance, and sweat, voguing represents the seizing of black and brown queer space, space that often provides nourishing moments of survival and expression for marginalized people who are told every day they don't get a seat at the table.

Even as voguing has spread through our everyday lives, from

YouTube to Nike and from major art institutions to liquor brands, voguing is always about survival. Lasseindra notes that Paris is the real scene of Europe because of the way brown people struggle there every single day—being kicked out of their homes, out of their families and communities, and all this while under constant attack from the state. Voguing offers a place of confidence. Not just a place of refuge or a "safe" space—a place of confidence. Voguing is not choreography but an expression and a bold embrace of self-acceptance. When you've been marginalized, this is a form of creative expression you feel from your soul and beyond. And like most creative work created under extreme duress, voguing offers us a personal challenge to go to the next level of ourselves.

"Don't Hate Us 'Cause We Fabulous"

900 Words on Prince

"Excuse me . . . are you Prince?" the hotel concierge asked me.

At first I thought he was joking, the kind of slightly homophobic jab I've grown used to hearing over the years, so I laughed as I said, "No, I'm not Prince," with a tone of obviousness.

"Are you *sure*?" he doubled down. I couldn't believe it. Had he never seen a picture of Prince?

Over my lifetime I've admired many black divas and pop singers, from Tina Turner and Little Richard to Beyoncé and Lenny Kravitz, but Prince's fierce, androgynous aesthetic completely changed my approach to my own body. Prince also made me queer. He was proof to my teenage mind that living outside the box is sexy, a kind of magic. Prince, for me, represented freedom.

On April 21, 2016, I boarded a flight from London to New York for a special performance studies conference at Yale organized by my dissertation advisor. I hadn't been back to New Haven since I graduated in 2012, so I was eager to see old faces and to go to all my old hot spots—BAR (the bacon and red onion pizza is to die for), 116Crown . . . and I really couldn't wait to get a piece of Lithuanian coffee cake. As the plane touched down at JFK, still rolling down the runway, I took my phone out of airplane mode and was showered with a barrage of messages, from WhatsApp to Facebook, with the news that Prince died. Wait, what? I immediately felt numb. It was a shock to me because Prince was still so young, so active, and I guess I had believed he would outlive all the rest of us. I had left London in a world with Prince in it. Six hours later he was gone.

When I used to pump around the streets of Ferguson, Missouri, a place you know of now only because of the 2014 riots, the place where I spent a small chunk of my early childhood years, kids who wanted to be mean called me "Prince." I'd walk down the street really feeling good about myself and people would just yell, "Hey, Prince!" laughing, pointing, sneering. Even when I lived in New York City and actually even until this day, people still yell "Prince" at me as a homophobic insult. Over the years I started associating the word Prince with faggotry—not Prince's own faggotry but mine.

But for the longest time I just didn't get it. I didn't understand how anyone could think that comparing me to Prince was an insult. Do people really think that insulting the way I dress by comparing me to one of the greatest artists of all time is going to hurt my feelings?

If you were black and in America during the 1980s and 1990s, of any age, you knew about Prince. Your family members loved Prince. You put Prince on at house parties, holidays, fish fries, BBQs, and birthdays. Your mom loved Prince. Your grandmother loved Prince. Your aunties and uncles loved Prince. But there was always something "not quite" about him, something unlocatable, dangerous, extravagant, fabulous. This is for sure what drew me to him. He was an outcast, a style rebel, who helped me feel free. In my family the term everyone uses to describe suspected gay people—though, of course, not *me*—is *funny*. Well, that or *artistic. Different.* It's a way of noticing the big old faggot in the room, looking him right in the face, without actually having to tell anyone the news. Prince allowed me to live as an open secret. Flamboyant as he was, he also gave me the space to play with my own sense of queerness, to be queer right now, to feel that it is okay to be "different," "funny." I was fascinated that he was able to be so famous, so celebrated, so loved—and yet utterly queer. From a very young age I was obsessed with what Prince did to blackness and masculinity. His androgynous aesthetic changed how I thought about my own body and he helped me connect to queerness. Prince gave me permission to wear heels, sequins, and earrings, and now I don't need permission from anybody.

Prince was more than a musical genius. I discovered him at a time I was playing the starring role in the feature film *Closeted Black Teenager,* and I remember thinking back then that he was so weird, so strange. But fascinating. Unlocatable, artistic, fabulous, a no-no. Music superstars have a way of living on through album rereleases, costume parties, and biopics, and Prince will certainly live on at purple dance parties all around the world. But his legacy will also continue on in every queer person of color who discovers him for the first time, who sees in him a kind of style inspiration, a "plan b" to replace the dominant script. His legacy will always be musical but his unique sense of style will also help generations of queer people of color to learn to love their difference. And when I listen to all my favorite Prince tunes or every time his music comes on at a party I will whisper, "Thank you." Thank you for setting me free. Thank you for helping me accept my identity as a black gay faggot, diamonds, pearls, and all.

1. Zachary Woolfe, "A Convergence of Blood, Sweat, Tears and Tchaikovsky," *New York Times,* May 20, 2012, accessed June 22, 2017, http://www.nytimes.com/2012/05/11/arts/music/young-concert-artists -with-hahn-bin-at-alice-tully-hall.html?_r=0. See also madison moore, "Iconoclassical: Hahn-Bin, the Violin Virtuoso with a Twist," *Interview,* March 3, 2011, accessed June 22, 2017, http://www.interviewmagazine .com/music/2011–03–10/hahn-bin/print/.

2. "Hahn-Bin at Carnegie Hall," *Today Show,* YouTube video, April 22, 2011, accessed January 27, 2016, https://archive.org/details/WBAL_2011 0422_110000_Today.

3. moore, "Iconoclassical."

4. Francesca Royster, *Sounding Like a No-No: Queer Sounds and Eccentric Acts in the Post-Soul Era* (Ann Arbor: University of Michigan Press, 2012), 4.

5. "Hahn-Bin at Carnegie Hall."

6. Raja Gemini, "I'm obsessed with this!" Facebook, March 22, 2015, accessed January 27, 2016, https://www.facebook.com/RajaOfficial /posts/1060962013920159.

7. "A Star Is Born: Newest Fashionista Famous for WTF Factor," *Coconuts Bangkok,* March 23, 2015, accessed January 27, 2016, http://bangkok .coconuts.co/2015/03/23/star-born-newest-fashionista-famous-wtf-factor -video.

8. Charlie Campbell, "The Mixmaster of Fashion," *Time,* October 6, 2016, accessed June 22, 2017, http://time.com/collection-post/4518801 /apichet-atirattana-next-generation-leaders/.

9. Gemini, "I'm obsessed with this!"

10. Craig Owens, "The Medusa Effect; or, The Spectacular Ruse," *Art in America,* January 1984, 104.

11. Michael Warner, *Fear of a Queer Planet: Queer Politics and Social Theory,* ed. Michael Warner (Minneapolis: University of Minnesota Press, 1993), xxvi.

12. Richard Wright, "Blueprint for Negro Writing," in *Within the Circle: An Anthology of African American Literary Criticism from the Harlem Renaissance to the Present,* ed. Angelyn Mitchell (Durham: Duke University Press, 1994), 103.

13. Adolf Loos and Michael Troy, *Why a Man Should Be Well-Dressed: Appearances Can Be Revealing* (Vienna: Metroverlag, 2011), 28; Simon

Doonan, *Eccentric Glamour: Creating an Insanely More Fabulous You* (New York: Simon and Schuster, 2008), xix.

14. Sarah Lewis, *The Rise: Creativity, the Gift of Failure, and the Search for Mastery* (New York: Simon and Schuster, 2014), 11.

15. Maya Angelou, "Still I Rise," in *And Still I Rise* (London: Virago, 1986), 41.

16. Robin D. G. Kelley, *Freedom Dreams: The Black Radical Imagination* (Boston: Beacon, 2003), 158.

17. Greg Tate, *Flyboy 2: The Greg Tate Reader* (Durham: Duke University Press, 2016), 334.

18. Royster, *Sounding Like a No-No*, 8–9.

19. Amrou Al-Kadhi, *Define Gender: Victoria Sin* (London: NOWNESS, 2017), online.

20. Laura Mulvey, "Visual Pleasure and Narrative Cinema," *Screen* 16 (1975): 11.

21. Roberta Smith, "Critic's Notebook; Standing and Staring, yet Aiming for Empowerment," *New York Times,* May 6, 1998, accessed January 27, 2016, http://www.nytimes.com/1998/05/06/arts/critic-s-notebook -standing-and-staring-yet-aiming-for-empowerment.html.

22. Thorstein Veblen, *The Theory of the Leisure Class: An Economic Study of Institutions* (Oxford: Oxford University Press, 2007), 11.

23. For more, see David J. Getsy, *Abstract Bodies: Sixties Sculpture in the Expanded Field of Gender* (New Haven: Yale University Press, 2015), especially xii; and Susan Stryker, Paisley Currah, and Lisa Jean Moore, "Trans-, Trans, or Transgender," *Women's Studies Quarterly* 36 (2008): 11.

24. T. L. Cowan, *GLITTERfesto,* accessed June 29, 2017, http://tlcowan.net /glitterfesto/.

25. Shaun Cole, *Don We Now Our Gay Apparel: Gay Men's Dress in the Twentieth* Century (Oxford: Berg, 2000), 88.

26. Bill Cunningham, "Ahead of the Game," *Details,* March 1983, 51, Downtown Collection, Fales Library and Special Collections, New York University.

27. Martin Manalansan, "Queer Dwellings: Migrancy, Precarity, and Fabulosity" (keynote address presented at the Seventh Annual Feminist Theory Workshop, Duke University, March 23, 2013), accessed January 27, 2016, https://www.youtube.com/watch?v=mdMUBO3ZvLc.

28. Carol Tulloch, "Style—Fashion—Dress: From Black to Post-Black," *Fashion Theory* 14 (2010): 276.

29. Gap, "Let your actions speak louder than your clothes," September 18,

2014, accessed January 27, 2016, https://twitter.com/gap/status/5126
47270878412800,

30. Gap, "Gap Inc. Reports November Sales Result," accessed January 27,
2016, http://www.gapinc.com/content/gapinc/html/media/press
release/2014/med_pr_GPS_Sales_1114.html.

31. Veronique Hyland, "Apparently, People Don't Want to 'Dress Normal,'"
New York, October 23, 2014, accessed January 27, 2016, http://nymag
.com/thecut/2014/10/apparently-people-dont-want-to-dress-normal.html.

32. Isha Aran, "Gap's Blah 'Dress Normal' Campaign Doesn't Get the Irony
of Normcore," *Jezebel*, October 22, 2014, accessed January 27, 2016,
http://jezebel.com/gaps-blah-dress-normal-campaign-doesnt-get-the
-irony-o-1649345286; Sapna Naheshwari, "Gap Has a Problem: Its 'Dress
Normal' Campaign Is Way Too Normal," *Buzzfeed*, October 22, 2014,
accessed January 27, 2016, http://www.buzzfeed.com/sapna/gap-has
-a-problem-its-dress-normal-campaign-is-way-too-norma#.sdrwDya60.

33. Sianne Ngai, *Our Aesthetic Categories: Zany, Cute, Interesting*
(Cambridge, MA: Harvard University Press, 2012), 4, 133.

34. Patricia Field, telephone interview by author, July 29, 2014.

35. Herbert Blau, *Nothing in Itself: Complexions of Fashion* (Bloomington:
Indiana University Press, 1999), 37, 9.

36. Cathy Cohen, "Deviance as Resistance: A New Research Agenda for the
Study of Black Politics," *De Bois Review* 1 (2004): 39.

37. Susan Sontag, "Notes on Camp," in *Against Interpretation and Other
Essays* (London: Penguin, 2009), 277.

38. Jack Babuscio, "The Cinema of Camp (AKA Camp and the Gay
Sensibility)," in *Queer Cinema, the Film Reader,* ed. Harry Benshoff
(New York: Routledge, 2004), 120.

39. John Berger, *Ways of Seeing* (London: Penguin, 2008), 9.

40. Susanne Bartsch, email interview by author, August 20, 2014.

41. Dick Hebdige, *Subculture: The Meaning of Style* (New York: Routledge,
1988), 18.

42. Ibid., 17–18.

43. *Oxford English Dictionary,* 2nd ed., s.v. "fabulous."

44. Tavia Nyong'o, "Unburdening Representation," *Black Scholar* 44 (2014):
77.

45. *Oxford English Dictionary,* 2nd ed., s.v. "fabulousness."

46. Tracy Clayton, "22 Animals Who Are Like YAAAAAAS!" *Buzzfeed*, October
17, 2013, accessed January 27, 2016, http://www.buzzfeed
.com/tracyclayton/22-animals-who-are-like-yaaaaaaas#.yaPpwzkzB.

47. I have heard these terms in queer night worlds, particularly in the house ballroom scene, but also in the fashion industry itself. During my time as a summer fashion assistant at the Condé Nast publication *Women's Wear Daily,* where I participated in countless photo shoots, photographers, stylists, and makeup artists all used these terms to describe the creative work they produced. Often, to encourage the model, the lead stylist would say, "Work!" while loud dance music played in the background.

48. For more, see Kimora Lee Simmons, *Fabulosity: What It Is and How to Get It* (New York: Regan Books, 2006). Martin Manalansan's new work on fabulosity (not yet published) also references this text.

49. "Book Yourself Fabulous," accessed January 27, 2016, bookyourself fabulous.co.uk.

50. Chris Koo, "Chris Koo—'Crazy in Love' Dance Cover," YouTube video, 2:35, a Beyoncé dance cover video, posted by Chris Koo, October 14, 2013, accessed January 27, 2016, https://www.youtube.com/watch ?v=mdiGBl6yngw.

51. B. Scott, "S1: 190; I Went to the Doctor Today!" YouTube video, 3:28, a confessional video about the power of hair, August 7, 2008, posted by B. Scott, accessed January 27, 2016, https://www.youtube.com/watch ?v=mi5J4YhkxN8.

52. For more on black speech as a practice of "signifyin(g)," see Henry Louis Gates, *The Signifying Monkey: A Theory of African-American Literary Criticism* (Oxford: Oxford University Press, 1998).

53. See especially Joseph Roach, "Sweating Blood: Intangible Heritage and Reclaimed Labor in Caribbean New Orleans," *Performance Research* 13 (December 2008).

54. E. Patrick Johnson, "SNAP! Culture: A Different Kind of Reading," *Text and Performance Quarterly* 15 (1995): 129, 132.

55. Roach, "Sweating Blood," 148.

56. Tulloch, "Style—Fashion—Dress," 276.

57. RoRo Morales, telephone interview by author, October 24, 2014.

58. Diana Taylor makes a strong case for pairing classical archival research with the "repertoire" of experience as a performance studies method. For more, see Diana Taylor, *The Archive and the Repertoire: Performing Cultural Memory in the Americas* (Durham: Duke University Press, 2003).

59. Ngai, *Our Aesthetic Categories,* 29.

60. Peggy Phelan, *Unmarked: The Politics of Performance* (London: Routledge, 1993), 6.

61. Ibid., 7, 10.

62. See Valerie Steele and Daphne Guinness, *Daphne Guinness* (New Haven: Yale University Press, 2011), 26.

63. Michaela angela Davis, "Resistance," in *Black Cool: One Thousand Streams of Blackness,* ed. Rebecca Walker (Berkeley: Soft Skull, 2012), 64, 62.

64. José Esteban Muñoz, *Cruising Utopia: The Then and There of Queer Futurity* (New York: New York University Press, 2009), 99.

65. See William Dean Howells, "An Opportunity for American Fiction," *Literature: An International Gazette of Criticism,* April 28, 1899, 361–62.

66. Leonard Silk, *Veblen: A Play in Three Acts* (New York: A. M. Kelly, 1966), 33.

67. Veblen, *The Theory of the Leisure Class,* 11.

68. Ibid., 106–7.

69. John Marshall Holcombe Jr. to Joseph Dorfman, September 8, 1932, Joseph Dorfman Papers, Columbia University, New York.

70. Veblen, *The Theory of the Leisure Class,* 107–8.

71. For more, see Elizabeth Currid-Halkett, *The Warhol Economy: How Fashion, Art and Music Drive New York City* (Princeton: Princeton University Press, 2008).

72. Michael Goldhaber, "Attention Shoppers," *Wired,* December 1997, accessed January 27, 2016, http://www.wired.com/wired/archive/5.12/es_attention.html.

73. Pierre Bourdieu, "The Social Space and the Genesis of Groups," *Theory and Society* 14 (1985): 731.

74. Pierre Bourdieu, "What Makes a Social Class?" *Berkeley Journal of Sociology* 32 (1987): 13.

75. Fiona Buckland, *Impossible Dance: Improvised Social Dance as Queer World-Making* (Middletown, CT: Wesleyan University Press, 2002), 37.

76. Walter Benjamin, *Illuminations: Essays and Reflections* (New York: Schocken Books, 1955), 223.

77. Andy Warhol, *The Philosophy of Andy Warhol: From A to B and Back Again* (New York: Houghton Mifflin, 1975), 77.

78. Marcel Mauss, *The Gift: Forms and Functions of Exchange in Archaic Societies* (London: Cohen and West, 1966), 10, 11.

79. Ibid., 10.

80. François Boucher, *Le vêtement chez Balzac: Extraits de la Comédie humaine* (Paris: Editions de l'Institut français de la mode, 2001), 14.

81. Honoré de Balzac, *Old Goriot,* trans. Marion Ayton Crawford (London: Penguin, 1951), 30, 31, 32.

82. Ibid., 50, 51.

83. Susan B. Kaiser, *Fashion and Cultural Studies* (London: Bloomsbury, 2011), 30.

84. Erving Goffman, *The Presentation of Self in Everyday Life* (Garden City, NY: Doubleday, 1959), 59.

85. Carolyn Cooper, interview by author, London, January 13, 2015.

86. Chimamanda Ngozi Adichie, "Why Can't a Smart Woman Love Fashion?" *Elle*, February 20, 2014, accessed January 27, 2016, http://www.elle.com/life-love/personal-style/personal-essay-on-style-by-chimamanda-ngozi-adichie.

87. Jack Halberstam, *The Queer Art of Failure* (Durham: Duke University Press, 2011), 6.

88. Valerie Steele, "The F Word," *Lingua Franca,* April 1991, accessed January 26, 2016, http://www.wiu.edu/users/mfbhl/180/steele.htm.

89. Hal Foster, *Design and Crime and Other Diatribes* (London: Verso, 2002), 18–25.

90. I owe my approach to eccentricity in part to Eve Sedgwick's essay "Paranoid Reading and Reparative Reading; Or, You're So Paranoid You Probably Think This Essay Is about You" — really an eye-opening must-read — in which she describes the obsession queer and feminist theory has with studying the surface to uncover unknown oppressions. "Paranoia has by now become less a diagnosis than a prescription," she writes. In other words, there's more to life, theory, and great ideas than pessimism and negativity. What about joy? What do we have to say about exuberance? Moreover, it's important to realize that a pessimistic approach to theory is raced and often removed from the everyday. Life is already pessimistic for brown, queer, and trans folk, so why invest more time and energy into what's wrong? Why not focus on what marginalized folks are doing right, and how *that* offers a critique of the systems that oppress us? See Eve Kosofsky Sedgwick, *Touching Feeling: Affect, Pedagogy, Performativity* (Durham: Duke University Press, 2003), 126.

91. Guy Debord, *Society of the Spectacle* (New York: Zone Books, 1994), 14.

92. Lars Svendsen, *Fashion: A Philosophy* (London: Reaktion, 2006), 37.

93. For more on sumptuary laws, see Caroline Weber, *Queen of Fashion: What Marie-Antoinette Wore to the Revolution* (New York: Henry Holt, 2006); and Yuniya Kawamura, *Fashion-ology: An Introduction to Fashion Studies* (Oxford: Berg, 2005).

94. Jean-Jacques Rousseau, *The Social Contract and Discourses* (New York: E. P. Dutton, 1950), 136.

95. Mary Wollstonecraft, *Vindication of the Rights of Woman: With Strictures on Political and Moral Subjects* (1792) (University of Oregon, Renasence, 2000), https://scholarsbank.uoregon.edu/xmlui/bitstream/handle/1794/785/vindication.pdf.

96. Rhonda Garelick's *Rising Star: Dandyism, Gender, and Performance in the Fin de Siècle* (Princeton: Princeton University Press, 1998) offers a compelling account of the nineteenth-century dandy and its relationship to consumer culture and media. Monica Miller's *Slaves to Fashion: Black Dandyism and the Styling of Black Diasporic Identity* (Durham: Duke University Press, 2009) offers a similar narrative historical account of the dandy, with a specific focus on the history of the black dandy, a history that had never been told.

97. Oscar Wilde, *The Picture of Dorian Gray* (London: Penguin Classics, 2012), 22.

98. Jean-Christophe Agnew, "Coming Up for Air: Consumer Culture in Historical Perspective," in *Consumption and the World of Goods,* ed. John Brewer and Roy Porter (New York: Routledge, 1994), 22.

99. Georg Simmel, "Fashion," *American Journal of Sociology* 62 (1957): 545.

100. Anne Hollander, *Sex and Suits: The Evolution of Modern Dress* (New York: Knopf, 1994), 21.

101. For more, see Goffman, *The Presentation of Self in Everyday Life.*

102. RuPaul, *Lettin' It All Hang Out: An Autobiography* (New York: Hyperion, 1995), foreword.

103. Virginia Postrel, *The Substance of Style: How the Rise of Aesthetic Value Is Remaking Commerce, Culture, and Consciousness* (New York: Harper-Collins, 2003), 9, 14, 70.

104. Kelley, *Freedom Dreams,* 2–3.

2. How to Work a Look

1. "@gugueyes, paparazzi shot by @dustyrebel I sure love going to whole foods casual as fuck but still slaying shoppers in a look," Instagram, September 14, 2015, instagram.com/p/7n8vdxp7Ki/?taken-by=gugueyes and instagram.com/p/7l9djzhVcL/?taken-by=dustyrebel.

2. Minh-Ha T. Pham, *Asians Wear Clothes on the Internet: Race, Gender, and the Work of Personal Style Blogging* (Durham: Duke University Press, 2015), 231.

3. Roland Barthes, *The Language of Fashion* (London: Berg, 2006), 41.

4. See Miller, *Slaves to Fashion*.

5. Krista Thompson, *Shine: The Visual Economy of Light in African Diasporic Aesthetic Practice* (Durham: Duke University Press, 2015), 13.

6. *Details*, December–January 1983–84 double issue, Downtown Collection, Fales Library and Special Collections, New York University.

7. Ashley Mears, *Pricing Beauty: The Making of a Fashion Model* (Berkeley: University of California Press, 2011), 75.

8. Sapna Maheshwari, "Exclusive: The Hairstyles Abercrombie Has Deemed 'Unacceptable,'" *Buzzfeed*, September 3, 2013, accessed June 23, 2017, https://www.buzzfeed.com/sapna/exclusive-abercrombie-hairstyle-rules-add-to-strict-look-pol.

9. Benoit Denizet-Lewis, "The Man Behind Abercrombie & Fitch," *Salon*, January 24, 2006, accessed June 23, 2017, http://www.salon.com/2006/01/24/jeffries/.

10. *Gonzalez, et al., v. Abercrombie & Fitch Stores, Inc., et al.* (2005), 03-2817 SI 04-4730, 03-2817 SI 04-4731.

11. Dwight McBride, *Why I Hate Abercrombie and Fitch: Essays on Race and Sexuality* (New York: NYU Press, 2005).

12. Ngai, *Our Aesthetic Categories*, 47.

13. Mulvey, "Visual Pleasure and Narrative Cinema," 11.

14. Morales, interview.

15. Buckland, *Impossible Dance*, 36, 37, 38.

16. Leo GuGu, interview by author, New York, April 1, 2012.

17. Anne Hollander, *Seeing through Clothes* (Berkeley: University of California Press, 1993), 451.

18. Muñoz, *Cruising Utopia*, 97, 99.

19. Carolyn Dinshaw, *Getting Medieval: Sexualities and Communities, Pre- and Postmodern* (Durham: Duke University Press, 1999), 12, 49–51.

20. Mister Wallace, telephone interview by author, October 20, 2014.

21. Thompson, *Shine*, 10.

22. Blaqueer, "The Fat Boi Diaries: Why Selfies?" personal blog, March 16, 2013, accessed June 23, 2017, https://blaqueer.wordpress.com/2013/03/16/the-fat-boi-diaries-why-selfies/.

23. Chaédria LaBouvier, "Why Chimamanda Ngozi Adichie's Beauty Campaign Matters," *Elle*, October 21, 2016, accessed June 22, 2017, http://www.elle.com/beauty/news/a40177/chimamanda-ngozi-adichie-boots-beauty-campaign-why-it-matters/.

24. Amy Cakes, interview by author, Los Angeles, November 7, 2014.

25. Michael Warner, "Publics and Counterpublics," *Public Culture* 14, no. 1 (2002): 50, 62.
26. Hollander, *Seeing through Clothes*, 451.
27. Warner, "Publics and Counterpublics," 81.
28. Rebecca Zurier, *Picturing the City: Urban Vision and the Ashcan School* (Berkeley: University of California Press, 2006), 6–7.
29. *Fresh Dressed*, directed by Sacha Jenkins (2015; New York: Samuel Goldwyn Films, 2016), DVD.
30. Richard Powell, *Cutting a Figure: Fashioning Black Portraiture* (Chicago: University of Chicago Press, 2009), 4.
31. Miller, *Slaves to Fashion*, 221, 181, 194, 1.
32. Agnès Rocamora and Alistair O'Neil, "Fashioning in the Street: Images of the Street in the Fashion Media," in *Fashion as Photograph: Viewing and Reviewing Images of Fashion*, ed. Eugénie Shinkle (New York: I. B. Tauris, 2008), 186.
33. Ted Polhemus, *Street Style: From Sidewalk to Catwalk* (London: Thames and Hudson, 1994), 7.
34. Ibid., 10.
35. Brent Luvaas, *Street Style: An Ethnography of Fashion Blogging* (London: Bloomsbury, 2016) is the first ethnography of street style blogging, though certainly not the first book about street style. Combining theory and practice, *Street Style* emerged out of Luvaas's own Philadelphia-based street style blog called *Urban Fieldnotes*, and a central highlight of the book is a robust collection of those images. Over the course of the rich narrative Luvaas focuses as much on the *how* of street style as on the *business* of street style. What's missing, though, are stories about how people take to the street to offer up creative, queer poetics of themselves—how they use the wide openness of the street to wear their own versions of the world. What's missing is how style, beauty, race, and queerness intersect on the street.
36. Sophie Woodward, "The Myth of Street Style," *Fashion Theory* 13, no. 1 (2009): 84.
37. Hebdige, *Subculture*, 17–18.
38. Pham, *Asians Wear Clothes on the Internet*, 224–26, 225.
39. Cakes, interview.
40. Pham, *Asians Wear Clothes on the Internet*, 227.
41. "Instant Fabulousness!" KlubKidVintage, accessed June 22, 2017, https://www.etsy.com/listing/128077556/sale-studded-wool-beret-medsmall?ref=shop_home_active_31.

42. Wayne Koestenbaum, *Jackie under My Skin: Interpreting an Icon* (New York: Fourth Estate, 1995), 23.

43. One example of this anti-fashion line of critique is Scott Herring, *Another Country: Queer Anti-Urbanism* (New York: NYU Press, 2010). On the whole, *Another Country* offers a much-needed counterargument to the story that all queer people want to be urban, that all queer people love New York City, and that all queer people everywhere want to move to the big city. Where Herring loses me, though, is in an anti-fashion, manifesto-like chapter, "Unfashionability," that rips into something he calls "queer chic." Queer chic, to his eyes, forces assimilation of a kind rooted in a toxic norm-inducing masculine look. What he points to, I think, is how certain (usually masculine) fashion codes become the norm, especially in many gay male circles. We don't have to look any further than the example of Abercrombie & Fitch, for instance, to see what Herring points to here. He shades, and I agree, a normative system in which desirability is scored according to how well you embrace the latest fashion trends. But what he overlooks is that fashion is actually the Barthesian industrial system of codes and signs that manages what we are able to purchase at the mall and when. *Style,* on the other hand, is much more personal, and it's about how people express themselves without regard to trends or norms or what the fashion system says is popping.

44. Mister Wallace, interview.

45. Roach, "Sweating Blood," 143–44.

46. David Halperin, *How to Be Gay* (Cambridge, MA: Harvard University Press, 2012), especially 362, 366, 357.

47. Thompson, *Shine,* 35.

48. Ibid., 25, 43.

49. *Poor Little Rich Girl,* directed by Andy Warhol (New York, 1965), DVD.

50. David Dalton and Nat Finkelstein, *Edie: Factory Girl* (New York: powerHouse Books, 2007), 4.

51. David Grazian, *On the Make: The Hustle of Urban Nightlife* (Chicago: University of Chicago Press, 2008), 96.

52. Ibid., 104, 107.

53. Susanne Bartsch, "How Do You Get Ready for a Night Out?" *Interview,* July 1991, 42.

54. Caroline Dinshaw et al., "Theorizing Queer Temporalities: A Roundtable Discussion," *GLQ: A Journal of Lesbian and Gay Studies* 13, nos. 2–3 (2007): 182.

55. David Grazian, *Blue Chicago: The Search for Authenticity in Urban Blues Clubs* (Chicago: University of Chicago Press, 2003), 63.

56. Christine Whitney, "Work the Look: Switch to Party Mode," *Harper's Bazaar*, December 7, 2012, accessed June 23, 2017, http://www.harpers bazaar.com/fashion/trends/g2399/day-to-night-dressing-1212/?slide=1.

57. Kathy Peiss, *Cheap Amusements: Working Women and Leisure in Turn-of-the-Century New York* (Philadelphia: Temple University Press, 1987), 66–67, 63.

58. "Club Kids," *The Joan Rivers Show*, YouTube video, 5:10, February 20, 2006, accessed September 29, 2012, http://www.youtube.com/watch ?v=aAm1RcsCOEg.

59. Frank Owen, *Clubland: The Fabulous Rise and Murderous Fall of Club Culture* (New York: St. Martin's, 2003), 130.

60. *Party Monster*, directed by Fenton Bailey and Randy Barbato (2003; Los Angeles, CA: DEJ Productions, 2003), DVD.

61. Michael Alig, quoted in Owen, *Clubland*, 129.

62. Susan Heller Anderson and David Bird, "New York Day by Day— Unofficial Party in Corlears Hook Park," *New York Times*, November 2, 1985.

63. madison moore, "Don't Ever Stop the Party," *Splice Today*, July 29, 2011, accessed June 22, 2017, http://www.splicetoday.com/pop-culture/don-t -ever-stop-the-party.

64. "Scenes from L.A.'s Kookiest Dance Party," *Papermag*, January 21, 2013, accessed June 22, 2017, http://www.papermag.com/scenes-from-las -kookiest-dance-party-1426753107.html.

65. moore, "Don't Ever Stop the Party."

66. Gregory Alexander, telephone interview by author, September 11, 2014.

67. Ibid.

68. Georg Simmel, "The Metropolis and Mental Life," in *The Blackwell City Reader*, ed. Gary Bridge and Sophie Watson (Oxford: Wiley-Blackwell, 2002), 11, 14.

69. Muñoz, *Cruising Utopia*, 182.

"I Create My Own Space" Interview

1. Michel Foucault, *The History of Sexuality: An Introduction* (New York: Vintage Books, 1990), 84.

3. Up in the Club

1. For a brief, lively profile of Berghain, including a rich discussion of its architecture and the club's history and placement in queer culture, see Luis-Manuel Garcia, "Draft Profile: Berghain/Panorama Bar," *LMGM Blog*, July 6, 2010, accessed June 22, 2017, https://lmgmblog.wordpress.com /2010/07/06/draft-profile-berghain-panorama-bar/. For a full discussion of the dynamics of the nightclub, see Garcia, "Can You Feel It, Too? Intimacy and Affect at Electronic Dance Music Events in Paris, Chicago, and Berlin" (PhD diss., University of Chicago, 2011).

2. To celebrate ten years of art, music, and club culture at Berghain the club held an exhibition in the summer of 2014 in one of its mammoth-sized unused spaces. The show featured work primarily by people who work for the venue, many of them artists and photographers, and others who are closely associated with the club. For more, see Berghain OstGut GmbH, *Berghain: 10* (Berlin: Hatje Cantz, 2015).

3. Tallkobben, "In Berlin atm, tried getting into Berghain 5 times already," Reddit, July 16, 2015, accessed June 22, 2017, https://www.reddit.com /r/Techno/comments/3dke7n/in_berlin_atm_tried_getting_into_berghain _5_times/.

4. Thump, "How to Get into Berghain. Maybe. Hopefully," February 25, 2015, accessed September 11, 2017, https://thump.vice.com/en_us/article/pg8 dqb/how-to-get-into-berghain-maybe-hopefully.

5. Benedikt Brandhofer and Leif Marcus, "Photos of People Who Didn't Get into Berghain," *Vice*, April 14, 2015, accessed January 22, 2016, http:// www.vice.com/en_uk/read/photos-of-people-who-didnt-get-into-berghain -berlin-club-876.

6. Max Wunderbar, "How to Get into Berghain: Berghain Door Policy Explained," accessed January 22, 2016, http://getintoberghain.com/.

7. Alexis Waltz, "Nightclubbing: Berlin's Ostgut," *Red Bull Music Academy*, accessed January 22, 2016, http://daily.redbullmusicacademy.com/2013 /09/nightclubbing-ostgut.

8. Malfunktion, "Daniel Wang talks about Berghain," Facebook, April 8, 2013, accessed January 22, 2016, https://www.facebook.com/noitknuf lam/posts/329977240457999.

9. Ibid.

10. Danuta Dramowicz, "Is There a Line at Berghain?" accessed January 22, 2016, https://itunes.apple.com/gb/app/is-there-a-line-at-berghain/id 915399160?mt=8.

11. Tobias Rapp, *Lost and Sound: Berlin, Techno and the Easy Jet Set* (Berlin: Innervisions, 2010), 142.
12. Charles Baudelaire, "Crowds," in *Paris Spleen*, trans. Louise Varese (New York: New Directions Books, 1970), 20.
13. Victor P. Corona, *Night Class: A Downtown Memoir* (New York: Soft Skull, 2017).
14. Grazian, *On the Make*, 63.
15. Sarah Thornton, *Club Cultures: Music, Media, and Subcultural Capital* (Hanover NH: University Press of New England, 1996), 12.
16. Burt Helm, "How the Bouncer of Berghain Chooses Who Gets into the Most Depraved Party on the Planet," *GQ*, July 25, 2015, accessed September 11, 2017, http://www.gq.com/story/berghain-bouncer-sven-marquardt-interview.
17. Rapp, *Lost and Sound*, 144.
18. Thilo Schneider, "Conversation with Wolfgang Tillmans," in Berghain OstGut GmbH, *Berghain: 10*, 31.
19. Thornton, *Club Cultures*, 114.
20. Jan Kedves, "Conversation with Sarah Schonfeld," in Berghain OstGut GmbH, *Berghain: 10*, 85.
21. Malfunktion, "Daniel Wang talks about Berghain."
22. Schneider, "Conversation with Wolfgang Tillmans," 32.
23. Lewis Erenberg, *Steppin' Out: New York Nightlife and the Transformation of American Culture, 1890–1930* (Chicago: University of Chicago Press, 1981), xiv.
24. Ibid., xi–xii, 23, 5–6.
25. Ibid., 5–6.
26. Stanley Walker, *The Night Club Era* (Baltimore: Johns Hopkins University Press, 1999), 89.
27. "Miss Kelly in Court on Mother's Charge," *New York Times*, May 23, 1915.
28. Kedves, "Conversation with Sarah Schonfeld," 85.
29. Thomas Onorato and Glenn Belverio, *Confessions from the Velvet Ropes: The Glamorous, Grueling Life of New York's Top Doorman* (New York: St. Martin's Griffin, 2006), 14, 208.
30. Richard Schechner, *Between Theater and Anthropology* (Philadelphia: University of Pennsylvania Press, 1985), 10.
31. Garcia, "Can You Feel It, Too?" 282, 288, 287.
32. Grazian, *On the Make*, 16.
33. Dietmar Hipp and Anna Kistner, "No Foreigners: Nightclubs Accused of Racist Door Policies," *Spiegel*, September 13, 2013, accessed November

28, 2017, http://www.spiegel.de/international/germany/german
-nightclub-door-policies-accused-of-racism-a-922149.html.

34. Caroline Lowbridge, "Jermain Jackson: *The Voice* Winner Was Barred
    from Own Party," *BBC News,* June 3, 2015, accessed January 22, 2016,
    http://www.bbc.co.uk/news/uk-england-32883122.

35. "Felix Da Housecat Denied Entry at Berghain, Accuses Club of Racism,"
    Fact, February 21, 2015, accessed January 22, 2016, http://www.factmag
    .com/2015/02/21/felix-da-housecat-denied-entry-berghain-unleashes
    -rant-twitter/.

36. Ben Malbon, *Clubbing: Dancing, Ecstasy and Vitality* (London: Routledge,
    1999), 64.

37. Robert Roth, "NY Club Scrutiny Draws Liquor Board Fire," *Billboard,*
    December 17, 1977, 68.

38. Jen Heger, "Racism Run Rampant? NYC Hot Spot 1OAK Accused of
    Banning Black Women from Club," *Radar Online,* July 31, 2014, accessed
    June 24, 2017, http://radaronline.com/exclusives/2014/07/1oak-new
    -york-celebrity-club-racism/.

39. Andy Towle, "New Gay Bar REBAR in NYC's Chelsea Neighborhood
    Accused of Racist Door Policy," *Towle Road,* April 17, 2017, accessed
    June 24, 2017, http://www.towleroad.com/2017/04/rebar-gay/.

40. Enid Nemy, "The Last Word at Discos Belongs to the Doormen; Education
    Backgrounds 'To Create Something' above the Crowd," *New York Times,*
    August 31, 1979.

41. Thornton, *Club Cultures,* 23–24.

42. For more on Lois Long, see Joshua Zeitz, *Flapper: A Madcap Story of Sex,
    Style, Celebrity, and the Women Who Made America Modern* (New York:
    Crown, 2006).

43. Let me point out that doors have appeared throughout the history
    of modern and contemporary art, perhaps most famously in Marcel
    Duchamp's *Door: 11 rue Larrey* (1927) and in his iconic last work, *Etant
    donnés* (1946–66).

44. See José Muñoz and Celeste Fraser Delgado, *Every Night Life: Culture
    and Dance in Latin/o America* (Durham: Duke University Press, 1997).

45. Sarah Thornton's recent work, for instance, has shifted toward a focus on
    the dynamics of the contemporary art world. See Sarah Thornton, *Seven
    Days in the Art World* (New York: Norton, 2008). See also Donald N.
    Thompson, *The $12 Million Shark: The Curious Economics of Contempo-
    rary Art* (New York: Palgrave Macmilan, 2008).

46. Thornton, *Club Cultures,* 3.

47. Langston Hughes, *The Big Sea: An Autobiography* (New York: Hill and Wang, 1963), 244–45.
48. Jimmy Durante and Jack Kofoed, *Night Clubs* (New York: Knopf, 1931), 176.
49. Erenberg, *Steppin' Out,* 117.
50. "A Souvenir of the Waldorf Astoria," Waldorf Astoria Papers, New York Historical Society, New York.
51. Erenberg, *Steppin' Out,* 34.
52. "A Souvenir of the Waldorf Astoria."
53. Lloyd Morris, *Incredible New York: High and Low Life from 1850 to 1950* (Syracuse: Syracuse University Press, 1996), 234, 235.
54. Ibid., 237.
55. Burton Peretti, *Nightclub City: Politics and Amusement in Manhattan* (Philadelphia: University of Pennsylvania Press, 2007), 4.
56. Durante and Kofoed, *Night Clubs,* 107.
57. Hughes, *The Big Sea,* 253.
58. Ibid., 225.
59. Nicole Fleetwood makes this point especially well in *Troubling Vision: Performance, Visuality, and Blackness* (Chicago: University of Chicago Press, 2011).
60. Rent party cards, September 14, 1929, March 18, 1955, May 9, 1929, Langston Hughes Papers, James Weldon Johnson Collection in the Yale Collection of American Literature, Beinecke Rare Book and Manuscript Library, Yale University, New Haven, CT.
61. David Levering Lewis, *When Harlem Was in Vogue* (New York: Vintage, 1982), 107.
62. Hughes, *The Big Sea,* 233.
63. Peter Shapiro, *Turn the Beat Around: The Secret History of Disco* (New York: Faber and Faber, 2005), 8.
64. Alan Jones and Jussi Kantonen, *Saturday Night Forever: The Story of Disco* (Chicago: A Capella Books, 2000), 209.
65. Roth, "N.Y. Club Scrutiny Draws Liquor Board Fire," 68.
66. Vanessa Grigoriades, "Régine's Last Stand," *New York,* April 19, 1999, accessed January 23, 2016, http://nymag.com/nymetro/nightlife/bars clubs/features/883/.
67. Pat Hackett and Andy Warhol, *The Andy Warhol Diaries* (New York: Warner Books, 1989), 22.
68. Bryan Palmer, *Cultures of Darkness: Night Travels in the Histories of Transgression* (New York: Monthly Review, 2000), 13, 19, 17.

69. Bret Easton Ellis, *Glamorama* (London: Picador, 2011), 27.

70. Bret Easton Ellis, *Glamorama* (New York: Vintage, 2000), 312.

71. Marvin Taylor, *The Downtown Book: The New York Art Scene, 1974–1984* (Princeton: Princeton University Press, 2006), 17.

72. Michael Musto, *Downtown* (New York: Vintage, 1986), 7.

73. Taylor, *The Downtown Book*, 20.

74. *Details*, June 1982, Downtown Collection, Fales Library and Special Collections, New York University.

75. Joseph Roach, *It* (Ann Arbor: University of Michigan Press, 2007), 1.

76. *Details*, November 1983, Downtown Collection, Fales Library and Special Collections, New York University.

77. Daniel Boorstin, *The Image: A Guide to Pseudo-Events in America* (New York: Atheneum, 1980), 57–60.

78. *Details*, May 1984, Downtown Collection, Fales Library and Special Collections, New York University.

79. Christie's, "Warhol Questionnaire: Carmen D'Alessio," accessed January 27, 2016, http://warhol.christies.com/warhol-questionnaire-carmen -dalessio/.

80. *Details*, November 1983, Downtown Collection, Fales Library and Special Collections, New York University.

81. *Details*, December–January 1983–84, Downtown Collection, Fales Library and Special Collections, New York University, 20.

82. Pascal Gielen, "The Art Scene: An Ideal Production Unit for Economic Exploitation?" *Open* 17 (2009): 14.

83. *Details*, July 1982, 5, Downtown Collection, Fales Library and Special Collections, New York University.

84. Brian Massumi, *Semblance and Event: Activist Philosophy and the Occurrent Arts* (Cambridge: MIT Press, 2011), 2–3.

85. *Details*, March 1983, Downtown Collection, Fales Library and Special Collections, New York University.

86. *Details*, June 1982, Downtown Collection, Fales Library and Special Collections, New York University.

87. Ibid.

88. Grazian, *On the Make*, 13.

89. Christie's, "Warhol Questionnaire: Carmen D'Alessio."

90. Henry Post, "Heart of Darkness," *New York*, May 3, 1982, 25.

91. Leslie Bennetts, "An 'In' Crowd and Outside Mob Show Up for Studio 54's Birthday," *New York Times*, April 28, 1978.

92. Tim Lawrence, *Love Saves the Day: A History of American Dance Music Culture, 1970–1979* (Durham: Duke University Press, 2004), 269–71.

93. "Steve Rubell Obituary," *Los Angeles Times*, July 27, 1989, 26.

94. Andy Warhol and Bob Colacello, *Andy Warhol's Exposures* (New York: Grosset and Dunlap, 1979), 50.

95. Truman Capote, Steve Rubell, and Bob Colacello, "Steve Rubell: In the Height of the Night," *Interview*, February 1979, 33.

96. Shapiro, *Turn the Beat Around*, 154.

97. There are certainly better and more interesting clubs in nightlife history than Studio 54, which surely doesn't need any more coverage. I'm thinking of places like Paradise Garage, the Loft, and the Warehouse, among many others. But my interest in 54 has to do with how it brought the terror of the tight door to a fever pitch. It was also a space that paid exceptionally close attention to theatrical design, was in a former television studio, and plugged into notions of celebrity culture.

98. Anthony Haden Guest, *The Last Party: Studio 54, Disco, and the Culture of the Night* (New York: William Morrow, 1997), 25, 26.

99. Roland Barthes, *Incidents* (Chicago: University of Chicago Press, 2010), 120, 124.

100. Ernest Leogrande, "Studio 54, Where Are You?" *New York Daily News*, April 26, 1977.

101. Peretti, *Nightclub City*, 102, 112–13.

102. Bob Colacello, "Oh Carmen!" *Interview*, April 1977, 42.

103. Andy Warhol and Pat Hackett, *POPism: The Warhol '60s* (Orlando: Harcourt, 1980), 367–68.

104. Andreas Killen, *1973 Nervous Breakdown: Watergate, Warhol, and the Birth of Post-Sixties America* (New York: Bloomsbury, 2006), 140.

105. Shapiro, *Turn the Beat Around*, 206–7.

106. Haden Guest, *The Last Party*, 42.

107. Marc Benecke, quoted in ibid., 59–62.

108. *Oxford English Dictionary*, 2nd ed., s.v. "hype."

109. Michael Musto, quoted in Haden Guest, *The Last Party*, 59.

110. Nemy, "The Last Word at Discos Belongs to the Doormen."

111. Walker, *The Night Club Era*, 60.

112. For more, see J. Jack Halberstam, *In a Queer Time and Place: Transgender Bodies, Subcultural Lives* (New York: New York University Press, 2005).

113. Jonathan Crary, *24/7: Late Capitalism and the Ends of Sleep* (London: Verso, 2014), 8.

114. Muñoz, *Cruising Utopia*, 65.

115. madison moore, "Nightlife as Form," *Theater* 46, no. 1 (2016): 56.

116. Ibid.

117. Joshua Javier Guzmán, "Notes on the Comedown," *Social Text* 32, no. 4 121 (2014): 60.

4. What's Queer about the Catwalk?

1. Richard Dyer, "In Defense of Disco," *Gay Left,* Summer 1979, 20.

2. "Supermodel (You Better Work)" chart history, *Billboard,* accessed April 10, 2016, http://www.billboard.com/artist/369236/rupaul/chart.

3. Beyoncé Knowles, Kasseem "Swizz Beatz" Dean, Makeba Riddick, Angela Beyincé, and Solange Knowles, "Get Me Bodied," *B'Day* (Columbia Records, 2006).

4. Mark Anthony Neal, "Sold Out on Soul: The Corporate Annexation of Black Popular Music," *Popular Music and Society* 21 (2008): 121–24.

5. "Soul Train Babies!!! OWWW!!!" YouTube video, 2:08, January 26, 2014, posted by Darrell J. Hunt, accessed April 10, 2016, https://www.youtube .com/watch?v=gY1gzvkkBGQ.

6. Vjuan Allure's Facebook page, accessed July 20, 2017, https://www .facebook.com/vjuan.allure.1?hc_ref=ARQWIX503wm_P1OiPX8nbPOKn -0lyA85hMSnDsK4SVSjly19CmlZYuiVOeo7mydbOYc.

7. Foucault, *The History of Sexuality,* 84.

8. Brian Schaefer, "Vogueing Is Still Burning Up the Dance Floor in New York," *New York Times,* July 23, 2015, accessed June 24, 2017, http:// www.nytimes.com/interactive/2015/07/22/arts/dance/20150726 -vogue.html?_r=0.

9. Joseph Roach, *Cities of the Dead: Circum-Atlantic Performance* (New York: Columbia University Press, 1996,) 256, 206.

10. On March 3, 2016, Escuelita announced it would be closing after a nineteen-year run in Hell's Kitchen. See Michael Musto, "Rip Latin LGBT Dance Club Escuelita," *Paper,* March 3, 2016, accessed April 9, 2016, http://www.papermag.com/rip-lgbt-dance-club-escuelita-1637308305 .html.

11. "FKA Twigs & Robert Pattinson @ Vogue Knights," YouTube video, accessed April 9, 2016, https://www.youtube.com/watch?v=oEEVMWO003k.

12. Marlon Bailey, *Butch Queens Up in Pumps: Gender, Performance, and*

Ballroom Culture in Detroit (Ann Arbor: University of Michigan Press, 2013), 161.

13. "FKA Twigs & Robert Pattinson @ Vogue Knights," YouTube video, 1:01, November 10, 2014, accessed April 9, 2016, https://www.youtube.com /watch?v=p6TT98XEEsc.

14. *Butch Queens Up in Pumps: Gender, Performance, and Ballroom Culture in Detroit,* by performance studies scholar Marlon Bailey, is the first book-length study of American voguing and house ball culture. The text is unique in that Bailey positions himself both as an ethnographer and as a participant who has a certain love of voguing culture, and the book feels familiar to anyone who has ever been to a ball. Throughout, Bailey breaks down the elements of voguing and of the local vogue scene in Detroit, his discussion stretching from the specificity of black queer language, showing how slang terms like *sickening* and *ovah* come to be positive and celebratory, to the critical importance of the commentator. Most other texts about voguing have focused on the film *Paris Is Burning,* such as *Paris Is Burning: A Queer Film Classic* (Vancouver, BC: Arsenal Pulp, 2013), by Lucas Hilderbrand, or are photo books meant to capture the residue of fabulousness made possible through costume, such as *Legendary: Inside the House Ballroom Scene* (Durham: Duke University Press, 2013), by Gerard Gaskin, and *Voguing and the House Ballroom Scene of New York, 1982–92: Photographs* (London: Soul Jazz Records, 2011), by Stuart Baker and Chantal Regnault. But I admit to being especially pleased about Bailey's work because finally, I thought, there is now a book—a document—written by a black queer person about the importance and value of black queer space and the stories of people who survive and thrive there. "Write *my* story," one voguer told Bailey at a function. *Butch Queens Up in Pumps* answers Muñoz's call for "critical idealism," showing that while we cannot and should not ignore the systems that keep marginalized bodies disenfranchised, we should devote just as much if not more time to thinking about how they use pleasure, aesthetics, and play to face that duress in their search for another world.

15. madison moore, "To Be Able to Blend: Does 'Realness' Still Belong in Ballroom?" *Out,* April 7, 2017, accessed June 24, 2017, http://www.out .com/news-opinion/2017/4/07/be-able-blend-does-realness-still-belong -ballroom.

16. Julianne Escobedo Shepherd, "Nah, Rihanna: A History of 'Vogue' Exploiting Queer People of Color," *Jezebel,* January 13, 2015, accessed

April 9, 2016, http://themuse.jezebel.com/nah-rihanna-a-history-of
-vogue-exploiting-queer-peopl-1679218615.

17. For more on infectious rhythms, see Barbara Browning, *Infectious Rhythm: Metaphors of Contagion and the Spread of African Culture* (New York: Routledge, 1998).

18. Paul Gilroy, "' . . . to be real': The Dissident Forms of Black Expressive Culture," in *Let's Get It On: The Politics of Black Performance*, ed. Catharine Ugwu (Seattle: Bay, 1995), 16.

19. Bill Zehme, "Madonna: The *Rolling Stone* Interview," in *Madonna: The Ultimate Compendium of Interviews, Articles, Facts and Opinions*, ed. Rolling Stone (New York: Hyperion, 1997), 106.

20. Baker and Regnault, *Voguing and the House Ballroom Scene of New York*, 116.

21. Tim Lawrence, "A History of Drag Balls, Houses and the Culture of Voguing," in ibid., 5.

22. *Oxford English Dictionary*, 2nd ed., s.v. "fierceness."

23. Foucault, *The History of Sexuality*, 95.

24. Muñoz, *Cruising Utopia*, 1.

25. José Muñoz, *Disidentifications: Queers of Color and the Performance of Politics* (Minneapolis: University of Minnesota Press, 1999), 23.

26. John Howell, "Voguing," *Artforum International*, February 1989, 9.

27. Jennie Livingston, *Paris Is Burning*, directed by Jennie Livingston (1990; Burbank, CA, 1990), DVD.

28. Jonathan David Jackson, "The Social World of Voguing," *Journal for the Anthropological Study of Human Movement* 12 (2002): 26.

29. George Chauncey, *Gay New York: Gender, Urban Culture, and the Makings of the Gay Male World, 1890–1940* (New York: Basic Books, 1994), 278, 246, 258.

30. Hughes, *The Big Sea*, 273.

31. Chauncey, *Gay New York*, 263.

32. In *The Scene of Harlem Cabaret: Race, Sexuality, Performance* (Chicago: University of Chicago Press, 2009), Shane Vogel makes a strong case for how the nightclub circuit of the Harlem Renaissance period was a space for expanding ideas of race and sexuality.

33. Joe Brown, "Underground Cinderellas," *Washington Post*, August 4, 1991.

34. Howell, "Voguing."

35. Jesse Green, "Paris Has Burned," *New York Times*, April 18, 1993.

36. Jennifer Dunning, "An Exotic Gay Subculture Turns Poignant under Scrutiny," *New York Times*, March 23, 1991. Even though scholars have

taken an interest in voguing since *Paris Is Burning*, there are as yet few scholarly monographs on the subject. This lack of scholarship has to do with the nature of the ballroom scene as a deeply underground culture that is difficult to penetrate for two reasons. The first is that though many clubs have voguing nights, the vogue balls themselves are typically not advertised widely outside of the ballroom community, and when they do occur they frequently do not begin until very late. Second, the ballroom community itself is especially wary of the production of another *Paris Is Burning*, making it difficult for ethnographers to win the trust of the community.

37. Philip Brian Harper, "The Subversive Edge: *Paris Is Burning*, Social Critique, and the Limits of Subjective Agency," *Diacritics* 24 (1994): 91, 99, 92.

38. Jackson, "The Social World of Voguing," 31.

39. Sedgwick, *Touching Feeling*, 125–26.

40. bell hooks, *Black Looks: Race and Representation* (Boston: South End, 1992), 149, 147.

41. Bailey, *Butch Queens*, 132.

42. "Getting Scammed by My Boyfriend's Ex (ft. Joanne the Scammer)," YouTube video, 6:00, posted by Superwoman, December 16, 2016, accessed June 24, 2017, https://www.youtube.com/watch?v=wPm UqWkMN1I&t=99s.

43. BRIC, Jennie Livingston, and JD Samson, "Petitioning BRIC Arts Media Celebrate Brooklyn!" Change.org, accessed April 9, 2016, https://www .change.org/p/celebrate-brooklyn-bric-jennie-livingston-and-jd-samson -cancel-celebrate-brooklyn-bric-s-screening-of-paris-is-burning-end-the -exploitation-of-the-ballroom-community-and-tqpoc-parisisburnt-shutit down.

44. Kiddy Smile, Skype interview by author, March 29, 2016.

45. Julianne Escobedo Shepherd, "New York Is Burning: Vogue's Move from Ballroom to Limelight," *Red Bull Academy*, May 22, 2013.

46. Vjuan Allure, telephone interview by author, August 10, 2012.

47. "How to Get Chopped at a Ball," Facebook, accessed April 9, 2016, https://www.facebook.com/TheOnlyMikeQ/posts/485638344862710.

48. Allure, interview.

49. Lasseindra Ninja, telephone interview by author, December 23, 2014.

50. Escobedo Shepherd, "New York Is Burning."

51. See Kath Weston, *Families We Choose: Lesbians, Gays, Kinship* (New York: Columbia University Press, 1997).

52. Marlon Bailey, "Gender/Racial Realness: Theorizing the Gender System in Ballroom Culture," *Feminist Studies* 37 (2011): 367.

53. Baker and Regnault, *Voguing and the House Ballroom Scene of New York*, 196.

54. For a rich history of black women and beauty pageants in the twentieth century, see Maxine Leeds Craig, *Ain't I a Beauty Queen? Black Women, Beauty, and the Politics of Race* (New York: Oxford University Press, 2002). See also Nichelle Gainer, *Vintage Black Glamour* (London: Rocket88 Books, 2015); and Deborah Willis, *Posing Beauty: African American Images from the 1890s to the Present* (New York: Norton, 2009).

55. *The Queen,* directed by Frank Simon (1996; New York: First Run Features Home Video), VHS.

56. Johnson, "SNAP! Culture," 125.

57. Baker and Regnault, *Voguing and the House Ballroom Scene of New York*, 114.

58. Lauren Berlant, *The Queen of America Goes to Washington City: Essays on Sex and Citizenship* (Durham: Duke University Press, 1997), 223.

59. Bailey, *Butch Queens*, 128.

60. For a lively discussion of the commentator in ballroom culture, see ibid., 156–64.

61. Ninja, interview.

62. Allure, interview.

63. The majority of the videos demonstrating voguing on the Internet are curated by Ballroom Throwbacks.

64. Allure, interview.

65. Bailey, *Butch Queens*, 161.

66. Allure, interview.

67. Bailey, *Butch Queens*, 58, 69.

68. RuPaul, "Step It Up," *Realness* (RuCo, 2015), CD.

69. moore, "To Be Able to Blend."

70. Ibid.

71. Bailey, *Butch Queens*, 56.

72. Allure, interview.

73. Escobedo Shepherd, "Nah, Rihanna."

74. Brian O'Doherty, *Inside the White Cube: The Ideology of the Gallery Space* (Berkeley: University of California Press, 1999), 14.

75. Mic Oala, interview by author, Berlin, August 19, 2014.

76. Ninja, interview.

77. Smile, interview.

78. *Proletarian French Voguers, Vice*, March 20, 2014, accessed June 24, 2017, https://www.youtube.com/watch?v=WK0udmxZam0.

79. Smile, interview.

80. Ninja, interview.

81. Oala, interview.

82. Zoe Melody, interview by author, Berlin, February 6, 2015.

83. Georgina Leo Melody, interview by author, Berlin, February 6, 2015.

84. See Bailey, *Butch Queens*, 61–64, for a full description of the performance categories.

85. Oala, interview.

86. Zoe Melody, interview.

87. Ninja, interview.

they say it takes a village to raise a child, and if that's so, then you 245 definitely need a galaxy to write a book! The things they don't tell you in graduate school. These pages reflect a global network of artists, performers, curators, drag queens, musicians, fashion designers, DJs, club kids, stylists, and creative renegades. They are also the result of friendship and community building in that special way that queer work makes possible. I am thankful to have been invited to share versions of this material at Performance Space Sydney, Ryerson University, Amherst College, Reed College, Eilean Shona, the Barbican, Tate Britain, the University of Oxford, Yale University, Washington University in Saint Louis, University College London, Virginia Commonwealth University, the University of St. Andrews, King's College London, and the Center for Lesbian and Gay Studies at the CUNY Graduate Center. Each invitation was an opportunity to learn and grow from those communities, and to push the work forward.

Huge thanks to Jeff Kahn for inviting me to perform new work at Performance Space Sydney. It was my first time in Australia, but hopefully not my last! The lovely Kate Bredeson asked me to develop aspects of this project in a residency at Reed College, and the critically fabulous Kaj-Anne Pepper asked me to be a guest judge at the 2014 Critical Mascara: A Post-Realness Drag Ball, hosted by the Portland Institute for Contemporary Art. This was an experience that wed theory and practice and helped me see and do fabulousness in real time. Nearly nothing powers you through writing like seeing your research in action—and having the heels to match.

I would not have been able to write this book without the guidance of Joseph Roach. The first time I met Joe, whom I was drawn to as a graduate student at Yale because of a book he wrote about eighteenth-century celebrities and the "it" factor, he asked me what I wanted to study and I had no idea what to say. Then he asked what I liked to do in my spare time and I told him I liked to go shopping, dance, and read fashion magazines. "Go study that," he said. "Those aren't *real* topics!" I insisted, but he assured me otherwise. Over the years Joe has not only shown me that my interests at the intersection of popular culture, queer studies, and performance studies are "real topics," but his searching questions, encouragement, and general enthusiasm about this project have opened up avenues in my work that I would not have thought to pursue. How can one person be so smart?

It's telling that Daphne Brooks would shape a project on fabulousness because she is a floating vision of Nanette Lepore; the first thing I said when I met her was, "You are *fabulous!*" Daphne has always encouraged my work and has pushed this project forward by reminding me to slow down. I admire Daphne so much, especially the way she navigates the spaces beyond academia, a model I'm trying my best to emulate. When this project was in its infant, dissertation stage, Paige McGinley was an ideal mentor because she is excited about unconventional ideas. She listens and knows how to tell you what you are really trying to say. When I asked her if I should dance to Tina Turner during a talk I gave on Tina at the Association for Theater in Higher Education annual conference, she was all, *yes*. In the French department, my first home at Yale, Maurice Samuels was an ideal mentor—he still is—and if it wasn't for Maurie, who let me pursue my interest in fashion in his courses on the nineteenth-century realist novel, I wouldn't have known that Balzac was just as interested in fabulousness as I am.

The American Studies Program was extremely supportive of this research when it was in dissertation form. Kathryn Dudley, Joanne Meyerowitz, Matthew Jacobson, Alicia Schmidt Camacho, and Laura Wexler were especially encouraging. Vicki Sheppard and I gossiped every week about pop culture, fashion, and models—and *America's Next Top Model* in particular. After conversations with her I always came away with new ideas that would move my work forward. Gregory Eow, then a fabulous librarian at Sterling, always wanted me to tell him more. Pat Cabral, in the Office for Diversity and Equal Opportunity, was like a mother to me when my own was a thousand miles away. Dean Michelle Nearon was always an advocate and a great listener, and I thank her for all the times I showed up at her office just to vent. Michael Morand believed in me from the very beginning, and I am indebted to his friendship and continued support . . . and to his fabulous colorful sock collection. You have to see it to believe it.

This would be a remarkably different book if I had not been fortunate enough to move to London to join the European Research Council–funded Modern Moves research project based out of King's College London and led by Ananya Jahanara Kabir. Moving to Europe was a surprise plot twist that has given this book a whole new dimension, and I am forever indebted to Modern Moves and to Ananya especially for her mentorship and for offering me such a life-changing experience. Thanks too to the rest of the Modern Moves family—Helena, Ania, Elina, and Leyneuf—for all the support, not to mention the dancing, dinners, strawberry tarts, and Indian food. A special shout-out to Leyneuf for her colorful catsuits!

King's has been a wonderful place to develop this work. In the Department of English Alan Reed, Mark Turner, John Howard, Richard Kirkland, and Sebastian Matzner have all been especially supportive. Thanks to Pelagia Pais and the Arts and Humanities Research Institute for including me in the 2015 Arts & Humanities Festival on Fabrication, where I gave the lecture of a lifetime on Beyoncé. They moved the earth to get me a wind machine for this particular performance lecture. I'm dead serious.

To my Berlin family: thank you for being so creative, weird, and queer. In Berlin, by now my other home, my girl Mic Oala has been the best friend, even when I was messy and almost totally falling apart. She makes me smoothies, lets me play in her clothes, and most important she introduced me to the Berlin voguing scene. Through her I was able to judge the Tit Bit Ball at Südblock in February 2014 and then the Berlin Voguing Out Festival in December 2015, both experiences that have deeply impacted my understanding of fabulousness as a transnational queer aesthetic. I am fond of Mic and am thankful for her friendship, spirit, and encouragement. Plus, her peanut butter chicken is off the hook. Blee-bloo-bloop! Thanks too to the rest of my Berlin family for all the food, dancing, and conviviality, especially Luis-Manuel Garcia, Christina, Kirk, Mika, Joey, Wool, Leon, Alinka, Thomas, Ando, Lauren, and all the people whose names I don't know or can't remember but who I always see and talk to on a dance floor somewhere. Shout-out to Ando for drinking opulent cocktails with me "upstairs," and a special shout-out to my girl Shaun J. Wright for his fabulousness, the "twirls," and for helping "Mother Feeling It" keep it together that one time when things got *really* real. Thanks to Georgina Leo Melody and the House of Melody for the runway workshops, which taught me a lot about performing fabulousness in a German context.

Thanks to my ballroom girls: Lasseindra, Vjuan Allure, Mother Steffie, Kiddy, and all of the Paris girls for their creativity, friendship, and showing me the way.

I also want to thank the faculty members in the Department of Theater and Dance at the University of Richmond where I was a Council for Faculty Diversity postdoctoral fellow for two years. The department was extremely encouraging. Thanks in particular to Dorothy Holland, Johann Stegmeir, Patricia Herrera, Chuck Mike, Matthew Thornton, Mari-Lee Mifsud, Timothy Barney, Paul Achter, and Nicole Maurantonio.

Tom Sellar, editor of *Theater* magazine, invited me to share some of this work first in an article on the contemporary dancer Trajal Harrell and second in another piece connecting art and nightlife. Luis-Manuel Garcia edited a special issue of *Dancecult* and included my early work on the importance of doing queer nightlife as a way of framing and understanding it. And Karen Tongson and Gus Stadler published my early theorizations of fierceness in an article on Tina Turner and fierceness in the *Journal of Popular Music Studies.*

Conversations and interviews with a number of scholars, artists, and performers have added greatly to my understanding of fabulousness, nightlife, and culture. They are, in no particular order: Ben Barry, Vjuan Allure, Alok Vaid-Menon, Michael T., Dan Beaumont, Gavin Butt, Soyica Diggs Colbert, Eric Lott, Nick Salvato, Cherie Lily, Hahn-Bin/Amadéus Leopold, Elliot Powell, Tom Sellar, Kyle Geiger, Travis Alabanza, Lauren Sohikian, Gregory Alexander, Loren Granic, Erik Lamar Wallace, James Ellis, Anthony Apitchou, RoRo Morales, Faun Dae, Kaj-Anne Pepper, Amy Cakes, Leo GuGu, Jelly Wet Taco, Diana Dae, Susanne Bartsch, Mic Oala, Sandrien, Georgina Leo Melody, Zoe Melody, Zero Melody,

Sophie Yukiko, Olaf Boswijk, Lasseindra Ninja, Pierre Hache, Fred Moten, Shaun J. Wright, Christina Wheeler, Patricia Field, Ramdasha Bikceem, Katya Moorman, Max Allen, E. Patrick Johnson, Caroline Weber, Melissa Blanco Borelli, Tavia Nyong'o, Scott Poulson-Bryant, Christopher Grobe, Luis-Manuel Garcia, Dimitri Krebs, Wendy Steiner, Khadijah White, Sue-Ellen Case, Jack Halberstam, Koritha Mitchell, Karen Tongson, Casey Mullen, Tommy DeFrantz, Deborah Paredez, Chioma Nnadi, Lucy Silberman, Simonez Wolf, Cody Allen, Michaela angela Davis, Guy Trebay, Jimmy Webb, Kayvon Zand, Steve Lewis, Daniel Kersting, Aymar Jean Christian, Aleksey Kernes, Sharon Needles, Andrew WK, Julie Baumgardner, Louise Bernard, and Greg Foley.

Thanks to everyone who booked me for a lecture or a DJ performance, especially Christopher Grobe, Julia Fawcett, Ben Barry, Jeff Khan and Nik Dimopoulos, Lee Adams, Lee Dyer, and Isis O'Regan. Ben Barry is one of the most inspirational and forward-thinking scholars I know, and he has supported my work from day one. The critically fabulous Pepper Pepper has supported my work from the beginning, and I am extremely grateful for their friendship and approach to the world. In 2017 Roya Amirsoleymani invited me to Portland as a guest artist scholar for the Time-Based Art Festival at the Portland Institute for Contemporary Art, a stellar experience. A huge thanks to Roya and to PICA for supporting me, and to Pepper again for creating that bridge. Guy Farrell let me stay in his house for two weeks!

To Chris Lavergne, Russ Smith, and Zach Stafford—thank you for believing in my voice. Sheri Pasquarella believed in me from the beginning and took me to Marquee in New York for the first time! Rizvana Bradley and Melissa Blanco Borelli were vital to my social life in London and have always been supportive of my work, even when I felt like giving up.

Whenever I went to Trash and Vaudeville in New York the inimitable Jimmy Webb always gave me a massive discount though I never asked for it, and I'm always inspired by his wisdom, his laughter, and that rock and roll sensibility. Cherie Lily invited me to host a party with her at Santos Party House in New York City, one of the first moments when I got to experiment with the gap between the theory of queer nightlife and actually doing queer nightlife.

To my amazing housemates at "The Gransden"—Piotr, Kate, Sarah 1, Sarah 2, Etienne, Lindsay, Ander, Marine, and Mathieu—you guys all saw me burning the midnight oil working on this book at the kitchen table for years. Whenever you asked how it was coming along, I just grunted. But now we can finally have that book party!

Sections of these chapters have appeared in a range of scholarly journals, although they have been reworked here. Portions of the chapter that is now called "Up in the Club" were published in "Nightlife as Form," *Theater*, January 2016, and in "Looks: Studio 54 and the Production of Fabulous Nightlife," *Dancecult: The Journal of Electronic Dance Music Culture*, May 2013. And portions of what's now "What's Queer about the Catwalk?" were published in "Tina Theory: Notes on Fierceness," *Journal of Popular Music Studies*, March 2012, as well as in "I'm That Bitch: Queerness and the Catwalk," *Safundi: The Journal of South African and American Studies* 18 (2017).

I am fortunate to have been supported by close relationships with friends, family, and colleagues who have in some way been part of this galaxy. I see you, Aymar Jean Christian, Courtnee "Woo" Phillips, Telicia Nicole, Mic Oala, Billy Haworth, Sheri Pasquarella, Brandy Butler, Katrena Moore, Ando, Paul Mac, jonny seymour, Jon McPhedran-Waitzer, Julie Baumgardner, Elinor Pinke, Lorenz Koenig, James Ellis, Isis O'Regan, Dimitri Krebs, Jeff Khan, Aymar Jean Christian, Vladimir von Dittersdorf, Guy Farrell, Seth Christman, Daniel Kersting, Michael Morand, Adam Watkins, Shaun J. Wright, and Tina Williams. A special thanks to Dimitri, Aymar, Tina, Ando, and Adam, who all watched me foam at the mouth about this project nearly every day for years. Aymar and Adam have been like brothers to me.

To Daniel Kersting: I'm sorry.

An extremely special thanks goes to my editor Joe Calamia. Not only did he believe in the project from the start, but he "got" the intervention I was trying to make right from the jump. He always pushed me to do my best and was there for me even when on the inside I felt like giving up, not because I didn't want to do the project but because of my own battle with depression. Depression tears even the things you care about the most right out of your hands, but Joe never let me give up. My copy-editor Robin DuBlanc sees everything, and I am thankful for her eye and help with cleaning up the manuscript.

At Massie & McQuilkin, Ethan Bassoff took a very early interest in me and in the development of this project, and I thank him for taking the first step.

Writing a book is a lot like rearranging your room. You pace around taking things out but then get lost finding things you forgot you had, sorting through a keepsake box that's clearly way too full yet you can't bear to throw any of it away. Eventually you get everything out and into the hallway only to realize, damn, you have a lot of stuff. So you just stare at the pile with an overwhelming feeling of dread, wondering how you're going to get it all back in. But you do get it all back in, and when what seems like an eternity later all the pieces are right where you want them, you stare at your new, clean, rearranged room with a special pride that you did it.

To my grandmother Delores Moore: I know you still don't really understand what I'm doing, but the only thing that matters now is *I'm done*.